Praise for

KNOCKED UP ABROAD

"Knocked Up Abroad floats and jabs, amuses and disturbs, informs and questions. At the heart of it is a true and lovely heart. Ultimately as scary as it may seem to leave one's home country, one never really leaves home at all.

No, home is a place first lived in a womb then carried in arms then held by hands. Home is family and family is home."

- Hubert O'Hearn, By the Book Reviews

ABOUT THE AUTHOR

Lisa Ferland is an epidemiologist by training who discovered that she had other interests beyond her formal degree—mainly the interesting cultural differences in child rearing practices worldwide. When she is not behind a computer, she can be found outside playing with her children or tackling the never-ending pile of laundry. Born and raised in the United States of America, she currently lives in Sweden with her husband, two children, and their loveable barky dog.

Knocked Up Abroad

◆ ◆ ◆ ◆ ◆

Stories of pregnancy, birth, and raising a family in a foreign country

Lisa Ferland

For my children, Calvin and Lucy, who teach me how to be a better person every day.

ISBN 978-0-9970624-0-3 (Print)
ISBN 978-0-9970624-1-0 (eBook)

Cover design by Emelie Cheng
Photography by Sandra Jolly

CONTENTS

FOREWORD

Naomi Hattaway, founder of "I Am a Triangle"

When I created the Facebook group called "I am a Triangle," I originally felt it would be a place for 30–50 people to congregate online, share experiences, and provide support for one other. I believed in the early days it might be a catchall for a handful of individuals who had experienced life abroad and wanted to talk about it from time to time. What I did not expect was that in just a few months' time, the group would collect over 3,300 amazing people from all over the world—and that number is still growing—who all share at least one thing in common: life abroad.

Triangles are described as being individuals from one country (Circle Country) who move to another one with a very different culture, known as Square Country. Over time, they are molded and shaped by their experiences and they become a Triangle. The "where they came from" melds with the "where they moved to," and they are permanently changed. They cannot become exactly like residents of the Square Country, where they live, and they will no longer be exactly as they were when they left Circle Country.

My own experience with life abroad first began in 2009 when I said, "Why not?" to my husband's question about whether I would consider moving to New Delhi, India for his career. Our overseas adventure continued as we found ourselves moving to Singapore after three years in India. However, our adventures abruptly ended in 2012 after a combination of events—I suffered from a common tropical illness, and my husband's job position had turned into too much travel and too many hours at work.

We found ourselves quickly immersed back in life in our passport country, and the true culture shock began as we felt we no longer belonged. Whether you choose to repatriate or it is something you cannot control, the potential for depression and feeling as though you don't belong is something not often talked about; however, it is something many struggle with as part of their repatriation reality.

I wrote a blog post discussing the ins and outs of repatriation in September 2013 after struggling with my own "repat blues" for about a year. The response to that blog post was overwhelming, and in an effort to help the thousands of people who emailed me on the topic, I created the Facebook group in October 2014. Living overseas and, ultimately, the discussion of "coming back home" is a topic that is so important to so many. I am honored to be a part of a thriving community that offers support and encouragement to others on a daily basis.

The "I Am a Triangle" Facebook group has provided a springboard for many amazing things to happen, one of which was an opportunity for many of the contributors of this book to connect in the first place! You are about to read the amazing stories of mothers (and two fathers!) who have pushed outside of their comfort zones in their quest to redefine their idea of parenthood. They all did so while living abroad in unfamiliar locations, without the comfort of extended family and lifelong friends by their sides.

We are all on a quest to "find home," and somehow along the way, we discover communities where our families can truly thrive and flourish. Regardless of whether you yourself have given birth abroad, plan to in the future, or simply want to sit down with stories that will inspire and warm your heart, you are welcomed into a community who knows that home is defined, quite simply, as that place where you find your family.

Naomi Hattaway is married with three littles (one in elementary school, one in middle school, and one who has left the nest and is now working full time). After living abroad, she now resides in Northern Virginia and continues to enjoy making an impact—even if only with a small corner of her world—for the better. She founded a relocation and real estate company called 8th & Home at http://8thandhome.com and enjoys assisting families with their own efforts to "Find Home."

INTRODUCTION

Living abroad is stressful. Being pregnant is stressful. When you experience both simultaneously, you are "knocked up abroad."

The idea for this book was born after receiving feedback on one of my articles about birthing abroad in a foreign, unfamiliar culture and medical system. I then posed a question in the "I Am a Triangle" Facebook group. I asked the members of the group how many women had had interesting or unusual experiences while giving birth abroad. The flood of responses that came from that simple question reinforced what I already knew—not only are birth stories fascinating but the additional contextual layers of foreign languages, cultures, and medical practices result in unusual situations for pregnant women. Even more so, after the birth these families must constantly navigate their foreign country to achieve things deemed as simple nuisances in their home countries. Things like registering a child for school or taking a baby to the doctor are slightly more difficult when one is unfamiliar with the system.

The women who contributed their stories to this book persevered despite countless barriers to birth their children in a foreign and unfamiliar environment. Most often, they welcomed their babies into this world in ways they had never imagined, without the supportive network of friends and family. The two fathers who contributed chapters write about what life is like with the shoe on the other foot. They experienced the life that every mother wishes their husband could appreciate—what life is like when Dad is solely responsible for the children and household duties and experiences the struggle to balance it all.

This book contains a collection of stories of adventures, misadventures, challenges, and joys that mothers and fathers experience while living abroad and raising a family. Each story, like each birth experience, is uniquely told through the lens of differing social contexts that each woman must navigate to obtain the best possible care for themselves and their unborn children. The culture clashes experienced while birthing abroad are numerous and frequently provide new obstacles to hurdle on the path to birth.

Parents of toddlers must learn the new social, parental expectations of their new foreign surroundings while juggling foreign languages, customs, and practices.

Throughout the creation of this book, interacting with parents from all over the world, it became clear to me that there is no one road to happiness and no one successful method for creating a family. At any moment, parents around the world are tackling the same issues of sleepless nights, finding and preparing food for dinner, educating their children, and passing along family traditions in infinitely various ways.

Knocked Up Abroad contains the stories of parents who have left the familiar for the unknown, embraced a little bit of adventure, and discovered who they wanted to be as parents—not as defined by their home or local cultures, but by blending all of the various influences in their lives.

- Lisa Ferland

SECTION I

KNOCKED UP ABROAD

CHAPTER 1

THIS WOULD BE REALLY FUNNY IF IT WASN'T HAPPENING TO ME

Mirren Childs
Nationality: United Kingdom
Knocked up in: Harbin, China

Pinned to my fridge is a postcard, which reads, "This would be really funny if it wasn't happening to me." It was given to me more than a decade ago by a dear friend with a dry sense of humor, with whom I was sharing an apartment as we navigated the trials and tribulations of the dating world in our thirties. However, there have been other periods of my life since then when it seemed to capture perfectly the zeitgeist of the moment. This is the story of one such time.

It was a cold evening in January 2008 when my husband, Peter, called me at work to tell me that his company had offered him the chance of a two-year secondment, a temporary transfer to a new position, to China. Initially I was dubious. We had been married for less than two years, together for four, after a long friendship and a tortuous road to romance, and for the first time ever I was starting to feel settled in our adopted city of Edinburgh. We had been trying for a baby for around a year but to no avail, and as my 40th birthday—and his 50th—loomed ever closer, we were each secretly beginning to doubt whether it would ever happen for us.

"I thought it sounded...fun?" offered my husband, after a pause. "An adventure. Don't you think it would be nice to have an adventure together? If—you know—the baby adventure isn't going to happen for us?"

He had a point. However, I had a vivid memory of the Chinese art-house movies I had enjoyed as an undergraduate, in which someone always seemed to be trudging through a 20-foot snowdrift, and I told him so.

"Where in China?"

It turned out that the job was in Harbin, in Heilongjiang Province in northern China, just a few hundred miles from the Russian border. A glance at the BBC Weather website for January showed temperatures of 5 °F (-15 °C) by day and -22 °F (-30 °C) by night.

"It's an adventure?" he said, with a hopeful smile.

I looked at him, looked at the screen, looked back at him, and shrugged.

"Okay," I said.

Seven months later, after a weeklong exploratory trip to China in May, a struggle to find an international shipping agent who had even heard of Harbin, let alone who was prepared to ship there, and a chaotic move, I was on a KLM flight from Edinburgh via Amsterdam to Shanghai. I would meet up with Peter at his company's head office before we flew on to Harbin a few days later. He had arrived a week earlier to get settled in and to find us an apartment. This he had done—sending me photos for approval— with the help of his assistant/interpreter, a young Chinese lad who went by the name of Kevin.

Our new apartment in Harbin was huge, angular, futuristic, and startlingly white, and—the Hello Kitty beaded curtains notwithstanding—its similarity to the Starship Enterprise didn't end there. The Chinese love for gadgets and elaborate, showy light fittings with pointless multiple settings were replete throughout. The 36-bulb red, white, and blue light fitting in the lounge could be illuminated in no fewer than 12 different configurations. We dubbed the kitchen light's default setting "the disco jellyfish." The shower was a walk-in, standalone blue transparent pod with eight water jet settings, a light, a built-in radio, and probable teleportation powers. Better still, we got to put the washing machine in the bathroom—a wildly exotic idea for British people!

Harbin as a whole seemed every bit as crazy. Especially for us, coming from a country full of old buildings and a city mostly built in the 18th and 19th centuries, the space-age Chinese architecture was dazzling. Our apartment was located in the out-of-town business district, all of which was spanking new and mostly unfinished. Vast swathes of many Chinese cities have this brand-new-partly-finished feel, but we had never seen architecture quite like it before. For example, the so-called Dragon Tower, or the monstrous red diamond which formed the intersection between two offices, or the strange public art resembling molecular structures which adorned everything from traffic roundabouts to the car park at the nearby Carrefour (the French supermarket chain without which expats in China would probably starve). Everything—roads, shopping malls, and restaurants—is on a vast scale, only amplified by the big blue skies that seem to stretch the horizon to the point of bursting.

The center of Harbin is older, built by Russian immigrants in the early 1900s when the Trans-Siberian railway—which ends there to this day—was born. The city still retains a strong Russian identity, which is very atypical of Chinese cities. The city's architectural centerpiece is, arguably, the gorgeous St. Sophia Cathedral, built in the Russian Orthodox style. Inside, it is now a somewhat poorly kept museum, with a display of interesting photographs (captioned, sadly, in Chinese only) documenting the genesis of the city, but the outside is Lonely Planet cover–worthy, especially in winter. The few westerners there are generally Russian, as indeed we were assumed to be by every Chinese person we met.

As in most Chinese cities, a passing attempt at embracing English can be seen in the many bilingual signs around the place, though these are often entertainingly impenetrable. We grew rather fond of the "Poet Beauty Salon" (where presumably you go in looking normal and come out resembling Lord Byron), the "Proper Ty and Casual Ty Company" (obviously flexible in their dress code), and the classic "The Trepang Monopolizes the Shop" (no idea). However, it is still common to see municipal signs in Russian as well, sometimes at the expense of English.

Make no mistake, Harbin is a winter city. The Siberian temperatures (for that is nearly what they are) that I saw that January night from the relative warmth of our Edinburgh apartment make Harbin not only a growing winter sports destination but also home to the world's most famous ice and snow festival. From late December to late January every year, a huge park known as Sun Island on the far bank of the Songhua River, and the frozen surface of the vast river itself, are covered in hundreds of elaborate snow sculptures created by artists who travel from all over the world to exhibit there. More impressive still are the gigantic, life-size architectural structures made from blocks of ice, lit from within by colored glass tube lights, which transform Harbin into a frozen Disneyland on an epic scale.

There is, of course, a summer as well. The extreme climate means that temperatures in summer consistently climb to the low 80s °F (low 30s °C), and a vibrant café culture exists from May to August along the banks of the Songhua and throughout the city's network of small lanes. But we arrived at the very end of August, moving into September, and the thermometer has a long way to drop from the summer high to the winter low, which begins with snows in mid-November. The result is that in the fall, the temperature can, and regularly does, drop by 18 °F (10 °C) increments from one week to the next.

In the third week of September, Peter had to return to the UK for a week to rectify a problem with our visas, which placed us in imminent danger of deportation less than a month after our arrival. Left alone on our Starship Enterprise, I began to feel the cold. Not outside. Outside was a fairly balmy 66 °F (19 °C)—pretty much a warm summer's day in Scotland—but inside, especially in the evenings, was a different matter.

The government policy is to centrally control the heating of all new homes and public buildings north of the Yangtze River. This heat is switched on permanently for six months of the year, October 20 to April 20. Once on it can, with some difficulty, be adjusted (although we found this out way too late) or even turned almost to zero; not that you'd want to, though—it gets so cold in winter that a five-liter bottle of water left on an unheated internal balcony can turn to a solid block of ice overnight. What the heat *cannot* be, however, is switched on in advance. Not even if there's an unseasonal cold snap. Or if your apartment happens to be so well insulated (because it needs to be) and so shielded from sunlight by the surrounding high buildings that *not one glimmer of warmth* from the mild autumnal blue skies filters through into your space-pod of freezing death.

Thus, in some bizarre inversion of all the laws of nature, the coldest time of the year by far in sub-Siberian Harbin—indoors anyway—is mid-September to mid-October. People wear coats in the office. They wear thermal underwear and long johns. Actually, they wear these all year round, just in case, but in late September they complain about the cold. By contrast, mid-April is the season for throwing open the windows to let out the stifling heat. Really, it's stifling all year round because in winter your apartment is heated to 81 °F (27 °C), *day and night*, and the restaurants and shopping malls even more so. You need an extra chair or shopping cart simply for all of your outdoor clothing. *Except* for that month in the fall.

Peter arrived back from Scotland in the final week of September with his shiny new visa to find me huddled on our Chinese landlord's spectacularly large and spectacularly uncomfortable leather sofa, wearing three sweaters, a scarf, gloves, and a giant double foot warmer. He, who professes never to feel the cold, laughed at me...the first night. By the second night, he was doing the same.

We looked at each other, and I said, "There has to be a better way to keep warm."

And thus our son was conceived, a result of Chinese governmental heating policy.

Of course, we didn't know that then. By that stage, we had been "trying" to conceive for almost two years, but in a very relaxed manner (no temperature charts or the like). I had mentioned our lack of success, in passing, to my doctor in the UK some months before the China job arose and was somewhat alarmed to find our "case" instantly transferred onto some kind of infertility conveyor belt without my having requested any such thing. My husband had been even more alarmed to find himself being quizzed about his fertility when visiting his family doctor because of a throat infection. Our reactions to this had been so visceral that we had concluded that, while we both loved the idea of having a baby, it wasn't an all-consuming priority for us. If it happened, it happened. If it didn't—as was looking increasingly likely—we'd...go to China.

I say all this by way of explaining how, despite us not using contraception, by that October the possibility that I might actually get pregnant was the furthest thing from our minds. So much so that when I had a strange, untimely, and exceptionally light period a couple of weeks later—while we were back in Shanghai sorting out my spouse visa—I put it down to the stress caused by the move and the visa situation. Either that, or it signaled the foothills of the menopause.

The disasters befalling us went from bad to worse when, at the end of the month, Peter was taken unexpectedly ill on a business trip to Beijing, and a few days later I was accompanying him on a hastily arranged flight to Hong Kong where he had to undergo a minor, but urgent and painful, operation. The surgery was scheduled for Monday at 1 p.m., and I had sat with him all morning, shivering in the over-air-conditioned ward. By the time he was wheeled away, I was ravenously hungry. My enquiries directed me to the hospital canteen, where I consumed a hearty British lunch of shepherd's pie or some such thing (one advantage of colonialism, I suppose). Midway through my meal, a member of the canteen staff approached me and offered me a free piece of cheesecake—I suspect it had been there all weekend. However, this didn't occur to me at the time and—never being one to turn down free food (and I was *very* hungry)—I accepted and ate it gratefully. It tasted perfectly fine.

Alas, it wasn't fine. Or I wasn't fine. Something, it became apparent as the afternoon wore on, was very *not* fine. For as I sat by my extremely drugged-up husband's side, my insides began protesting increasingly painfully until, at some point in the early evening, I exploded in both directions with the worst food poisoning I have ever experienced. I'll spare you the graphic details but it was *not* pretty. Since it happened when I was actually in a hospital, I was hospitalized as a result. They hooked me up to an IV, pumped me full of rehydration salts and antibiotics and anti-nausea drugs to stop the vomiting when I *still* couldn't keep anything down, not even water, after 36 hours.

I was very, very sick. I was in that bed for three whole days, staggering up intermittently only to wheel my IV to the toilet, endure a little more hell therein, and then stagger back to bed again to sleep, or vomit a bit more. Instead of me playing the supportive wife and hospital visitor, Peter ended up being the one visiting *me*, tottering painfully down from his room two floors above me, while we swapped trashy novels and tried to dodge the well-meaning but somewhat disturbing visits from the hospital's resident nuns.

It would have been really funny if it wasn't happening to me.

What nobody ever, at any point, asked me, was whether there was any possibility that I might be pregnant. They never tested for it, despite taking multiple blood and urine samples. It has taken seven years for it to occur to me that the reason for this was probably my age. In the UK, this question is standard for any female of childbearing age undergoing a medical procedure, but in China, a 40-year-old woman is more likely to be a grandmother than a mother.

Whatever the reason, I was never asked the question—to which I would have had to reply with a surprised, "Well, I doubt it, but I suppose technically it is possible"—and for the reasons which I described earlier, it didn't cross my mind to alert the doctors to the possibility. In truth, completely unsuspected by me, I was around three or four weeks pregnant at this point. Whether this caused my sickness, exacerbated it, or was purely incidental to it, I will never know. I only have the apparently perfect health of my son so far, and blind hope for the future, on which to trust that the drugs with which they blithely filled me did no harm.

The immediate result, however, was that when we finally made it back to Harbin in early November, shaken by our experiences but convinced that the worst was now behind us—and buoyed by the news that our shipped goods from home were finally scheduled to arrive after their 10-week journey from Scotland—and I missed another period, I was at first largely unfazed. It was the stress, I figured. The physical trauma. Maybe the drugs. My body was bound to be somewhat out of sync after everything it had been through.

Another week went by, and I Googled the side effects of the one drug I'd been given whose name I knew. Disruption to the menstrual cycle, it said. There. Nothing to worry about. Another week, and I casually mentioned to Peter that I hadn't had a period since before Hong Kong. (I still thought that I'd had one in Shanghai.) Maybe I should buy a pregnancy test, I half joked.

I was in denial. I drank. Our shipment arrived, and as Peter was still forbidden from heavy lifting, it fell to me, Kevin (the assistant), and a passing trash collector to carry our 27 heavy boxes up the final flight of stairs from the elevator door to our apartment. Elevators that don't quite go as far as you need them to are a common feature in China. This strenuous activity, I felt certain, would coax my recalcitrant uterus into doing its job.

But no. More days passed, and it started to feel less like a joke.

Scarcely believing I was even considering it, I consulted our Mandarin-English dictionary for the phrase for "pregnancy test." It gave me "pregnant" (*huái yùn*) but that was all. Google Translate wasn't any more helpful. I spoke no Chinese, and English speakers in Harbin were rare. Too embarrassed and too much in denial to ask Kevin—and with no wish to reveal the whole business to the entire staff of Peter's office, which would have been the result—I stutteringly confessed my fears to Peter one Sunday evening and begged him to come home from work—a five-minute walk away—the following lunchtime to accompany me to the nearest pharmacy and try to make them understand.

On Monday morning, the first snows of the year began to fall and kept on falling. Even in the harshest winters in the UK, we rarely see concerted and persistent snowfall, and any snow underfoot almost always stays wet and slippery. Not so in Harbin. The snow comes down hard and fast for around a week while the temperature hovers around the freezing point, but once it drops below 23 °F (-5 °C) or 14 °F (-10 °C) and stays there, the snow freezes solid and acquires the consistency of pack ice. The preferred winter footwear of women in Harbin is stiletto-heeled boots. The heels dig into the ice with a satisfying little crack and act like a mountaineer's crampons, enabling the wearer to walk at an efficient clip without slipping at all. It's an impressive sight to behold.

All this, however, I was yet to discover. Donning, instead, my Serious Walking Boots (whose textured soles instantly filled with snow, turning them effectively into flat skates with no grip whatsoever), the vintage 1960s fur coat that my mother-in-law had foisted on me despite my ethical objections (it works, I'm sorry to report), and the exorbitantly expensive and hugely impractical white, goose-down-filled ski mittens that I had purchased on the company's "cold weather clothing allowance," I gripped Peter's arm resolutely, and together, through the driving snow, we teetered, slipped, and slid the couple of blocks from our apartment to one of the (fortunately fairly ubiquitous) pharmacies which I had noticed on a previous exploration.

A middle-aged Chinese woman greeted us, smiling, from behind the counter. Tentatively, Peter tried the beginning of a "Do you have a…?" sentence and then looked at me.

"*Huái yùn…?*" I said and shrugged, indicating speculation.

The woman's beam widened.

"Aahh!" she said excitedly, pointing to my stomach. The Chinese love babies and are very keen on all things baby-related. "*Huái yùn? Huái yùn?*"

"No," I shook my head and shrugged some more.

"Don't know," Peter said in Chinese.

"*Huái yùn…??*" I tried again, exaggerating my pantomime of confusion.

The woman frowned and repeated her enquiry as to my pregnancy with a little more concern. *"Huái yùn?"*

"No!" I said again in frustration.

My eyes scanned the shelves full of medicines behind her, trying to identify a pregnancy test which I could point to, but everything was covered in Chinese characters, with no pictures and nothing at all that I could recognize.

Finally, in desperation, my eyes fell on the small pad of Post-it notes that the woman had before her. Chinese people in service jobs always seem to carry these, and they have a habit of scrawling down screeds of characters on them and presenting it to you if you don't understand what they're saying. This is a by-product of living in a country with several different languages with one mutually intelligible writing system, but they never seem to twig that it doesn't work for English or to comprehend that there could be anyone on earth who can't read Chinese.

I pointed to the pad and her pen with an enquiring look. Obligingly, she slid them across to me, and after a moment's thought, I drew a female stick figure (like that on the door of a ladies' bathroom) and, watching the woman's face, I then carefully added to my drawing a round pregnant belly, and finally—again checking her for understanding—a large question mark above the figure's head. Fortunately, punctuation in Chinese is one thing that is the same.

In stick-figure terms, a light bulb appeared over our friendly pharmacist's own head.

"Aaaahhhh!" she exclaimed, and turning, she reached down and produced what was recognizably a pack of two pregnancy tests from the shelf behind her, handing it to me with a beam.

"Huái yùn [something]?" (I never did find out the correct phrase.)

"Yes! Yes! *Xiè xiè! Xiè xiè!* [Thank you!]" I cried in extreme relief.

We slid and slipped and teetered our way back home again, both in a daze from the surreality of our situation. It took me a further 24 hours to pluck up the courage to take the tests—which were both, of course, indisputably positive.

"Well," I said to Peter as we both sat stunned, trying to absorb the news. It was November 19th, and we had been in China for less than three months.

"I guess I need to start taking folic acid again."

I had taken it dutifully for three months before we had first started trying for a baby, and for six months after, but as month after month went by, there had seemed little point in continuing, and I had stopped. But his family had a history of spina bifida, and I was suddenly alarmed at the realization that I was probably already a good few weeks—seven, as it turned out—into what could only be called an unplanned pregnancy, and I had done nothing to prepare my body. Leaving nothing to the vagaries of Google Translate this time, I asked Peter to subtly enquire from a friendly senior colleague who would know about such things what the appropriate word was. He duly returned from work with another Post-it, with the Chinese for folic acid written down in both characters and pinyin, so that we could pronounce it.

So, for the second day running, we navigated our way through the falling snow and slippery ice to the same pharmacy and presented our treasured Post-it to the same female assistant. She put on her glasses and read it solemnly, and then her face lit up.

"Aaahhh!!" she cried in delight, grinning wildly as she pointed triumphantly to my stomach. *"Huái yùn! Huái yùn!!"*

The discovery of the pregnancy sent me into a period of turmoil and fears over the next few weeks. The "China adventure" was supposed to be *instead of* the "baby adventure." I was dazed and terrified, thousands of miles away from home in a country where I didn't speak the language and knew almost no one. This was exacerbated by not so much morning sickness as the unfortunate revelation that my baby apparently demanded that I eat every two hours, or else I would collapse. We decided to travel home to the UK for the Christmas holiday, but on the morning of the day that we were due to fly to Shanghai (there are no international flights out of Harbin, except to Vladivostok), I noticed some blood spotting in my underwear.

Thus far, I had seen no doctor at all. Our medical insurers seemed unsure even where Harbin was, and were certainly unable to locate any English-speaking doctors. Furthermore, I was still, by my calculations, in the danger period for an ectopic pregnancy, and I was about to undertake a four-hour flight followed by a 12-hour flight the next day, so I decided I should get checked out with an ultrasound.

As luck would have it, one of Peter's female colleagues had a cousin who worked at the local maternity hospital. In the UK, trying to exploit such an advantage to jump the queue would be viewed very negatively indeed, but in China the maxim, "It's not what you know, it's *who* you know" (referred to as *guang xi*) is the bedrock of all business and human transaction. Later that morning I found myself accompanied by Peter's colleague, Li Jia, and her cousin, being ushered through room after room of resigned-looking Chinese women sitting patiently in waiting rooms in their winter coats in the under-heated, less-than-clean hospital. After presenting my passport and handing over the ever-necessary wad of cash, I was shown, through a final packed waiting area, into a large consulting room where several patients were already having ultrasounds on two or three other beds, all set at angles from each other for some degree of privacy. Li Jia's cousin propelled me toward the vacant bed.

A female doctor barely glanced up at me. I was instructed, via Li Jia's halting translation, to lift my clothing just so, and then the doctor swiftly and expressionlessly applied the scanner to my flat belly. I tried to sit up to see the screen, which was positioned such that the doctor and those standing could see it, but the recumbent patient couldn't. My shoulders were gently but forcefully pushed back down onto the bed.

The problem, I found out later, was that in China it is illegal for medical practitioners to reveal the sex of an unborn child to the parents because of fears of infanticide caused by the one-child policy. This law doesn't apply to foreigners, and in cosmopolitan cities like Shanghai, foreign mothers attending expat clinics are routinely told the sex of their baby unless they request not to know. But in Harbin they clearly didn't know this and had possibly never dealt with a foreign patient before. Since the baby's sex is indistinguishable at that stage, it would hardly have mattered—but rules are rules, and they say no looking at the ultrasound screen. The doctor continued her investigation for a few minutes, then, without looking at me at all, she barked something in Chinese to my companions.

"She see baby," translated Li Jia, deadpan. "Baby okay." This was the eloquent and professional report from my first ever ultrasound.

My mature and serene response, such was my continuing state of disbelief about the whole thing, was to sit bolt upright, craning my neck to see the screen, and exclaim incredulously, "What? You mean there's really one there?"

I was pushed back again, almost violently this time, but after some lengthy discussion, the doctor was finally persuaded to give me a printout of the results. I received a single sheet of paper with a tiny ultrasound blob picture, and a terse report, which was translated for me later as follows:

Finding: uterus anterior, enlarged size. Gestational sac intrauterine, measure 5x30mm. Crown-rump length 36mm, fetal heart pulsation visible, fetal limb bud visible. Both ovaries normal size and shape. CDFI: fetal heart blood flow visible.

Conclusion: pregnant uterus.

Single fetus.

Live fetus (gestational age nine weeks).

It was happening to me. And it really wasn't funny.

Mirren Childs relocated from Harbin to Shanghai, where she lived for six years, working as an actress and backstage with three expat theater companies. She moved back to the UK at the start of 2015 and now lives with her son in Yorkshire, England. She is studying for a master's degree in theater.

CHAPTER 2

WHAT TO EXPECT WHEN YOU'RE EXPECTING IN MALAYSIA

Jackie Wilson
Nationality: United Kingdom
Birthed in: United Kingdom and Malaysia

Getting knocked up and moving abroad seemed to be serendipitously connected for me. Back in late summer 2012, I was working in the office of a large UK dairy company, my two-year-old daughter, Holly, in part-time day care, when I received a text message from my husband, Colin, asking me to call him urgently.

Once you become a mother, any ominous message with expressed urgency will induce a *"what's happened to my baby?!"* panic. So, despite being in a team meeting, I excused myself to take the call.

The call was my husband announcing his promotion. A promotion that just happened to be about 6,000 miles away in Malaysia. I shouted at him not to be ridiculous and returned to the meeting, relieved mostly that Holly was okay. Over the course of that evening it all started to sink in. Our thought processes went from of course we wouldn't go, to maybe we should go, to of course we are going to go.

I should also add that at some point during the evening, I took a pregnancy test, and it was positive. This was not a huge surprise given our recent activity had been proactive in the pursuit of such an outcome; however, the timing was crazy. You couldn't make it up.

I was knocked up, and we were moving abroad.

Up until this point in my life, I'd never really considered myself as someone with big travel aspirations. I loved the UK. I loved the changing of the seasons, I adored London and the good old British seaside, and I was really settled in our little cottage in the suburban town of Chertsey. I didn't feel like I needed to find myself. Gap year travels were never on my to-do list. I actually found people's travel stories really dull, I'm ashamed to confess.

All that said, I was by no means fearful. I have always stood by the philosophy of saying yes to new experiences—a character trait that has lead to snowboarding down mogul-infested black diamond runs, running marathons, and cycling 60 miles (97 km) with a team of psychiatric nurses. Generally, I am a yes kind of gal.

The other notable thing was how perfect the opportunity was for our circumstances. I had hit the spot in my marketing career where it was time to either write another annual plan for a brand of cheddar cheese or push for a promotion to the heady heights of more general management. I wasn't desperately excited about either of those options, the latter certainly looking unlikely in light of Baby Number Two.

The reason for my waning interest in cheese was writing. During my first year of maternity leave, I'd started to write for local magazines and entered a few short story competitions, winning the runner's up prize in one of them. I had started to realize that everything I was good at in the field of marketing was linked to writing. Life had been throwing clues at me for the past 10 years that the written word was my thing. Now, here I was being offered the chance to go somewhere where I wouldn't have to flog cheddar cheese in order for our family to remain housed. I could write, risk free, and for nothing but pleasure if I wanted.

Then there was the second pregnancy to consider. I had found my indoctrination into the world of parenthood the first time around to be something I can only describe as massive. To say I was not prepared for the impact a child would make on my life would be a bit of an understatement. There is a cliché that goes around the parents-to-be circuit along the lines of life never being the same. I just took that as of course it won't be the same, I'm going to have an excellent kid, and I'll just do all the stuff I do now, just when she's not being cute. I was utterly thrown by the reality of this task. Perhaps because I'm a Libra, the fact of my character is that I do love balance. I thrived on the doctrine of working hard and playing hard. I was all over the concept of delayed gratification. I wanted to earn my fun, but once earned I'd cash it in fully, leaving a no-credit balance.

Holly arrived and there was no balance whatsoever, and it hit me like a train. I was terrified and utterly out of my depth. My permanent state of high anxiety led to a ridiculously low milk supply, resulting in a night's stay in hospital on the fourth day and a panic switch to bottle feeding. The guilt of this lasted for several years, and I still have flashbacks. I rarely slept despite Holly sleeping better than any baby I had ever heard of. I just couldn't stop watching her.

No question, I was head over heels in love with my gorgeous little hair bear, while at the same time broken into tiny pieces of physically and emotionally exhausted mom flesh. I am pretty sure this wasn't postpartum depression, but it was most certainly postpartum something.

When I finally let go of the life I once knew, around the 10-month mark, I vowed that should we be blessed with another baby, I would not let myself get that broken again.

So the opportunity to have my second baby with three months to prepare for the birth in luxury, with the possibility of live-in maids, lactation consultants, doulas, the warmth of the sun, and nothing to think about but my babies made it a done deal.

Telling people about the decision brought about a myriad of responses. My dad looked terrified, asking questions that made it clear he thought we were going into the heart of a war zone. My mother-in-law was devastated at the prospect of her beloved granddaughter being taken away. My best friend simply stopped talking to me for a while. My boss, having just returned from a holiday to Kuala Lumpur, gushed at how I would love it, telling me that Tiffany's was like a corner shop there. People generally fell into a camp of envying us or concluding that we'd gone stark raving bonkers.

Many implied that Colin was putting his career first and that I was selling out and giving up on my career. It hurt a bit that the writing dream wasn't really taken seriously and that people didn't see the strength in my decision that I felt I'd shown. To me, the decision I made was far from selling out; to me it was the bravest thing I'd ever done. The casting vote in the decision-making process was mine entirely, and everything from that point onward felt like it was the right one.

Cut to late October, when my husband and I—and a growing bump—were seated in our lounge, partaking in a two-day cultural orientation course with a lady called Pam. Here we learned how pointing in Malaysia was rude, and that necklines, such as the one I happened to be wearing, would be deemed sexually aggressive and inappropriate. We were also shown a bell curve graph indicating five phases we would encounter as part of our expatriation.

These were:

1. The Honeymoon/Excitement Phase
2. The Shock/Grief Phase
3. The Adjustment Phase
4. Re-entry Issues
5. The Acceptance Phase

I couldn't get past the word "grief." That was an emotion I wasn't keen to invite into my beautiful baby-making world. We spent an unscheduled portion of the course on this point, basically while I forced Pam into confirming that of course it doesn't happen to everyone and certainly not to types with the strength of character that Team Wilson were clearly demonstrating.

Now it is December 29 and I'm 24 weeks pregnant, standing in our empty Chertsey house and sobbing like a baby as a giant container carrying 97% of our entire material world chugs off down the road bound for Malaysia—considerably slower than our own journey would take. As I chucked my soggy tissue at the space where the bin used to be, I consoled myself with the theory that it was likely I'd just experienced my grief phase, so from now on we'll just do Phases One and Five, thank you very much. The baby, now revealed to be of the male kind, kicked me reassuringly, and the adventure began.

Here's what happened.

1. The Honeymoon/Excitement Phase (Including a Birth)

I did indeed find this phase exciting and with honeymoon qualities. Okay, the first week was a little bit scary, including tears in a supermarket, a fair bit of heat-and-bump-generated sweating, and a lot of swearing at a seemingly unfocused satellite navigation system. But mostly, we all forgot our jetlag in gaping mouthed trances at what was to be our new life.

Malaysia for the virgin expatriate is a bit of a gift. For those seasoned world explorers arriving from the glossier bubbles of Singapore and Dubai it was less so, but for a working class girl from the UK suburbs, it was the Emerald City. There we were, guided like royalty into a world of privilege like we'd never known. I actually cried as a squad of relocation professionals escorted us to our spanking new expanse of a condo, 29 floors up with the Petronas Towers sparkling directly in front and an actual palace to the right. Everything seemed to be made from marble, the pools were the size of minor lakes—and there were two of them, flanked with Jacuzzis and cabanas and overlooked by a state-of-the-art gym.

From this almost literal ivory tower, the real Malaysia seemed equally charming. In contrast to our sparkling accommodation patrolled by uniformed guards, the surrounding area was gritty to say the least. As you left the beautifully landscaped orbit of the condo, the paths became increasingly bumpy, the caliber of traffic more dubious, and the smells more, shall we say, authentic. It took a while to understand that the aroma of vinegary, rotting vegetable peelings was actually that of a durian, South East Asia's proclaimed "King of Fruits." I've still never dared to try one.

From the social perspective, things were equally wondrous. Following a number of Google searches along the lines of "expat mom KL HELP ME!" I had managed to find no end of places to go and people to see.

While I'm neither particularly shy nor any kind of social butterfly, making friends in an expat community when pregnant and with a cute and chatty toddler was, on the surface, one of the easiest things I've ever done. Conversations were set up: Where are you from? How long are you here? When is your baby due? How old is your daughter? Are you in oil and gas? A 90-minute playgroup session could pass in the blink of an eye. Skimming *How to Win Friends and Influence People* on the plane, I made mental notes to smile a lot and to remember to ask people about themselves. I was flying! Look at me, pregnant global superwoman! On many occasions I couldn't believe my luck. Often I would bob with bump around our gently heated, luxury condo pool with my daughter playing happily beside me, wondering if it was all a dream.

On the bump front, on the fourth day, Adeline, a lovely lady from the orientation company, took me along to a private hospital called Pantai to take a look and meet some obstetricians whom I might choose to deliver my baby. Having had my daughter in a UK hospital with a midwife I'd never met before nor seen since, this seemed both decadent and delightful. The first doctor we met was Dr. Premitha Damodoran. She made me laugh, drew some hilarious diagrams of lady bits, and my search was over.

I saw Dr. Premitha every couple of weeks in increasing frequency up until the birth. Every appointment included a full scan. Given the fact that a normal pregnancy in the UK will be scanned twice, this also seemed insanely decadent and delightful.

Then came the big moment. During my 38-week appointment, Dr. Premitha had a quick look where the sun don't shine and declared me to be four cm dilated. I'd felt nothing more than a little bit fidgety. Given the fact that my daughter arrived after two hours and seven pushes, the doctor offered to break my water manually the very next day, thus avoiding the prospect of my baby being delivered by a taxi driver. I had been warned on the mommy circuit that it was common to be pressured into scheduled Cesareans to enable efficient scheduling and also to avoid births on dates that included numbers thought to be bad luck.

Having my water broken, however, felt like a fairly innocuous intervention, and to know, albeit with less than 24 hours' warning, when my boy would arrive seemed like a wise choice. The crazy Kuala Lumpur traffic, unpredictable driving styles, and rain-induced traffic jams were not absent considerations in this choice.

And so it happened. The whole hospital experience, once through the doors of the place, was incredibly similar to the UK, with the key difference being the swiping of our credit card and every sentence shared with us ending in "*Lah,*" the untranslatable but statutory ending of a sentence for Malaysians.

"You wan chips *lah*?"

"You English *lah*?

"You very fat *lah*!"

While I'd been told of hospitals resembling five-star hotels, the birthing "suite" where my magic happened was almost identical to that of St Peter's Hospital in Chertsey, UK. It was all reassuringly clinical. There was no fine art on the wall, no plush cushions, and if the bed linen was anywhere close to 400-count Egyptian cotton, then I was in no position to notice.

My water was broken. A couple of hours of pacing the room to my birthing playlist—that lazily resembled my running one—and it was time to push. This is where it all turned into a bit of a pantomime. A colorful posse of nurses flanking Dr. Premitha surrounded me, celebrating each contraction with a monotone and speedy chorus of "harder, harder, longer, longer, longer" followed by abrupt silence and a sigh. Somewhere around the fifth go, I sensed an element of boredom creeping in for them and gave it a big one. And there he was. Meet Benjamin Hamilton Wilson, 7 lb. on the nose with a full head of hair, just like his sister. The chorus line disappeared for some chicken rice and 100Plus (*lah*).

Despite having a doctor of your own choosing, getting scanned so regularly, and all the benefits of a private hospital, giving birth in Malaysia drew me to the conclusion that having a baby was 90% mother nature and 10% location. A melon-sized skull leaving through a grape-sized exit is going to smart a bit wherever you are. I loved my first anonymous midwife as much as I loved Dr. Premitha for delivering my babies and repairing me very neatly. I slept not a wink on either first night regardless of surroundings, frankly because I'd rather gaze on my babies. If I had to do it all over again and had a choice, I'd say I'd toss a coin with regard to home or away.

Somewhere around the 37th sleepless night, however, the honeymoon ended.

2. The Shock/Grief Phase

Despite all the psychological preparation with Pam for avoiding this, it did actually happen with the full force of her prediction. In retrospect, I think I was subject to the head-on collision of several factors, this phase of expatriation being only a small part of it.

Of course, the wow factor of a sparkly new sunny lifestyle had to normalize at some point. On top of this, I had to deal with the realities that come with a new baby coupled with the challenges of this making it two highly dependent mini humans I was charged to look after. All of this in a foreign land with no family and what were at that point promising but only very nascent friendships to lean on.

After baby Ben was born, we had a run of seven consecutive weeks of lovely guests, my mom, my husband's mom, and my two best buddies. We all existed in a bubble of newborn cuddliness.

Then they left and took my sanity with them. I wanted it and them back!

And here's where it got a bit dark in the sunshine. For the next six months, I existed in a stressful state of permanent high anxiety. I never seemed to stop sweating, and suddenly it was unbearable; Ben never seemed to stop crying. The look of desertion and resentment on Holly's face never seemed to leave. I had to allow 20 minutes on both ends of every journey just to allow my brain to process everything I needed to do, which wasn't even that much.

The shine on our new Asian lifestyle was also beginning to dull, which I guess was Pam's point. Everything that was novel and exciting was becoming our new normal. The smiley friendliness of Malaysians was becoming a little bit less heartwarming. The simple fact being that they would smile at you regardless of the situation, rendering the underlying sentiment a little bit uncertain.

"We no have—*lah*!"—smile!

"No can fix your broken phone, no *boleh*!"—smile!

"You no can play on see-saw *lah*"—smile!

For a British person, the smile accompanying bad and sometimes ridiculous news just came across as insincere and mocking. When a smile accompanies everything, how do you know when it's real?

Food shopping became the bane of my existence. This deserves a graphical model in itself. Before Ben was born, the acquisition of groceries was an exciting challenge, bringing on a kind of hunter-gatherer mode that was quite rewarding. Hopping from supermarket to supermarket was interesting and went someway to filling the days.

With a baby, food shopping was reduced back to the functional, necessary task it should be. At this stage in the game, I had not yet properly adapted to family catering using local ingredients. Imported goods were liable to simply run out without warning, creating a cycle of jungle drums amongst expats, who would then bulk buy whatever they could find, exacerbating the problem further. Facebook post in the group "Expat Moms": "The Village Grocer in Bangsar Village has Quorn sausages!" Approximately 95 minutes later it wouldn't. Expat Angie from Bangsar South would, however, have a freezer full.

I once wrote out a process flow of all the stages in bundling my two kids into the car to go to a supermarket, and there were 32 steps. From clipping a baby seat onto the travel system to unclipping it, securing it with a seatbelt to pacifying my toddler with a snack or toy while securing the baby. All while being a hyper-anxious new mom in car parks as hot as furnaces on very little sleep in a foreign land. How could I ever have thought this was a good idea?

Around this time, Tesco, the UK's most popular supermarket at the time, was launching an online delivery service. This could've been the answer to my prayers. Unfortunately though, it was, like most other food supply options, only a partial solution. I concluded that Tesco's reason for being a popular supermarket was its ability to serve the mass market. British expats in Malaysia were not the mass market, and hence their requirements did not make a lucrative inventory. Teething problems of the new service meant a high probability of unwanted substitutions and sometimes for the delivery just not to arrive. Not a great situation for a mom down to her last three diapers.

Days had become a simple process of surviving with both children fed and intact until the time Daddy returned from work. Daddy, who was previously basking in the glory of the life he had provided for his family, was suddenly thrust into this state of guilt for wrenching his family from the warm bosom of the extended family who could've made this all better.

"We can go home if you want, Princess, you just have to say."
"Okay, can we?"
"No, I can do this."
"I want to go home."
"It's okay, today was quite good."
"I hate you!"

The irony of this time was that I was in a situation where huge amounts of help were available, accessible, and truly normal for expats and the wealthier locals. The most common situation was to have a Filipino or Indonesian live-in maid. The cost of this was ridiculous, equating to a monthly wage similar to what I used to get in a day for marketing cheddar cheese. You would see the helpers walking loops around the swimming pools with tiny babies in strollers. They would do nursery drop-offs. They would cart groceries up the hill. All this while polishing the condo granite to shine you never thought possible.

The trouble is, for a first-time expat, the idea of full-time or live-in help seems just a little bit absurd. We've all seen the movie *The Help* and smugly chastised the seemingly ridiculous and pompous characters. Then, as Brits, we have our well-mannered politeness to deal with on top of all this. How do we let a stranger into our lives to wash our pants, cuddle our new babies, and see us sometimes weep with despair? I went on a bit of a journey with this.

On arrival in Kuala Lumpur, we used an agency that supplied two Indonesian ladies to come to the condo every Wednesday to blitz it. I reveled, like many others in my abstention at first. "Oh no, I've not gotten a helper [chuckle], I'm not one of 'those' mothers spending their life in a beauty salon or on the tennis court, oh no! I am raising my own kids [smug smile]."

Shortly after Ben's arrival and the departure of our guests, I started to realize that approaching this like a martyr was actually going to break me. Without a helper, there would be no respite whatsoever. My mother-in-law was not going to pop around. My sister and her two offspring would never visit to provide a distraction for my toddler while we mommies discussed baby poo scenarios. I impressed no one with my dogged determination to refuse more help. I just became bedraggled and broken.

When my husband ran out of ironed shirts and I was retrieving soiled muslin cloths from the laundry basket, I bit the bullet and graduated to a part-time helper, a lovely Indonesian lady called Nurul, who would come for three mornings a week. She would take care of cleaning and laundry. I would focus on childcare and food provision. About six months later, I wanted a few more hours that Nurul couldn't do, so I switched to a Filipino lady called Anne who I still have now as I am writing this.

Now, over two years on, I've seen how a well-chosen helper can become a well-treated and well-loved extension of the expat family. The trouble is, I just don't really need it anymore. The irony of my helper journey is that I reconciled the logic of having more help far too late. The moms I know who had full-time help over their newborn months were the most content. If I judged them harshly, then the only person having a negative experience there was myself.

And so the chain of events that lead to my period of despair will never happen again. I won't be having any more babies, and I will never be a "newbie" expat again, so I can't learn from this experience.

What I would tell my younger self or someone embarking on this, however, would be this: What goes up must come down—be ready. Accept help—it's actually the strong thing to do, and more than anything, know that what goes down will also come back up again.

3. The Adjustment Phase

This is the part of my knocked-up-abroad life of which I am most proud. When Ben was to six months old, I had started to rebuild my broken self, and the dust was settling on a life that I had earned rather than been gifted. I'd started to run again; I was writing columns in magazines; Ben was in a nice routine. I was still sweating a lot, but I was coping. I was becoming more resilient, more resourceful and was starting to feel like I could cope with anything.

The biggest turning point was our attendance at the Great British Ball 2013, our first big night out since arriving in Kuala Lumpur. I was still carrying an extra dress size of baby weight but managed to borrow an amazing dress. I bought some sparkly disco shoes and had my hair and nails done. Okay, somewhere around 10 p.m. I leaned over and immersed my left boob in the chocolate pudding, but it created a laugh and a memory—the only downside was the stain on my friend's dress. Both babies also remained asleep for the babysitter, and I made it to midnight without turning into a pumpkin.

We ate, we danced, and we remembered who we were. I came back to life that night. I'd begun to trust Pam's graph, and I knew things were going to be okay.

4. Re-entry Issues

This phase was billed as the one where an expat would return for home leave or home permanently and feel resentment at not being received as traveling heroes.

So far, we've only done the fleeting and temporary leave part of this and for that we found no issues. We weren't expecting a hero's welcome, just some crumpets and chocolate. Ben was still only eight months old when we first went back to the UK, and our lives still revolved around him. It was Christmas, and we had a new baby that most people had never seen and a little girl that left the country as a squidgy toddler. We were welcome, heroes or not.

I imagine a final and permanent re-entry will be a bit tougher, but I'd like to think I have the kind of friends and family who would tell me to shut up and wind my neck in if I developed any Robinson Crusoe allusions. For my son Ben, who was born and so far has only lived in Malaysia, his re-entry is really an expatriation. I'll just keep an eye out for his Shock/Grief in Phase Two.

5. The Acceptance Phase

And now, here we are well into our third year of this crazy caper. Holly is about to start big school, Ben nursery. I have started to earn money for writing, and it feels like I am living a dream; whether it's *THE* dream or not doesn't matter—it's mine, and I love it.

There are still some days when Malaysian customer service will make me want to eat my own head (*lah!*). There are times when a canceled play date will make me feel temporarily alone in this world, and there are still times when I crave a crumpet and a run with a chilly breeze, but that's not expatriation—that's just life being life. I've felt lonely in the UK, and I expect one day I'll crave *nasi lemak* and *roti canai* for breakfast when faced with marmite on toast.

And that's my journey so far.

I was knocked up abroad. Now I'm a mother of two abroad. I've been knocked up in my home country, and I've been a mother of one there. The fact is, motherhood, irrelevant of location, is a huge deal! It takes your life as you knew it, smashes that to smithereens and lets you rebuild it into something even more amazing wherever and whoever you are. The pain of childbirth is universal. Babies don't sleep through the night wherever you are. A sick child will break your heart in a cold climate or a hot one. Having my babies was the hardest, yet most rewarding and wonderful thing I've ever done. Doing it abroad simply added an intense filter to it. The highs were higher, and the lows were a bigger drop.

Back on that fateful day in 2012, I'm not going to lie, I agreed to come to Malaysia because I thought it would make things easier, while giving my family and me an amazing adventure. Therein lies the truth of my experience. It made a certain period of my experience so very much harder, which made coming back from it so much more rewarding. I am so proud of myself for what I have achieved. I made Malaysia a beloved home with a hoard of friends after a period of blaming it for my potential downfall. I feel stronger than I ever have and like I can conquer anything.

And so to Pam, I'd say, "Babe, your graph was spot on, but the necklines and pointing? Really?"

Jackie Wilson was born in the UK and lived there without feeling amiss for 40 years before expatriating to Kuala Lumpur. She worked for nearly 20 years in marketing for classic UK food brands, including Twinings, Kingsmill Bread, and Cathedral City Cheddar Cheese, but always held tight to a dream of becoming a writer. The heavens seemed to align, and here, alongside numerous magazine articles, blog entries, web content, and a work-in-progress novel is evidence of a dream coming true.

CHAPTER 3

SHUFFLE, SHUFFLE, DUDE

Lana M. Ankarcrona
Nationality: USA
Knocked up in: Sweden

While enjoying a pleasant family trip on the California coast, I decided to be adventurous and bodyboard my five-month-pregnant self way out in the ocean. Read: the Pacific Ocean, dwelling place of terrifying Jaws-type sharks and other dangerous aquatic fauna. My husband and I were having a grand old time until I was met with a clamping sting as I landed heavily on my right foot. Being the mild, nondramatic person that I am, I instantly thought, *shark bite!* and started splashing and flailing toward the shore, trailing blood and surely with a herd of sharks in tow.

This was actually a valuable experience because we soon learned from my brother-in-law's very experienced surfer brother Zach, who happened to be on hand to examine my profusely bleeding foot, that it wasn't a shark bite at all. In fact, it was the result of an altercation with a stingray. He went on to explain that there is a special sort of gait one must adopt when ocean-walking (as if there was any thought in my mind of ever again taking a dip in an open body of water). This gait is referred to as the "shuffle." One must "shuffle, shuffle, dude" while walking through the sand, kicking it up and alerting the stingray that you are coming so they will presumably swim away. Based on my recently acquired expert experience, this is a farce and all stingrays have malicious intent, but I nodded wisely while receiving this information and was quickly shuttled home at breakneck speeds by my terrified husband.

Upon our return to the house at which we were staying, my brother-in-law's father Greg, also very experienced and wizened in the ways of terrible stingray creatures, took one knowing look and prepared a large bucket full of scalding water that I was supposed to stick my foot in to help draw out whatever vicious poisons might be in the wound. The next three hours were a blur as I slipped in and out of consciousness and teetered on the brink of certain death.

The only thing I can remember is Greg puttering around the house and muttering bemusedly, "Ya gotta shuffle, shuffle, dude."

Miraculously, I survived, although my foot has yet to regain full feeling along the left side and remains ever-so-slightly larger than the other. But I feel like I got off easy, all things considered. Stingrays are vicious, vindictive creatures. Don't let that adorable smile on their faces convince you of anything less.

Never forget: "Shuffle, shuffle, dude."

That traumatic, painful learning experience is how I adopted this mantra and have since applied this to all aspects of my life. Essentially, don't be afraid to kick up some dust while you move toward your ultimate goal, so it knows you're coming. Wouldn't want to sneak up on life and get a sucker punch to the face, now would you?

Which brings me to where I am at this very moment: aching back and twitchy legs, a sleep issue that I'm really trying not to identify as insomnia, and eight months pregnant. But, let's go back to the beginning so we're all on the same page...

A group of friends and I packed up our bags and trekked all the way from Bakersfield to Stockton, quite possibly the two most illustrious towns in California. Our pickup truck was packed to the limit, and my friend and I were stuffed up in the bucket seats in the back. Upon our arrival to Stockton, we did what any road-weary travelers would do: locate the nearest Starbucks for Wi-Fi, caffeine, and a clean bathroom. Don't judge; you know exactly what I'm talking about. Upon our arrival, we placed our order, and my other friend saw a man and exclaimed, "Oh my God, I know that guy! He's from Switzerland or someplace weird like that!"

She went on to explain how they had been introduced through mutual friends at another conference, and that he was really good at guitar, and so on (I wasn't paying much attention as there were more pressing matters at hand, like caffeine.) We introduced ourselves and raced through the pleasantries:

"Hi, my name is…"

"How's it going?"

"What's your name? One more time?"

"Okay…well, nice to meet you!"

And then we retrieved our drinks and left. As we were leaving, I asked my friend about the handsome "Swiss or someplace weird like that" dude:

"Okay, so what did he say his name was?"

"Daniel something…*crunch*"

"Daniel Crunch?!"

"What?! No, I almost ran into the curb. Thus, the *crunch.*"

And this is how Daniel became forever dubbed Daniel Crunch. The funniest part is that he didn't really understand the origins of his nickname until years later, despite several retellings of the story…Bless his heart.

Later on during the conference, Daniel and I struck up another conversation at the punch bowl, exchanged numbers, and our budding romance began. Over the next four years Daniel and I experienced a split, dated other people, and then we found our way back together again. During this time our paths kept crossing through our shared love of music as we competed in a national music competition together, worked together in church music ministries, and helped to organize a youth camp when I visited Sweden for three months during the summer of 2009.

It was during this summer that I realized I just couldn't deny it anymore—we had formed an inseparable bond; this was happening. Although it would mean uprooting my life and starting over, changing the dynamic of all of my friendships and family connections, and demand hours of paperwork and cause general inconvenience sorting through my entire life to that point, my usual pragmatism had no place in my decision *whatsoever.*

And I have never, ever looked back

This man has certainly worked his wily magic ways, because over the course of our 10 years together I do believe he has found a romantic corner hidden neatly away in the recesses of my heart. What began as a six-month fling with a strange Swedish boy (he wasn't from Switzerland at all!) turned into an additional couple of years of bargaining with myself and God and anything/anyone I thought could lend some insight, and imagining all the different reasons it would never work. This blossomed into a headlong tumble into what would later become one in a succession of many of the best decisions I have made in my life to this point.

The first few years of our marriage were a whirlwind. Adjusting to a new country and culture that is very effective at masquerading as "not very different" from my own was a slap in the face that I eventually recovered from (or not, depending on the day), and it took me the better part of three years to land. Stumbling from one cultural faux pas to the next, there were moments where I had to pause and just laugh at myself. To do anything else would have resulted in the most monumental pity party this world has ever known.

One of the biggest differences I noticed right away was the delicate art of making a friend. Making a Swedish friend involves a complicated process of casual encounters that lead to coffee dates that lead to dinners/lunches that lead to invitations home/elsewhere that eventually lead to a friendship. This formula is not to be deviated from in any way unless you happen to share a workplace or mutual friend, and in these cases, proceed with extreme caution. Do not pass go. Do not collect 200 dollars. You should approach a new acquaintance in Sweden as you would approach a skittish horse with a carrot, treating your new "friend" as a potential romantic interest. There's really no better way to describe it.

If you ever plan on visiting Sweden, you should really take this advice to heart, as it is hard won and backed by years of experience. I have puzzled out this special formula after a series of failed American-style attempts at connection. The results of which could best be characterized as an actual response I received after jumping the gun on someone, "Let's keep it casual..." as she backed away from me onto her bus home after what I had thought was a great girls' movie night at my place. You'd have thought I had just propositioned her right there in the street. Maybe I should have? Swedes are statistically much more open to casual sex on the first date than making a new friend at a coffee house. I won't even touch that logic. Having said all this, if you actually manage to break into these tightly knit social circles in Sweden, many of which have been in place since *gymnasium* (Swedish high school), you will have won yourself a friend for life. And I really mean for life. Your average Swede will prefer to maintain a handful of close friends rather than a large group of acquaintances. Once the connection has been made, you're golden. This makes the painstaking friend-making process worth it, somehow. I have heard it said that Swedish people make terrible strangers but amazing friends. I could not have put it better myself.

Shuffle, shuffle, dude.

Life went on, as it invariably does, and I began putting down roots in Sweden. I talked my way into a job as a barista at Espresso House, Sweden's answer to Starbucks, in addition to enrolling myself to *Svenska för invandrare* (Swedish for immigrants) courses, and began working on my Swedish. I sort of hit the ground limping at Espresso House with the basic Swedish I had picked up to that point, so I relied heavily on gesturing, facial cues, and visual aids. You would be amazed at how much can be communicated via body gestures as opposed to actual speech. I did get increasingly adventurous, however, and was popping off my limited Swedish at every opportunity. My old coworkers and I still laugh about the time I offered a customer a *sug*. While I was innocently spreading my fledgling Swedish wings and was trying to offer him a straw (*sugrör*), I was in actuality offering him a blowjob. At least I made him smile.

Around two years later I landed myself an administrative position with an international English school in Stockholm. This meant I now had a reliable salary, 25 days of paid vacation, a solid 8 a.m. to 4 p.m. schedule, and most importantly, the eligibility to go on the legendary year-long *föräldraledighet* (parental leave) without putting us in the poor house. I had officially landed on Planet Adult, which meant we could finally begin considering adding another person to our little family of two.

After about two years of feeling the baby itch, it seemed like perfect timing once my husband was on board during Christmas of 2014, but as soon as he said those words (you know, the succinct man-words that are of the baby-having variety) my insides went flippy, and I suddenly decided that I was not, in fact, ready to start a family. It was the farthest thing from my current reality and was not up for discussion. I mean, I'm living away from my family, my mother, friends, and support system, have not lived here in Sweden quite long enough, need more time under my belt at work, I haven't reached my goal weight yet, "Aren't there places to which we want to travel first?" and on and on and on.

Yes, I know. My husband is a saint.

But two months later, on Valentine's Day, Daniel's grandmother passed away. It was a beautiful, bittersweet passing, a lot of family sing-alongs, reunions, and looking back on sunnier days, which is extra special considering the sun never shines in Sweden during February. It's interesting how death can force you to face yourself. Suddenly all the excuses that seemed valid at the time just sort of fall away. Those things on which you build your entire foundation just sort of crumble, and you're left staring your bull straight in the face. While it felt strangely self-absorbed at the time to think of starting a family, looking back, I've come to realize that the distance between experiencing death and creating new life is not all that far. It was during this time that we both felt like we had the proverbial green light.

They said it would take several months at least. They were wrong. One month later we discovered we were pregnant. What!? *Shuffle, shuffle, dude.*

Att väntar barn (to await a child) in Sweden has been a most interesting experience, in that it was absolutely nothing like what I had been expecting at all. Singular. And heavy on the "waiting" part. To begin with, I have not seen an obstetrician or a gynecologist in the entirety of my pregnancy to this point. The Swedish medical system prefers to take things as naturally as possible, which means seeing a *barnmorska* (midwife) for all of your checkups all the way through to delivery. If my delivery is a healthy one with no complications, I might not see a doctor at all. I'm still not sure how I feel about that. I have always had a healthy respect for the American medical system, and the prospect of only seeing a midwife for my entire pregnancy initially felt a bit granola for my taste. But I am also of the lukewarm Earth Mother/half-hearted yoga practicing variety, so I quickly warmed up to the idea and congratulated myself on being so open-minded.

Unfortunately, my local midwife wasn't really interested in seeing me until my eighth week, but I came to terms with this because that meant I had plenty of time to read up on the entire pregnancy online. I was thoroughly informed for my first check-up. One could say a little too informed? My level of concern regarding several topics seriously outweighed my midwife's concern, which was simultaneously comforting and deeply disturbing. I can drink coffee? Some sushi is okay? Can I pat my head and rub my stomach at the same time? Wait, what's that? I'm not seeing you again for another couple of months? Hmmm. Can I get a second opinion?

Leaving the midwife's office, my husband and I were puzzled, but mostly elated at the new journey we would be taking together. The next few months were fairly uneventful, aside from an ill-timed (but at some moments, wonderful) trip to Budapest and a four-day sailing trip in my 13th week. All I can say about four-day sailing trips at 13 weeks pregnant is: **Not recommended**.

I was keeping my pregnancy a secret from basically everyone, apart from family and two of my colleagues at work. This was torture, but later I discovered it to be quite a good thing because the second the world hears of your pregnancy, you are Pregnant. All conversations and glances and advice and thoughts involving you are Pregnant. I came to realize that I was lucky to have a good five months or so of being Just Lana. Once that belly popped out, as well as the news, I became Pregnant Lana. This has been great fun, to be honest, but I can only imagine if we had broken the news earlier...I will just say from my experience, pregnancy became a bit longer once the news was out. All the extra talking and thinking about it somehow expands the wait time by four months. I don't quite know how that works out scientifically, but trust me. It's a fact.

Upon our return to Sweden from the stingray incident, I had three things to which I was looking forward: my 28th birthday, my first day back at work after the long vacation, and my third midwife appointment. Yes, you read that right. In my sixth month of pregnancy, I had seen a midwife all of two times and had exactly one scan. So I was really selling myself the "awaiting child" line to avoid thinking of all the worst case scenarios and horrible things that might have cropped up between my second midwife appointment and now. Plus, we can't forget my poor stung foot that was probably developing some sort of gangrene.

This midwife appointment was different than the others because my midwife was on vacation (welcome to Sweden). I had to meet with a different midwife who shall remain unnamed but permanently affixed to the top of my personal list of most hated people in the world. Before I go on, I should remind the reader that I am American and do not resemble anything close to the long, lean, Nordic physique you see strutting the streets of Stockholm. I have always been more of the curvy variety, and the way my body has responded to this pregnancy was no exception. After a very basic and, some (me) would say, cold rundown of my progress to this point, she instructed me to step on the scale to update my record. My weight had not been an issue with my primary midwife to this point in all of the two meetings I had had with her, so I stepped confidently on, assured of the fact that my baby had been growing along and my bump along with it. I was glowing. I was radiant. I was health embodied.

Boy, was I wrong.

There's a secret, lesser-known instructional book, *The Midwife's Book for Meanies* (please note: this book does not actually exist) that this particular midwife must have gained most of her knowledge from, because she really let it rip. In addition to really stressing the horror of the 9 kg (just shy of 20 lb.) I had gained to this point, she launched into a riveting monologue educating me on portion control, avoiding sweets, and recommending most of my nutritional intake to be derived from air. My claims on being fairly active with walking and whatnot didn't do much to appease her, as she practically chortled with mirth before launching into a "calories in, calories out" speech and how much more important it was to eat air rather than go for a walk.

Like I mentioned before: *Enemy of the State Numero Uno.*

After much nodding and inner-cheek biting, Daniel and I exited the office with whatever shreds of dignity I had left to muster, and I did what any reasonable, emotionally adjusted pregnant woman would do in this situation: I allowed myself to descend into the depths of despair and grabbed my phone for an epic texting frenzy with my mother and aunt (we have a special texting thread devoted to just this sort of therapy), during which they assured me that, "Yes, 19 lb. is a *very* reasonable amount of weight gain," and, "Of course, this woman is off her rocker and clearly an unhappy person," and all the other reassuring, and a bit mean-spirited, things that you need to hear to bring your spirits up.

I have since recovered and returned to my earlier state of Healthy Glowing Pregnancy Goddess, with momentary carb-loading glitches and wallowing in emotional pits of self-doubt, but I have heard from others that these are totally normal occurrences. I have since had several visits with my primary midwife, and she has taken my weight one or two times without batting an eye. She is now affectionately referred to as Angelic Fairy Godmother.

Another very Swedish experience is the *profylaxkurs* (birthing class). We recently completed ours in English, which was an amazing and humbling experience all rolled into one. Daniel and I are used to wowing bystanders with our "How We Met" story, but during the first session of this class it became clear the other couples were actor stand-in types that had been handpicked to put our story to shame. Amber and Henrik, (may or may not be their actual names) from South Africa and Germany respectively, met while on a goodwill trip to save whales in Antarctica. Noriko from Japan and Johan from Finland met while on a mission with the UN somewhere in the Middle East. Us?

"Ummm…we met at Starbucks?"

I know, right? Lame. Trust me, our full-length story in all of its glory would awe and inspire you to no end, but no way does it measure up to UN missions or whale-saving trips in Antarctica. These couples had to be imposters strategically planted to make us feel extremely ordinary. And the whale-savers were vegan to boot. Daniel decided we couldn't be friends based on this fact alone. As if they would really have time for us in the middle of their humanitarian efforts.

Disclaimer: The two other couples in the group with us were all actually quite lovely, and I look forward to hearing some good baby news from them any day now.

At the conclusion of this class, however, we found ourselves able to somehow rise above the obvious universal peer pressure and felt possessed of great knowledge and information. We've got a little folder with papers in it and everything. We are going to rock this delivery. We are thoroughly prepared and glowing with contentment and benevolence. What's that? Oh, yes, this is our first child. And?

Picking a birthing center in Stockholm has been an experience all to itself. Each one purports itself as the coziest, smartest, most welcoming and modern facility—one, in particular, offering a corner bathtub, a post-delivery congratulatory meal complete with candles and the Swedish flag, and a two-night stay with full medical and breastfeeding support from the on-site staff. And all of this for only 100 Swedish kronor a day (roughly $12). And did I forget to mention that all of my midwife visits and tests are free (thanks to the taxes I pay), and the time off work required to make it to those visits and tests is entirely paid. *Shuffle, shuffle, dude.*

I will never forget the moment of silent reverence that followed the answer to a question another international couple posed during an English tour of a birthing center. The father had asked about insurance and how to go about it, and how much a C-section would cost if it were deemed necessary. The nurse replied in somewhat of a confused manner, "Well, the delivery is free...and that includes the C-section if it is needed."

Compare all of this with my very American idea of birth to this point in my life: a long, brightly lit white corridor down which I am being wheeled, screaming my head off. A doctor comes in to check me in intervals and asks me to rate my pain using frowny or smiley faces. After delivering my child, we are presented with a bill for thousands of dollars and invited to kindly leave the hospital at our earliest convenience (and not to forget to use the wheelchair on the way out).

As I sit here in my 32nd week of pregnancy and look forward to the life-changing event that is ahead of me. I couldn't think of a better place to birth our first child. Sure, there will be family and friends missing from the scene, but the rest of the situation is looking pretty darn streamlined.

However, as one friend ever-so-gently reminded me a week ago, that baby is coming out one way or the other, regardless of the quality of healthcare I have access to and how many classes I have taken or the type of breathing I utilize to get me through each contraction. This is a process that has been enacted countless times before by women all over the world. More specifically all the amazing and strong women in this book, and at the end of each unique story, the same thing has happened: A child has been born.

Our bodies, as well as the baby, know exactly what needs to be done, and does it at the exact moment it needs to happen. This, apart from all the information made available to slightly spazzy expectant mothers such as myself, is most comforting. I can mentally prepare myself as much as I possibly can, but at the end of the day, my body and my baby will find the groove and get it done. And if my life story to this point has taught me anything, it is that life has a way of working everything out on its own, somehow.

Whether I am ready for it or not, it is coming at me at real-time speed, and I can choose either to fight it or kick up some dust as I figure out how to continue moving toward the goal. I just have to remind myself of the sage advice given to me after my near-death experience on the Pacific Coast...

Shuffle, shuffle, dude.

Lana Ankarcrona is an American who has left sunny California for the cold, harsh Nordics. She is a lazy linguist and avid reader of historical fiction. She has become quite fond of Swedish pastries but will never accept marzipan or licorice as actual food items. She makes her home with her Swedish/American husband in Stockholm, Sweden. She tries to document her life in Sweden on her blog "In My Honest Opinion" at http://lanaanka.wordpress.com.

CHAPTER 4

TOO MUCH ADVENTURE IN THE AMAZON

Lisa Ferland
Nationality: USA
Knocked up in: Ecuador

"Thanks for coming in today. Where are you going on your trip?" the travel nurse asked as I sat down with a folder of papers in my lap.

I had diligently printed off all of the requisite forms from the US Centers for Disease Control and Prevention advising me on the travel vaccinations I would need before entering the tropical rainforests for my upcoming adventure with my husband.

"Ecuador. We are going to fly into the capital, Quito, then take a bus into the rainforest where we will stay in a thatched roof hut for a few days, and then back out into the mountains to some beautiful volcanic hot springs," I told her excitedly.

The nurse clacked away on her keyboard and brought up all of the information on her screen.

"It looks like you'll need shots for hepatitis A, typhoid, and yellow fever. The map shows that you'll be staying in a yellow fever endemic area so you'll definitely need that one. You'll also need to take some malaria pills with you. Hang on a second while I'll go get everything."

The nurse left me alone in her tiny office to gaze pointlessly at the various travel posters she had tacked up on the walls. Pictures of a couple under Jamaica's famously Caribbean Dunn's River Falls, a family on safari somewhere in Africa, and a standard picture of a needle to remind me that these vaccinations were going to hurt.

The nurse returned with a tray of needles and started jabbing me one at a time in my left, non-dominant arm.

As she held the last needle poised over my skin, ready to jab, she asked me almost offhandedly, "Oh, by the way, are you by any chance pregnant?"

Her question made me pause. My husband and I had recently made the conscious decision to start trying for a baby. That discussion had only happened about three weeks ago—or was it four weeks ago? I couldn't remember, but surely we weren't pregnant yet. It was too soon for that, right?

"Well, we just started trying, but I haven't had my period so...perhaps? I really don't know," I replied.

She set down her needle and proceeded to ask me questions to which I had no answers. When had we started trying? What was the date of my last menstrual cycle? When was my next period expected? I didn't know the answers to any of her questions, and she seemed greatly dissatisfied with the ignorance I had of my own body and baby-making activities. I wasn't charting or logging our activities into any pregnancy app on my phone; we were just having fun. She was not comfortable sending me into the jungle without adequate protection against yellow fever, but vaccinating a pregnant woman was shown to result in disastrous birth defects.

"Call me when your period comes, and I will vaccinate you as quickly as possible. Here's my number." She sent me out the door with a sore arm and a bruised ego.

One week later, I still had no period, but every home pregnancy test (all three of them) yielded negative results. Was I pregnant or not? Ever the diligent nurse, she did not trust the negative home pregnancy test results without the appearance of a period. I returned to her office for a blood test to rule out pregnancy before she would consent to administering the final vaccination.

The next day, I received a phone call from the travel nurse, "Lisa, umm, I have never, in my entire career as a nurse had the pleasure of giving this news, but you are pregnant!"

I was four weeks pregnant with our first child—apparently too early for those home pregnancy tests to detect. One week later, I donned all of my mosquito repellent–enforced jungle gear and headed into the rainforest of Ecuador, prepared, or so we thought, for an adventure.

Flying in between the mountaintops of the highest capital city in the world, Quito, was a harrowing experience for our first trip to South America. The view from the passenger's window transitioned from a thick cloud layer to the appearance of mountains so close you could almost reach out and touch them. The city's buildings seemingly materialized out of the thin air, and the plane had to make a series of abrupt turns and a rapid descent to make a precise landing at the small airport. Even seasoned travelers hail this airport as one of the most terrifying in the world due to its mountainous surroundings, short runway, and low visibility with the ever-present cloud layer. Quito, at 9,350 feet (2,850 meters) above sea level, is at a higher elevation than some of the mountains I hiked in the Adirondacks during my college years. The air is thin, and some people experience altitude sickness immediately upon arrival.

We grabbed our backpacks and hopped on a bus to take us on dirt-packed roads that form a narrow ledge around the sides of the numerous mountains that act as huge barriers across the Ecuadorian landscape. You can't go over them, and you can't go through them, so you must drive around them. I couldn't enjoy the view on the bus ride as not only did the constant switchbacks make me feel nauseous but the precipitous drop-off on the side of the road made me think that at any moment, our driver could sneeze and our bus would veer off the cliff into the abyss below. The bus cabin filled with the smell of burning brakes as they were constantly being applied during the winding descent down the mountainside. I prayed, and I am not usually the praying type, that the brakes would not give way until our trip was complete. I had asked for an adventure, but this was more than I had bargained for, and we were still on our first day.

Somehow, I'm not sure how, but our driver's attention did not wander during the five-hour journey, and we arrived at a rural bus depot, if you can even call it that. It was a large dirt parking lot with many pickup trucks zooming around and groups of Ecuadorians waiting for their buses. We were the only people to get off at that stop, and we had no idea what to do next. There were no telephones to let our rainforest "resort" know that we had arrived, and cellphone service was out of the question. We were in the rainforest. I sat down with our bags as my husband set off to try his broken Spanish with the locals to find out where we should go, if anywhere.

A pickup truck drove up and stopped right in front of us. Being the only non-Ecuadorian people there, I suppose we stood out a bit, and it was obvious that we were American tourists in town. The local Ecuadorians were all about six inches shorter than I was, with dark features and dark hair. We were typically outfitted for the rainforest in our REI rainproof, SPF-50, and DEET-reinforced cargo pants, as most tourists are. More than likely, we looked ridiculous to the locals who donned T-shirts with 1980s pop cultural icons like Madonna and Michael Jackson—most likely not clothing dunked in mosquito repellant. A man jumped out of a truck, said nothing to us but grabbed our bags, and waved for us to climb into the bed of the truck. We clambered in and hoped that we weren't being kidnapped and held for ransom at a later date—something my in-laws had warned us of when we mentioned we were going to Ecuador. Among other things, it would be really embarrassing if my in-laws were right about their warning after we brushed them off as being unnecessarily cautious.

The truck dropped us off at our very authentic, Ecuadorian rainforest jungle hut resort where we were instructed to never, under any circumstances, drink the water from the sink or shower. The local water was from the river and was full of numerous amoebas and microbes that would result in major gastrointestinal distress if ingested. We were provided two glass jugs of water that we would need to ration throughout the day. *This is perfect*, I thought sarcastically. I had almost forgotten that my body was growing a new cluster of cells and that I was in the very fragile state of possible miscarriage as I was only five weeks pregnant. The unfamiliar surroundings were enough to take my mind off everything except pure survival.

Our thatched-roof hut had screened windows for walls that allowed for a beautiful 360-degree view of the lush rainforest. My husband heard a squeaking noise and discovered that we had bats in our hut. Properly terrified of rabies from an errant bat scratch or bite, we informed the resort staff about the bats' presence. I'm pretty sure they rolled their eyes at us as if to silently thinking, *We cannot possibly rid this jungle of all of its wildlife. Why did you come here, again?* Outside of our hut we saw leaf-cutter ants, tarantulas, snakes, pitcher plants, and every type of insect you can imagine. As a biologist, I was fascinated by the biodiversity that I was witnessing, but as a newly pregnant woman, there seemed to be an unending array of venomous or poisonous flora and fauna around every corner. The nearest medical facility was a five-hour bus ride back through the mountains, so it wasn't exactly the best place for a medical emergency.

One night, there was a massive rainstorm (we were in the rainforest, after all), and those screened walls did nothing, understandably, to prevent the rain from whipping through our hut. The wind was so turbulent that our sheer curtains were flying perpendicular to our bed as illuminated by the sporadic lightning streaking through the dark night. As the rain soaked my face and the thunder boomed around us, I pulled the covers over my head and prayed that the falling trees we heard crashing around us wouldn't land on us as we slept. When we awoke it looked as if a hurricane had torn through the forest. Palm leaves were scattered everywhere and a tall palm tree had crashed through the porch of the hut next door.

The remainder of our trip comprised the most stressful 10 days I have possibly ever experienced. Our itinerary was designed before we discovered I was pregnant, and things that had seemed like a fun experience back in the US seemed unnecessarily dangerous now that we were in Ecuador. We were taken by a local guide through the rainforest, and apparently he wanted to give us an authentic, native experience. We sampled a drink made from the masticated leaves of a local plant that was then spat into a bowl and allowed to ferment in the sun for four days. To not have drunk it would have been rude to the native tribe we were visiting, so I gave it a little sip like a good tourist should.

A six-hour trek through the rainforest yielded a few slips on steep rocks and mud—one that almost sent me tumbling into the raging river below. We hiked through a cave that had not only hundreds of bats (rabies again!), but a swiftly flowing river that we had to cross by swimming while clinging to an old telephone cord that was loosely tied to a hole in a rock to prevent us from being swept away into the depths of the cave. I wish I were making this up, but I think we lost count of how many times we could have died if just one thing had gone wrong. And I was doing this all with a fetus growing inside my belly. Our parents would have been pale with horrified disbelief if they had only known the myriad of potential disasters that could have befallen us on that trip.

After escaping the rainforest with all of our limbs intact and only a few insect bites, we gratefully got back on the death bus and took another five-hour journey through the volcanic mountainside to a new location. I cried with joy as we were given the keys to a hotel room with actual walls instead of screens, and a five-gallon jug of fresh water. The hot springs were a delight to relax in and calmed every nerve that had been frayed during our Amazonian trip. My husband hugged me and promised me that for our next vacation, we would skip the adventure and opt for something "boring" like a sandy beach with a swim-up bar or something equally not life-threatening. Little did we know that vacations, as we knew them, would forever change after the arrival of our baby.

We left Ecuador safely, through some miracle, and our baby survived the changes in elevation, exposure to the hot springs, and breathing air filled with bat feces just like millions of Ecuadorian babies do. It was my first experience, though not my last, being pregnant in a foreign country, and while I managed to avoid the need to access local medical services, doing so would have provided an entirely new set of challenges. Perhaps my newly pregnant state in the Amazonian context or the pregnancy-friendly malaria pills that gave me nightmares meant that everything only appeared to be scarier than it was in reality. Actually, I know that not to be true, because my husband admitted to also being terrified of our surroundings, and he didn't have the excuse of being pregnant. It was a trip that would have stressed out anyone—pregnant or not—and consequently was the last set of unnecessary risks that we have ever taken. We will gladly leave the rainforest to the brave explorers and globetrotters of the next generation.

Lisa Ferland lives with her husband and two children in the Swedish countryside, where they go on daily walks through the woods looking for either wild blueberries or mushrooms. She is an active proponent of free-range parenting, creative play spaces for children, and cultivating a life that is both active and healthy. Her adventures in Ecuador were only the beginning of travel for her then-unborn son.

SECTION II

BIRTHING ABROAD

CHAPTER 5

KNOCKED UP IN NAGOYA

Meika Weiss
Nationality: USA
Birthed in: Nagoya, Japan

We got married on a beautiful day in May, raindrops still clinging to blades of grass as the sun broke through the clouds to illuminate the fading tulips. We had expected our first year of marriage to include camping trips and road trips; I thought I might plant a garden in the backyard. But we had encountered a fork in the road ahead that wasn't on our map. Life was taking an unexpected turn.

Three weeks before our wedding day, my fiancé, Mike, and I drove my beloved black Volkswagen to a friend's house after work. It was early spring; the trees' tiny leaves were an innocent shade of green, and the smell of warm upholstery was still novel. I'd just parked in the driveway and was reaching for my door handle when Mike told me to hang on a minute. He spoke carefully.

"Dave can't go to Japan. He said something in an email to the customer—it's a long story, but they decided it wouldn't be wise to send him to work in a Japanese office." He paused, and in the back of my mind I registered the songs of birds that had just returned from their southern migration as my heart began to race. I knew what this meant.

"They want us to go."

A heartbeat elapsed, and I asked, "When?"

"Well, we'll need to go on a home-finding trip in about six weeks, but we won't have to move until August. If we say yes, though, things are going to start happening fast."

Six weeks! I did the math in my head. Three weeks until our wedding, followed by a week away for our honeymoon, then just two weeks back at work—did I have enough vacation time for this? Did it matter anymore?

I thought about the career I'd hoped to build. How would this trip affect those goals? I'd had a terrible work experience the year before that I was still recovering from. I'd made some hopeful connections in the past few months and had just begun a new internship, but my current job paid the bills. It wasn't a career I would miss. And I'd wanted to live overseas for as long as I could remember.

"Yes," I said. "Let's do it."

So we did.

After our honeymoon we took a whirlwind trip to Japan to find a new home—I never did go back to work after we returned. Between meeting with movers, dividing our just-combined belongings into groups (what would go in our sea shipment, our air shipment, or be covered with sheets in the basement), and getting the house that was suddenly ours, and not just his, ready for the friends who would be staying there while we were gone, there was too much to do and barely enough time to do it.

And seemingly suddenly we were there—taking trains rather than cars and trying to decipher which bottle on the supermarket shelf was the cooking oil.

We enjoyed quiet weekends together in that first year of marriage, but we spent our days apart—he at the office and I at home, trying to adapt to the idea that I—*I!*—was a housewife. Well, I thought, with all this time on my hands, and since I'm not working anyway, I suppose we might as well have a baby.

It was our first anniversary. My husband and I had planned to take the train from our townhouse to a love hotel downtown, and after checking in there to head down to Nagoya Port and the now-defunct Italian Village. We found sitting beside the fake canals drinking cappuccino comforting; it wasn't Japanese, so it felt like home. To our eyes, the ubiquity of love hotels was bizarre. It's just what it sounds like—a hotel that rents rooms for the purpose of giving couples a private place for intimacy. Some have themed rooms; others are more like regular hotels. All are discreet.

My husband and I giggled and dodged like freshmen skipping school as we walked up to the single entry door, our eyes alert for my husband's colleagues—we were really a little closer to his office than was comfortable. In the lobby, rather than the traditional bowing concierge we were greeted by a giant backlit display board with pictures of over a dozen rooms.

"Oooh, look! This one has a hot tub! Let's do this one," I said.

"Sure. Well, no, the light is out on that one; I don't think it's available right now. How does that one look? It has a hot tub, too," replied my husband.

"Yeah, that's good. Do you know what that kanji means? I think I've seen it before, but I don't remember."

We puzzled our way through our Japanese illiteracy and made our selection. Mike pushed the appropriate red button, and a bell sounded quietly behind us. We turned to see a white light slowly blinking above a hallway; as we entered the hallway we saw that there was a similar light beside an elevator. The doors slid open.

The elevator let us out on small landing with only two rooms, one of which had another white beacon guiding us in. The door was unlocked, and we fell inside, exhilarated by our success and still only half-believing that we were doing this.

Our neighbor, Mariko, was one of my very few friends in these early months. Although she was Japanese and had grown up near Yokohama, she had attended college and worked for several years in the States and had gotten married there—she understood both my culture and hers, and what it was like to be a foreigner. She was in Nagoya on an expatriate assignment, as we were, and in addition to being a friend and support was a priceless window into Japanese culture.

I'd confessed our crazy plan to her one day over tea. Her apartment was cozy and intriguing, and I enjoyed visiting. The best spot was at her *kotatsu* table—of similar size to an American coffee table, but with an electric heater attached to the bottom and a comforter sandwiched between that and the tabletop. I can't imagine a cozier spot to sit and have tea on a chilly day.

She leaned back and laughed when I'd told her we had gone to a love hotel over the weekend. Have you ever been to one of these places? I'd asked incredulously. It was crazy! She waved her hand noncommittally and grinned as she poured more tea. Then she carefully explained that normally, people do not stay at a love hotel for a whole night.

"Oh my gosh, there's a *tanning bed* in here!" I exclaimed as I peeked in the back room of the surprisingly large suite.

There was a hot tub with a TV, too, a drab view of an office building from the window, and a bedroom that was less exotic than I had imagined.

By then it was mid-afternoon, and we were getting hungry. We'd planned to drop off our things and head to the *Coco Ichibanya* around the corner for a late lunch of our favorite Japanese curry, then continue on our way down to the port.

It didn't take long for our plans to hit a snag.

The suite had two doors to the exterior. One door separated the hallway from the entryway, where a small strip of red carpet offered a place to leave one's shoes before stepping onto the tiled entry platform. This was the *genkan*, and wasn't unlike a Japanese home or guesthouse. In this case there was also an additional door separating the *genkan* from the interior rooms. My husband reached the door first. The tile was cool on my feet as I waited for him to go so I'd have room to get my shoes on.

"Huh," he said, "This is strange." He jiggled the handle.

I cocked my head in question.

He jiggled the handle again, and, ever the engineer, bent over to examine it.

"What is it? Is there something wrong with the door?" I asked again.

"Ah...I think it's locked." His examination of the door and its locking mechanism was becoming increasingly vigorous.

"Locked? From the *outside*? That can't be. Let me try."

It was locked.

Mike reached over to the keypad on the wall, covered in unfamiliar kanji, and started pressing buttons. Nothing happened. He pressed more buttons. I jiggled the handle. We were both getting a little tense.

"This is a fire hazard! They can't lock people in like this!" I was indignant.

Feeling defeated, we went back in the room, and he picked up the phone. He was much braver in this regard than I was; I hated the awkwardness of a conversation without recourse to gestures even more in Japanese than in English.

"*Mush-mushi...*" I could hear a woman's voice crackling on the other end of the line.

"*Hai, sumimasen, ano, 305 desu. Ano...watashi no doa ga...mondai desu.*" Room 305, he said in rough Japanese. My door is a problem.

This sort of situation really wasn't covered in our Berlitz language classes. Mike was off the phone now.

"She kept saying credit card. I think we're locked in here until we pay, and then when we leave, that's it. We can't go and come back."

We were trapped in a room we couldn't leave, and we didn't understand the rules. My first response was to flee, to figure out how to get the door open and get out as quickly as possible. But as we talked through the options, we decided that since we were already there we may as well settle in and—ahem—get our money's worth.

What had initially seemed like a blow to our carefully planned day soon revealed itself as a gift. Our first year of marriage had been filled with adventure, but also with long hours, big transitions, and accompanying stress. And now we were locked in a room with no distractions. I hadn't brought a book. We didn't have smart phones. It was just...us.

Four weeks later, we were arguing about whether a really, really, really faint pink line counted as a positive pregnancy test or not.

It does.

It was warmer now, and Mariko and I were sitting at the bistro table on my back patio. It was a pleasant place, with a postage-stamp lawn I mowed with our kitchen shears, set off from the common pathway by an evergreen hedge that was still growing in. We were drinking tea, and I remember looking down at the creamy brown liquid in my cup as we talked. She had shared her own exciting news with me a few months ago; today it was my turn.

"Soooo..." I said. "I have some news. I'm pregnant!"

"Oh!" she said, in delighted surprise. "That is wonderful! I am *very* happy for you!" Her eyes began to look suspiciously shiny and she waved her hand self-consciously in front of her face.

"I'm sorry," she said, "It's the baby. Ever since I became pregnant I am very emotional."

She had just found out that she would be having a little girl and was so very excited. We talked about how funny it was that our children were both being born in Japan but would be raised in America. Their American home wasn't far from ours, and we thought it would be fun for them to be friends.

I was 29 weeks along when my doctor had recently learned that my husband had been 9 lb.—over 4,000 g (!)—at birth, and was concerned that our baby would soon be too big to turn to a head-down position. He recommended acupuncture and moxibustion to help her find the right position. "I cannot explain why it works," he said, "but in my experience, it has been very effective."

Acupuncture I was familiar with; I could clearly picture somebody lying on a table with a dozen trembling antennae protruding from their forehead. Moxibustion, I learned, is an ancient technique that involves taking a small, cone-shaped plug of mugwort, setting it on an acupuncture point on one's skin, and burning it. The two practices have been used in concert for hundreds of years.

As I entered the clinic a few days later, I was directed up a staircase of sleek modern wood to a small room that smelled of incense. I walked in and lay down on the examining table. It was a pleasant space, tidy and somewhat dim. A friendly looking young woman wearing muted pink scrubs had me remove my socks and asked if my feet were often cold. And what about my hands? She asked. Do I suffer from headaches?

Questions answered, the woman got to work. She slid the hair-like needles into my shoulders, my hands and forearms, and my legs, ankles, and feet. The needles' pinch felt like a cross between a mosquito bite and the sting of a biting fly when they pierced my skin, some of them continuing to ache and some seeming to disappear.

"*Daijoubu?*" she asked as she circled around the table, "Are you doing okay?"

She went from point to point, gently rolling the small needles between her fingers so they spun in my skin. She took some needles out, had me turn on my side, and placed needles in my back. That was a relief; lying on my back at that point in pregnancy made me terribly lightheaded.

"*Hai*," I replied breathlessly, "yes." "*Daijoubu.*" I didn't have the vocabulary for nuance.

I breathed a sigh of relief as she removed the acupuncture needles. Then, she carefully placed a small amount of dark-colored herb in a few places on my body, most memorably on the outside edges of each pinky toe. A quick scratching sound, and the sharp smell of the match was followed by a sweet, heavy scent of burning herb. Tell me if it gets too hot, she said.

I took deep breaths, willing away the swimming feeling in my head. Being on my back and strong scents both made me lightheaded when I was pregnant, and this was like being in an incense-filled smoke tent.

I felt the heat in my toes, and just seconds later, "Ack! *Atsui! Atsui! Itai!*" The gentle warmth quickly became a sharp burn.

"It's hot!" I said, "It hurts!"

She ducked her head and apologized, and after quickly removing the hot herbs from my toes, she helped me slowly to sit up. I breathed deeply, slowly, waiting for the all-too-familiar floating feeling to pass.

I'd planned to visit a French friend who was on bed rest at the same clinic before heading home, but my instructions were sternly given: I was to return home right away and lie on my left side for the next six hours. My eyebrows shot up as I recalibrated my plans for that afternoon and evening.

I stepped out into the bracing winter air, turning right and left and making my way carefully down the wide subway station steps. My shoes were invisible beyond my belly as they padded heavily down the even concrete steps. The song announcing the train's arrival rang through the station as I descended to the lower level, and I jumped, as always, at the abrupt sounding of the train's horn as it pulled into the station. I felt inexplicably fragile, as the baby would fall right out if I moved too abruptly.

Shoes off, house slippers on. My husband was traveling, so I'd be entertaining myself this evening. I made some tea, grabbed some pillows, and settled in under the cozy green and white tulip quilt that had been a gift from my mom in high school. The day before, my friend Julie had providentially lent me the entire first season of *Sex and the City*, so my entertainment was taken care of.

By the end of the first episode the baby was restless in a way she'd never been before; first kicking, then stretching. I'd never felt anything like it. It seemed as though she'd decided to take up the yoga practice that I'd quit early in my second trimester when I'd realized that the fine-boned women in my prenatal class were unlikely to gain as much weight as I had in one leg—or maybe one foot. Yes, I was pretty sure the baby was doing downward dog. And now warrior two. Oof.

This hidden child took my breath away as she pressed into my lungs; until bedtime, my belly rolled like the waves I'd see back home on Lake Michigan after a storm.

The next day I had a doctor's appointment, with the obligatory ultrasound.

"Good news!" said the doctor, "The baby has turned!"

I already knew that, though. Sometime the evening before, as I watched the drama unfold between Carrie and Mr. Big, I became the crazy lady who recommends acupuncture and moxibustion to her skeptical friends for all their pregnancy ills.

My least favorite part of any appointment was the weight check. My Germanic frame and American habits were a poor fit for the Japanese culture of pregnancy and its recommendations to gain the smallest amount of weight possible. Every appointment was the same, "Your weight, it is too much. Please control." I should consider more sushi, I was told, or perhaps less fruit.

Mariko wasn't having a problem controlling her weight. Unfortunately, it wasn't because she was privy to cultural tricks that helped keep her slim. Unlike me, her morning sickness didn't go away at the three-month mark; if anything, it seemed to get worse. She was sick all day long, multiple times a day, barely able to eat and rarely feeling relief from her unsettled stomach.

She had invited me to enroll in her food delivery co-op and stopped by one brisk afternoon to translate a mysterious letter I'd gotten in the mail from them the week before.

"I told my doctor about my sickness at my appointment today," she said sadly. "He told me that I was acting too nervous and anxious, and that was making me sick. He said that I needed to relax for my baby."

I was furious that a modern doctor had the audacity to blame her for what turned out to be hyperemesis and told her that I thought her doctor was terrible. I think she knew that already, but sometimes we need someone else to affirm in us what we already know to be true.

It was Friday, and I was due to be induced on Monday. At 40 weeks and four days, I was more than ready to be done. I'd gone for a two-and-a-half-hour walk that day—less than the four hours my doctor recommended, but as much as I felt was reasonable. Still no baby. I was getting grumpy.

At 3 a.m. Saturday morning, I woke up to feeling something squeezing through my belly and lower back. It was similar to how my period cramps felt normally, but with a harder edge. My heart jumped. Baby!

I tried to get a few more hours of sleep, but I was far too excited. From the bedroom, I heard Mike push the green button on the bathtub control panel to fill it—beep!—followed a few minutes later by the tune indicating my bath was ready. I lumbered into the bathroom and for the next two hours stretched and breathed in the warm water.

At 9 a.m. we headed to the clinic. The small parking lot was conveniently empty, and we headed upstairs to the unfamiliar birthing floor. I exchanged my jeans and too-small maternity shirt for a pink gown then had another contraction; I put my arms around Mike's neck and stretched downward, looking without success for the comfortable position.

The next five hours were a repetitious blur, most of which I remember in brief vignettes. The cherry blossom pictures I'd printed out to use as focal points, as recommended by my vintage Lamaze video. Sending Mike out to the vending machine, again and again, to buy me more grape juice. My nurses murmuring to me that I needed to eat something to keep my strength up. The taste of dry Cheerios. Outside, the world carried on as though this were an ordinary day.

By 2 p.m., I'd had enough and asked for an epidural. Unlike American hospitals, epidurals aren't standard in Japan. Public hospitals often don't offer them, but it was an option at my clinic— just not the preferred option. After checking my dilation, my doctor reminded me of the conversations we'd had of a natural birth and told me that he would give my husband and I a few minutes to discuss and think this through. If I still wanted one at that point he would call a second doctor, and we could have it done.

At seven centimeters dilated, I was in the stage of labor known as transition—my body was wrapping up dilation and preparing me to push the baby out. It's the shortest, most intense stage of labor, and it doesn't normally take more than an hour or so. I could do that, I thought. I am an outlier. Now that I've given birth to three children, I understand that women are infinitely more variable than textbook descriptions suggest. Some give birth reliably at 38 weeks; some have 30-minute labors and birth in the car. I carry my children to 41 weeks, and my transition stage lasts three to five hours.

All I remember from these hours is Lois, my translator-turned-doula, looking in my eyes and helping me breathe. Mike pushed on my lower back with tennis balls until his hands went numb.

At long last, I was declared fully dilated and moved to the delivery room next door. The delivery chair was similar to the examination chairs I had become accustomed to in the course of my pregnancy. It held me in a semi-upright position, each of my legs supported separately by legs that swung out to the sides when needed.

And then...I waited. My doctor was occupied performing a C-section on the woman who had been laboring silently in the neighboring room all day, and I was told it would be better if I waited for the baby to work her way down anyway.

I focused my eyes on the electrical outlet on the other side of the room and watched the clock as the hands moved slowly from 6:00, to 6:05, to 6:10, and on along its face. 6:15. 6:20.

At 7 p.m. on the dot, my doctor came bursting through the side door from the other delivery room. "Okay!" he said in Japanese. "Where are we?"

And then I pushed, which was the most blissful sensation after having held back for so long. Something happened on the monitor—the baby's heartbeat?—and he told me to focus, that everything would be fine now, and that I should give a gigantic push to get the baby out next time. I did, and out slid a slippery little stranger, simultaneously tiny and tremendous.

She was perfect.

That night, I went to sleep in a comfortable bed, my baby in the nursery so I could get a full night's rest. My hip didn't cramp up once, and I could—oh, bliss—roll over onto my stomach without difficulty.

The five days I spent at the clinic after that were blissful. We received visitors: my Japanese teacher and friends from church, bearing flowers. Mariko came, too, her own baby like a little koala in a carrier on her chest. At just four or five months of age, she looked so big next to my tiny newborn. She *was* big, in fact; Mariko had been getting massages because her back was beginning to hurt from carrying the baby everywhere.

The weather was beautiful. Although the calendar said it was early February, Nagoya, Japan said it was early spring. Far from the deep snow we'd experience in our home state, when I opened my window and leaned out there were flowers blooming on the patio below and the smell of warm soil in the air. It was a day much like the one just a year and a half before, when this unexpected road unfolded before us. I had no idea how much joy or struggle was down that path on the day we said yes, but I wouldn't trade it for all the sushi in Japan.

Meika Weiss is a Michigan native who continued her birthing adventures after repatriating to her home state. Her second child was born in a wading pool in the living room, and her third more traditionally, in an American hospital. After she collected a full complement of birth experiences, she turned to applying her observations on how cities function in Japan, Taiwan, and Egypt to advocate for improved bike and pedestrian infrastructure in her own community. She can occasionally be found blogging at Traversing Tulip Lane. Her writing has also been featured on the Strong Towns blog.

CHAPTER 6

MOON MONTHS

Ember Swift
Nationality: Canada
Birthed in: China and Canada

The office is mauve and turquoise with a gray plastic desk. The tiles on the floor are cracked in several places and caked with the evidence of half-hearted mopping. I notice the trim of the doorframe is broken in two places, and the ceiling plaster is cracked in a jagged line near the window. This makes me think of incisions, and I repeat the word for episiotomy in my head in Mandarin. I involuntarily shiver.

In my hand is a four-page, painstakingly translated birth plan, and I'm fidgeting with it, knees jostling, and my husband puts his hand on top of my hand-knee-birth plan to stop the jittery jostle. I look up at him, annoyed. I'm annoyed with him at least 20 hours a day now. I distract myself from his presence, the silent forced motionlessness and the crack in the ceiling by repeating more of the vocabulary words in my head: *oxytocin, C-section, umbilical cord...*

When the doctor comes in, she hesitates mid-stride when she realizes there's a foreigner sitting in her office. Despite being a foreign-affiliate women and children's hospital in Beijing—with Canadian ties no less—the number of foreign mothers who use its services are few. It has something to do with its shoddy translators, likely, but I am conducting everything in Mandarin. Part stubbornness, part impatience with shoddy translation.

"Can she speak our Chinese language?"

This 50-plus-year-old doctor has directed her question at my husband whose response time is too slow for me, and so I respond ahead of him, pointedly finding her irises.

"Yes, she can."

She looks at me with a look I can't distinguish between surprise and amusement as she sits down at her desk, motioning for her trailing nurse to sit as well, beside her on the little stool against the wall, and I notice that it's the nurse's job to take notes while the doctor sits, relaxed, looking over my files.

There's a debate about my due date. I have calculated it several times. It's supposed to be January 1, but based on the size of the three-month fetus inside me, they recalculate it for January 8. This annoys me. She speaks quickly. I understand most of it, but the speed of her speech tells me she doesn't respect that its my second language. This annoys me too. Later, I'll wonder if she spoke that quickly as a form of respect, assuming I *would* understand, not doubting my language ability. That will be a rare moment of generosity in my overall annoyed pregnant state.

I really hate being pregnant.

She examines me and is gentle, and I try to remember that this should make me less annoyed, but it doesn't. When the appointment is nearly over—the first of what will be many—I turn to my husband, whose look of boredom annoys me further. I dramatically jostle the birth plan at him, but say nothing.

He clears his throat.

"My wife has some worries, doctor," he says, "Some things are done differently in her country than here."

He laughs apologetically, and I have to resist my Technicolor urge to slap him. Instead, I take over, my energy swatting him nonetheless, explaining that I have a birth plan, would she mind taking a look at it, and can I leave her a copy. She is giving me the look she gave me earlier, and I subtly register that I'm probably acting like a nervous lunatic, and she has seen a million controlling first-time mothers like me, but I hand her the birth plan anyway. I watch her flip through the pages casually, like it didn't take me two weeks to put it together with my compiled research, like it didn't take me ages to find example bilingual birth plans, and like I didn't work tirelessly doing diligent translation and language verification and then agonize over the order of the points for priority.

She has finished flipping before I can finish being annoyed.

"I will look this over, but I'm sure there won't be many problems. I'll let you know at our next appointment."

She asks me—directly—if I have any other questions, and I am so surprised that my plan won't be discussed in detail that I quietly deny that there are at least a hundred questions waiting to escape my teeth. My husband is already standing, and so I also stand, and then we are out in the dingy hall, and another first-time mother has slipped into the office behind me before I realize with an accelerated heart rate that my birth plan is no longer in my hands. It's on my hard drive, yes, but that hardly feels like a safe place for it right now. My husband grabs my empty hand casually, and this is perhaps the ultimate act that triggers annoyance, like he has no idea how unsafe and vulnerable the hand feels without the grip of the carefully printed and stapled document.

"See, I told you there'd be no problems," he says.

I respond sharply with, "She said she'd look at it, not that she'd follow it."

He kindly ignores me.

A week earlier, we had toured two other hospitals. The other two were in our neighborhood, but this one is a 15-minute drive away. We've decided on this hospital we'll use only because the first one was way out of our price range and the second one included an initial interview that made me so angry that I left the hospital lobby steaming with rage. I hit the sidewalk solo and sobbing, walking away from the humiliation without looking back despite my husband calling after me and my in-laws surely shaking their heads with the emotional instability of their daughter-in-law. I didn't know then that the hormones were attacking my patience. I just knew that the hospital "host" was condescending and disrespectful and hadn't once looked at me while speaking, as though my foreignness were tantamount to my invisibility. Our home was just a 10-minute walk away, but by the time I got there, I was embarrassed by my own behavior. Luckily for me, no one mentioned it. When I tried to apologize to everyone later on, my words were swatted away with the impatient sweet reassurances of "no need" and "don't mention it." In Chinese culture, there is no need to apologize among family. When hormones are involved, I consider this a bonus.

The real heart of the problem was this: I didn't want to give birth in a hospital. I wanted a home birth—an earthy experience with a midwife and a bathtub and massaged shoulders and candlelight.

Home births are illegal in China now. A big part of this is the one-child policy that forces families to register their births immediately. Hospitals take care of that. As a foreigner in China who is a temporary resident and whose children will have Canadian passports, I am not restricted by the one-child policy. But in China, it is also illegal to have dual citizenship. Only if we were to choose to give our children Chinese citizenship (a crazy choice considering Canada's free education and health care) would I then be subject to this policy.

Frankly, I think the biggest reason against home births in China is economic. Hospitals are big business in a country with so many people. Even with the majority of the women giving birth just one time in their lives, there are hundreds of millions of one-time mothers in China. That's a lot of money for hospitals. It's a socialist capitalist system, after all. They may say it's about health and safety since there's no home-birthing system in place like there is in Canada, but that's the socialist veneer over the capitalist agenda.

Add to this the fact that C-sections are much pricier than a vaginal birth, and they're the most common, accounting for about 60% of the births in the country. First-time mothers are often told that it's "too painful" to give birth naturally, that their hips are "too narrow," or that they simply won't have the strength. I was shocked to learn these things.

What I wanted was a natural birth. No drugs. No interventions of any kind. Chinese people looked at me like I was a swollen contradiction: a modern Westerner wants an old-fashioned birth? I was up against an entire country and birthing trend: Little Canada versus Massive China. I would have preferred a forest and a hut. The further along I grew in my pregnancy, the more I wanted as far away from the modern chaos of Beijing as I could get—a city filled with almost as many people as my whole country.

But, we were doing it. There. In a hospital. We were now officially patients of the Mary's Women's and Children's hospital of Beijing, that semi-private Canadian-affiliate establishment that would allow my husband in the room while I gave birth, unlike the basic Chinese hospitals that still refused men entrance to the gynecology wings. It was still the 1970s in China in so many ways, despite the calendar declaring 2012.

On a subsequent visit to the Mary's Women's and Children's hospital, a young nurse tells me that I should not be vegetarian throughout my pregnancy because I will starve my child.

Two months later, the same barely 20-year-old nurse tells me that I have gained too much weight and that I should control my eating. I remind her that my vegetarian diet was supposed to starve the baby. She looks at me confused. She has forgotten her own rhetoric.

They weigh the mothers at the hospital. The waiting room is filled with plush, Barney-purple armchairs holding bulbous baby-filled humans and their bored companions—mostly older women, presumably mothers-in-law and mothers, but occasionally men engrossed in their cell phones or staring at the wall-mounted television screen that plays silently in one corner. The weigh-in scale is at one end. The nurse's desk is at the other.

A mother steps on the scale. The nurse yells across the room asking how much the mother weighs. The mother yells the amount back. The pen scratches the chart. The mother sits down. Another mother stands, is weighed, her blood pressure is also checked, then she is dismissed back to the plush purple chairs until the doctor is ready.

Another mother stands, is weighed.

I am the next mother. I stand. I walk to the scale. I stand on the scale. I am yelled at. I yell back, obediently. She asks again. I have to yell it twice. She notes my spiking weight with an intake of breath. She scratches the chart with her pen. An older woman nearly swallowed by plush purple whispers to the pregnant lady beside her, loudly enough for me to hear that foreigners are fatter than Chinese people. It's normal, she says. I step down. I allow myself to be swallowed by my own purple chair. My husband doesn't look up from his phone.

Fifty-five pounds later and I have twinges on New Year's Eve. I knew I was always right about the due date. I am pleased with myself. I have secured a doula who is a long-time American expat, whose Chinese is excellent, and who also has a Chinese husband and two kids. She is not technically legal, but the hospital nods knowingly when I declare that "my friend" will also attend the birth. She will come in the morning, she says, and meet us at the hospital.

"Go when your contractions are three to five minutes apart," she says. "In the meantime, try to get some rest."

I don't. I sit in the bathtub. Then I lie wide-eyed in the bed as my husband snores. He has gone into a narcoleptic anxiety sleep after already panicking and gathering up our things and placing them by the door, just like in the movies. My eyes rolled in time with his pacing.

It's morning on January 1 and I'm rolling on a big birthing ball in the hospital, but they have told me that I'm still only one cm dilated, and they have left me alone. I feel silly to be at the hospital and progressing so slowly after eight hours already. The light bulbs dangling from angular metallic brackets in the ceiling over the bed have started to seem like contemporary art. The way the shadows splinter off their form fracturing the gray and white speckled drop ceiling tiles between contractions seem metaphoric for the pain, almost foreboding, like they're a sign of things to come.

They are.

Another eight hours later and I am still only one centimeter dilated. The baby, once said to be in perfect position for a quick birth, is still head down but seems to be butting my lower back with every wave. Robyn, the doula, and my husband are each pushing on my back with each contraction or helping me count through them. I am still hugging the birthing ball. I am losing hope.

Twenty hours later and the pain is dulling. I sleep between contractions. They have left us alone and are no longer checking in on us every 20 minutes. It's dark outside. Somehow the day has passed. Robyn is asleep on the room's futon couch, and my husband is asleep on the floor as I rock through the contractions and go back to sleep for 10-minute intervals.

Thirty hours later and I'm only one and a half cm dilated. They are adhering to my birth plan. They're offering no drugs. My water hasn't yet broken. They tell me to keep going with flat eyes and indiscernible facial features hidden by face masks. I don't know it then, but I have unknowingly lined all their pockets with a superfluous day in the hospital. "Add fuel," they say, literally, but it means "don't give up," or "you can do it," and I suddenly feel very annoyed to be birthing in my non-native language.

I complain loudly to Robyn in English. She nods. I'm grateful for her.

Thirty-five hours later and I'm at five centimeters. The back and tailbone pain are so excruciating that I start to consider the extremes. A C-section. Just cut the baby out of me. Just kill me and take the kid. How hard would that be? Just release me from the waves of torture that fill my entire skull with shadow, spilling me from sanity into nightmare, the ink of pain staining my blood black. I am done. I am over this. I can go now.

I ask for an epidural. I feel like a failure, and I cry as they take me out of my private laboring room and put me in the clinical birthing room, tilt me on my side, and insert the tube into my back. I've betrayed myself, my own wishes, and as the screaming inside of me slowly quiets, I start to breathe normally again, sleep washing up to find me. I also permit myself to stop crying, stop blaming myself, stop all commentary whatsoever. I check out. I sleep for two hours.

They stop the drip when I'm almost fully dilated. They break my water. The rush of contractions comes back to me just before I am being tasked with pushing, and I have been forced onto my back, the very position I had resisted, but the time between contractions is too brief, and I can't get up. The hospital bed is too narrow for alternate positions; I can't get out of this one, can't crawl under the dresser filled with surgical instruments that I see to my left, supported about a foot from the ground on four wooden legs. The space beneath would fit me were I not to have this huge growth on my stomach and an extra 50 lb. on my limbs. Head turned to the left between pushes staring at it longingly, I imagine myself there, focusing on the shadow that falls under it, beckoning me to hide, animal-like, away from the fluorescent lights and the room filled with too many masks topped with eyes I don't recognize.

They tell me to stop yelling. To quiet down. I yell louder. I hate them all.

My doctor had January 1 off. She suddenly appears between my knees at the final hour. It's now January 2 because of this marathon labor. She's come back for me. I feel better. I love her. I love everyone.

When they see the baby in the birth canal, they start talking about how *lihai* I am, which means tough and strong and I realize that they're not complimenting me but marveling at me and Robyn explains that the baby is posterior, is coming out facing upward, and I'm birthing her that way, which explains the slow labor and the back pain, but I don't know that yet. I just know that it had better come out of me quickly no matter which way it's facing, and I wish they would damn well pull the thing out already instead of marveling at its position.

A woman comes by my head. She asks me where I am from. I glare at her. My husband answers that I am Canadian. She compliments my Chinese even though I have not spoken to her and says, in broken English, that "Canada is good place," and then asks me in Chinese how long I have been in China. I look at her with the blank contempt of someone being singled out for her cultural difference in the most inappropriate time possible. I ignore her question. Seconds later she is shooed away by the other doctors. She is the technician in charge of the baby when it's out, I am told later, and I am relieved I didn't have to bark at her. I wish I had memorized her eyes so that I can point my finger at her later, but all I can remember of her are her shoes and the sound of her scuttle. When it's all over, I will wonder if I was too rude and should apologize.

There is one more push and a rush of relief, and the baby is placed on my chest immediately, just like my birth plan requested. It is squirming, and I am speaking English to this little creature, more kitten-like than human, calming it, telling it Mommy's here, that it's okay, that there's nothing to worry about. There is no crying, and in a flash they are all chirping at me—the doctor, the nurses—in high-pitched Mandarin, to suck out its nose (I do) and pat its back (I do), but the baby has calmed and is breathing visibly, and they remark to each other that they rarely see a baby emerge without crying. There's a moment of stillness that hovers over us. I haven't checked its sex yet, and I don't think to do so until my husband asks, and then the blanket they have placed over its squirming anxious arrival is lifted to reveal her. Our daughter.

She is only taken away for a moment to be weighed and to have her vitals checked. She cries, then, but there is no suctioning or immediate inoculation or eye washing or the myriad of other things I worried would be done to her before she had even bonded with me. Robyn is monitoring and confirms that the plan has been followed. She is returned quickly. Then they leave me alone with just Robyn and my husband, our daughter nurses, almost immediately, and I am crying and on the phone with my parents and crying some more.

I am a mother. I am a mother. I am a mother.

I am sitting in our red sling-back IKEA chair, breastfeeding my daughter. After my 42-hour labor and a few days recovery in the hospital, I was whisked back to our apartment, dressed in polar layers despite the dry and nowhere-near-Canada cold of Beijing in January. I have been placed on house arrest, aka moon month duty. In Chinese, it's roughly translated as "sitting out the month," and it's a postpartum tradition that women will not leave the house after giving birth for at least a 30-day moon cycle. I have agreed to it, having been talked into the health benefits of allowing myself to rest, allowing myself and the baby to be catered to, allowing the meals and cleaning to be done by others. It was a no-brainer.

My mother-in-law is a woman I don't quite know well yet. She's a strong wind of personality, tunneling on high speed through our narrow apartment rooms with her opinions, almost viciously generous with cleaning and cooking, officiously directing either the consumption of the food she has made or the instruction to never mess up the part of the house she has just tidied or else.

She hovered over me during the first week as I breastfed, as I struggled to get the latch right with my shallow nipples. She even reached forward and tugged on my left nipple once, to my amazement, in an attempt to help it grow longer, which was simply not going to happen with a tug. Eventually, the baby figured it out. She was smarter than both of us.

The border crossings in this household are so numerous. They do not stop at culture and language. There is no privacy. There is no personal space.

Right now, it is the third week, and my own parents have arrived, ready to help, and our apartment is brimming with well-meaning kindness, but spilling over with suffocation. My mother-in-law has stopped hovering during feedings, mercifully. I barked once, showed my fangs, and she backed off. My own mother is a breath of fresh air from across the oceans. She caters but holds back, calmly offering thoughts and support, leaving me alone instinctively when she can see me start to bristle.

As I sit here, still 30 pounds overweight and finally healed from the small stitch necessary after my baby came out "sunny-side up," all I can think about is exercising. I have just been served my requisite moon month meal of millet congee with papaya chunks, green veggies and lotus flowers, egg and tomato, and steaming rice. Thanks to being vegetarian, I have avoided the pig feet soup and oxtail blood porridge (etc.) that usually typifies the postpartum diet. It doesn't make me eat less, however, as this food is delicious and nutritious, and I am ravished every day thanks to breastfeeding and sleeplessness. I am so grateful for the food.

My mother-in-law has encapsulated my placenta and is feeding it to me like a medication. I am taking it. I feel strange to eat my own ground-up pregnancy organ and wonder if this is the ultimate in non-vegetarianism or if it even counts, since it came out of me and nothing died. Quite the opposite in fact: Something was born. It's so incredibly disgusting tasting, even in capsule form, that I have to hold my breath and follow up each capsule with a spoonful of honey. It will be six months before honey doesn't taste like placenta capsules. I have just licked the honey spoon clean, but I can feel the ghost of the capsule's passage in my esophagus. I want to go downstairs and find something else to cover the taste.

The baby is asleep, and I gently stand, feeling my hips still angled strangely, walk gingerly to the crib and place her in, and then quietly tiptoe from the room and descend the apartment stairs to the first level where the family is sitting, trying to converse, tripping over gestures and props. There's an audible sigh as I join them— the new-mother-turned-translator—and both sets of parents begin speaking to me at once to explain their current conversational dilemma, each set thinking nothing of speaking over the other set; each only hears the other's language as noise.

Somehow, I determine the problem and summarize the whole affair in two sentences in each language, my minimalist translation technique saves my sanity, and they all laugh, relieved to finally understand, happy to no longer be pursuing the ordeal of conversing. The subject drops. I take up the floor.

"I think I can start walking now," I say, tentatively. My husband emerges from his cell phone–coma and looks up, frowning. "I don't mean outside," I add, hastily, "I just mean the stairs."

My parents are confused as I'm speaking Mandarin, and I quickly translate. They nod in silent support. My mother has already marveled at my resolve. Even explaining to her that I am not following it strictly except for the part where I remain indoors and don't consume cold foods, she shook her head with disbelief. I bathe, I play on the computer, I read, I have friends over, I said. I am a postpartum party girl. She laughed with sympathy creeping into the corners of her eyes.

"You can't enter the wind," my husband says, stressing that it's my joints that will suffer, but I won't know it until I'm old and then I'll always remember that I failed to care for myself when I had the baby.

"There's no wind in the stairwells," I say, "And I'll bundle up."

We are on the sixth floor. There are 84 steps leading up to our door. No elevator. My parents, in their sixties, have confirmed that their knees are no longer young.

I witness an open Chinese conference on the matter between my husband and his parents. I am not consulted, of course. I am spoken about as though I'm not there. I wait, my irritation shimmering under a patina of patience. I smile awkwardly at my parents. The Chinese judgment committee trio examines my stance and reluctantly agrees to 20 minutes per day, as long as I dress in my polar layers, as long as I don't emerge from the building into the outdoors, as long as I go slowly. I am amazed that I have won this battle. I nod.

The walks begin.

In 20 minutes, I can go up and down the stairs 10 times at first. My hips scream. Eventually, I make it to 18 times, not quite mastering a full descent and ascent in one minute. My hips stop hurting. I amuse myself with a stopwatch and podcasts. I do this for the next seven days straight until I am released, into the January sunlight.

Alone.

No one told me that the baby wouldn't be allowed out. No one mentioned that Chinese tradition of keeping a baby indoors for the first three to four months of their lives is considered so normal that on the few occasions when I loudly insist on taking *my* newborn out in her equally thick layers of fleece and down-filled puffed clothing, the reaction from strangers and neighbors alike ranges from stark amazement to open scolding.

By the time my daughter is six months old and I am heading to Canada to reunite with my parents and other family members, I am so relieved to be released from my ever-hovering in-laws and the unspoken Chinese rules of parenting that I barely wave goodbye to them at the airport when our family of three slips through the international gates. My daughter is happily against me in the carrier. I am still 10 lb. overweight, and I've started to consider the extra weight my protection against Chinese judgment.

A week after being back in Canada, I miss my mother-in-law's cooking.

A year later and I am pregnant again. Surprised. I'm back in my old jeans and no longer breastfeeding and finally running again. We had just started talking about possibly having another, but my eggs acted before my doubt could reanalyze the decision. It is all happening. Again. Sigh. I remember how much I hated being pregnant.

I decide to do it all differently. I want a natural birth. Period. I want a midwife. I want to be in a home environment. I want it to be in English.

Canada.

The midwives are amazing. I need no birth plan. I see them in the summertime at five months, happily discover the baby's sex in advance (not allowed in one-child policy China to avoid unnecessary abortions), and schedule a return to the midwifery clinic in the late fall when the kids and I—daughter on the outside, son on the inside—will return to Canada for my ideal birth. My husband will join us closer to the due date.

I have to switch midwifery clinics in the fall. The Toronto housing situation falls through. We don't have a place to live, and I arrange to birth at my parent's house three hours north of Toronto while they're in their winter home in Florida. They agree over the phone, anxiously. I meet new midwives at 36 weeks. My pregnancy has gone by so fast because I haven't had time to focus on how much I hate being pregnant. A toddler is a time sucker. I love her for that. I have two appointments with the midwives, but the second one never happens. My son starts knocking on my cervix for release nine days early. My husband isn't in Canada yet. I call my best friend, and she drives at top speed from Montreal. I leave my daughter with my cousin.

I am in my parent's house alone. I light a fire. It doesn't take. I do various yoga moves and stretches, rocking myself with my head on the floor. I relight the fire. I fill up the tub. With crackling logs as my soundscape, my body takes me into a new dimension in which the contractions are journeys into the cellular center of my being, like waves that I must surf, like lights that I have to both swallow and extinguish simultaneously.

I finally reach my husband on the phone, waking him from a

deep sleep. He is scheduled to leave the next day. He will miss the birth, and I cry with the loneliness of this fact, letting tears echo their splashes in the open palm of bath water. I am being cradled by warmth, I say to my cells. I am okay. I am fine.

Breathe.

Two hours later and the midwives have arrived, and my best friend is holding my hand, and I am breathless in the firelight, swirling with the immediacy of a birth in a home space, my ancestors staring back at me from the frames held up by wall hooks, watching me about to extend their family tree by a new bud.

He is not posterior. I do not need intervention. I feel the widening of his doorway viscerally. I feel the transition like an arched passage. I give birth on all fours and catch him between my legs like a slimy football and gather him to my chest as I spin to collapse on my back and there is nothing but peace. He is my son. He is in my arms. I am fine and held by the power of women and the magic of motherhood, once again.

This time, only 14 hours from the first twinge. Too easy.

It is the coldest winter on record in 25 years, snow piles reaching halfway up the sliding glass doors off my parent's living room, and the car regularly won't start. My husband is insistent that we should never live in this <expletive> country.

He has just tried the car again and likely flooded it with his impatience. He is at the front door, stomping the snow off his boots, swearing. I am feeding the baby on the couch. Our toddler daughter is playing with toys on the living room floor. We are alone, a brief respite from regular visits by extended family and friends, and he takes this opportunity to rail into my parents. They are scheduled to come up and meet their grandson for a few days at the end of January. Our son will be over a month old then. The moon month will be over.

"They don't care about us. They just left us here. They still haven't even met their grandson!"

"They care! They call every day." I say this defensively. I remind him that I encouraged them to stay away. I remind him that it was my request.

"Exactly. You're so selfish!" He flings this like a snowball, slapping me with its icy impact.

"You are as selfish as they are," he continues. "They want to stay where the weather is nice and they leave us here to fend for ourselves, and you think everything's fine. If we were in China, my parents would be caring for us, and you know it."

He keeps missing my point—that space is what I wanted, time to bond as a family of four and not a family of six, like it would be with his parents around, constantly invading and interfering. For him, that's normal. For me, this is normal. I had thought he'd share in my nesting fantasy, that he'd cuddle into the closeness of it, cooing at his new infant son while cradling his daughter and kissing his wife. I had thought wrong.

"You're just mad because you have to do more. I'm healing, and there's a new baby. You just don't like to cook and do housework."

He ignores this. He didn't come to take care of me, and I know that. He's a terrible caregiver. He resents the implication that it's his job, too, despite the moon month being his tradition that he, once again, insisted I adhere to. In this weather, I don't mind staying indoors, but I still miss his mother's cooking, and I still would love him to massage my shoulders. Even once.

He has navigated a grocery store alone, with limited English. He came back with products I have never seen before. He has tried to fix the car. And failed. He has shoveled a walk for the first time in his life and needed verbal instructions. He discovered what it feels like to have your nostril hairs freeze. He hates the snow. He wants to move to southern Thailand permanently, <expletive>.

I sit back into the couch. My daughter is now up beside me trying to distract me from the argument that she feels is coming even if she doesn't understand it. The tension hangs in the air. She is waving a book in my face saying, "Mommy, read!" and I open it for her, absently trying to think of the best thing to say and failing to come up with anything. I am terribly under-slept, and my brain is a mumbling numbness of birthing hormones. The encapsulated placenta pills that I found a company to make for me do not seem to be helping. They're still disgusting. The so-called clarity they're supposed to offer hasn't been forthcoming.

I begin to read to my daughter. As I read in English, my Chinese brain is trying to think about ways to dispute this moon month, to argue it away because, after all, we are not in China, and I can handle the cold temperatures, and I crave a crisp walk in the fresh air with my baby against my chest, hidden under winter coat, older baby bundled up on the sleigh, tugged behind on the packed snow. I crave it even more than I crave my mother-in-law's no-nonsense caregiving. I wonder why she never passed this trait onto her son. I wonder why he doesn't see that this is supposed to be his job, too. He's also a new parent. He also has a new baby son.

He storms away to soothe himself with his computer sound wave music files, and I glance at the calendar, looking forward to the end of the moon month in just 10 days. There is no stairwell to walk up and down, but I am relieved to have not ballooned as much in this pregnancy. Just up 35 lb. this time and now just 25 to lose, and I am much less anxious about them, knowing they'll mostly melt away eventually, and even if I still hang onto a few, they'll be a decent souvenir from this amazing experience of birthing two human beings in my late thirties.

The book is finished, and my daughter is bored and goes off to seek other toys. Her brother is sleeping in the cradle. I rise from the couch and start to make dinner and as it comes together easily I realize, with relief, that there is quiet in my head.

Out the kitchen window is the open Canadian deep blue sky of dusk decorated with fluffy white clouds, pines swaying in the breeze, stubborn winter blue jays coming down to steal the birdseed (that I made my husband put out this morning), their blue wings a brave streak of living color against the purity of white snow. I feel my breath, held, my body balanced at the kitchen sink as I stare out the window. Even though we will go back to our home overseas in just a month's time, to the clang of Chinese culture and trays of steaming food from the generous older generation bursting in with all their traditional ways imposed upon me, I know it is just family love of a different hue. It will come in on a different wing but will be just as breathtaking.

The evening light glints off the snow crystals like stars carpeting the ground. I let them glitter into me. My shoulders relax. No matter where we are, I know my home. It is here. This is my country. These are my roots. Now, I will pass them on.

Twice.

Ember Swift is a Canadian musician and writer who has released 11 albums since 1996 and is the author of the award-winning blog "Queer Girl Gets Married." She is also a longtime contributing writer to several publications and websites, including Beijing Kids Magazine, Herizons Feminist Quarterly, Mami Magazine, and the website InCulture Parent. She is currently working on a larger memoir project. She and her husband and two children live primarily in Beijing, China but make regular trips back to Toronto, Canada. For more information, please visit http://www.emberswift.com.

CHAPTER 7

TWO CHILDREN, ONE INTERNATIONAL MOVE, AND A BABY

Ersatz Expat
Nationality: Ireland
Knocked up in: Kazakhstan and Malaysia
Birthed in: Malaysia

I n most countries you buy a pregnancy test in the supermarket. Not so in Kazakhstan. Before you have the joy of looking at those two blue lines, you have to wait in line at the pharmacy and ask the pharmacist for a test. The phrase, "Can I have a pregnancy test please?" had never come up in our Russian lessons, and it was not one you could ask someone to tell you without getting into all sorts of questions and discussions. Luckily Google Translate delivered the goods and, wonder of wonders, the pharmacist understood me the first time! The tests don't come in convenient cartridge packets, just little strips that look like the pH paper you use at school.

Just before I got those two long-awaited lines that told us our third baby was on the way, we had found out that we were moving from Kazakhstan to Malaysia. This meant a change in insurance provider and a potential loss of maternity coverage, so the first thing I had to do was call to arrange to continue it on a private basis for the last two months of pregnancy in order to cover the costs of delivery. Fortunately, our insurers were agreeable to this, and I could cancel the private policy at any time rather than then being locked into an annual contract.

Insurance issues sorted for the time being we then had to negotiate the Kazakh maternity system. Their maternity schedule is actually much better than the one in the UK (where I had my previous two pregnancies) because all meetings are with a doctor rather than just a midwife (we had to pay extra to get OB coverage of the pregnancies as this is not standard in the UK). Because I was leaving the country mid-pregnancy, however, they decided not to book me in to the system but rather just meet with me on an ad hoc basis for scans and when necessary. My local clinic had English-speaking doctors, and one went with me to every OB hospital appointment. However, they were not, on the whole, a lot of use as the kind general practitioner they sent with me had no obstetric experience at all and did not know the relevant terminology in either English or Russian. As a result I spent a lot of time learning Russian terms in order to be able to glean something from the meetings. My OB from the UK very kindly sent my notes over with advice on the medication I would need to take, which I translated for the Kazakh doctors.

Kazakh doctors are very big on pills and herbal remedies, and they love prescriptions—a visit for a simple case of tonsillitis will see you leaving the doctor's office with at least five different types of pills, and at least one of these will be some sort of herbal remedy. During pregnancy, however, they seem to avoid prescription pills wherever possible. They were rather bemused by my UK prescriptions for the various pills and potions I had to take in the first trimester including aspirin, high-strength folic acid, progesterone, and others. They put this down to my foreign quirks and decided to add various herbal remedies on top. I did what I always do: smile, say thank you, and then ditch the woo stuff— there was no way I was feeding our unborn baby some valerian root!

Unlike my usual OB, my Kazakh doctor never once checked my blood pressure or urine but was obsessed with my weight. I gained very little during pregnancy, so they were most concerned. They were rather blasé, however, when at 16 weeks our youngest daughter developed a strange rash they thought was fifth disease. They tested my blood for rubella, which I knew I had been vaccinated for, but did not run a check for fifth, and I don't know if

I have ever had that particular childhood disease! When I developed a fever, they advised against bringing it down with paracetamol (I was, inevitably, given some herbal remedy), and I had to tell the pharmacist I was buying paracetamol for my husband in order to be able to get some. I never like taking stuff when pregnant, but with my first two I was always advised that a fever would do more harm than the tablets needed to get rid of it.

The scans were a bit of a letdown in Kazakhstan. They were very thorough with all the measurements, and I was provided with an array of print outs (in Russian) of growth measurements and observations; there was, however, no facility to print pictures. I know that this is not the primary purpose of a scan, but we have a full set of scan photos (monthly to six months, biweekly to eight months, and weekly thereafter) for my first two pregnancies, so it was a shame not to have the same for this baby. My husband took a few fuzzy shots of the screen on his phone, but it was not really the same.

My Kazakh colleagues at work had some very strange ideas about pregnancy and found my own attitudes toward it equally baffling. They would not allow me to lift chairs, and the school nurse told me off for wearing high heels—both of these activities were, I was told, guaranteed to harm the baby. Another colleague told me that my husband should stop drinking beer as it would harm the baby. Given that his biological contribution was at that stage complete, I am not quite sure of the logic of this, but as neither of us are big drinkers, it was no skin off our noses. Funnily enough, pregnant Kazakh women have no objection to enjoying a stay in a hot tub or a session in the *banya* (sauna), which are complete no-no's in the UK.

During the first two trimesters, my husband and I were busy running around Astana doing our best to sort out all the myriad of things required for an international move. We sorted the packers, sold the car, and spent many hours of our lives getting the requisite export certificates for our two pets. We made the mistake of thinking that we were on top of it all when our insurance decided to throw a spanner in the works.

A lady from the insurers' Dubai office (which handled Kazakhstan) called me to book the doctor who would be managing the baby's birth. This baby was to be delivered by a planned C-section, and it would be my third operation. The nurse (who was English) said that as I lived in Kazakhstan I would have to go to the UK to deliver. This would have been fair enough as the hospitals in Kazakhstan are not the best place for a repeat C-section. It took me some time to explain that I would not be in Kazakhstan but in Malaysia, on the island of Borneo, where the hospitals and doctors were capable of performing the operation I needed. She proceeded to lay into me over the telephone. I was lectured for 10 minutes. I was told that I was an irresponsible parent; a third C-section was a highly dangerous operation that could only be performed in certain hospitals. I should have thought about that before becoming pregnant apparently! I was both upset and bemused by this telephone conversation. After our older daughter was born, I checked with our OB who confirmed that there were no problems with either of my previous operations. Both had healed well, and I could happily go on to have at least two if not more C-sections extremely safely.

The nurse was not having any of it. She told me that insurance would only cover me for birth in the UK. I asked about alternative options in Kuala Lumpur and Singapore but was told that the hospitals there were not up to standard. This was a disaster for us. Our older children, aged seven and five at the time, would move with us to Borneo in June. If I had to return to the UK for delivery, we could all travel back there in July, but my husband and children would have to return to Borneo in August for the start of the new school year. My husband was the new principal of the school, and it would be impossible for him to take leave, and the whole process would be very disruptive for the children. To add to the nightmare the British Passport Office told me that as an Irish national, I could not apply for a passport for our new daughter. It would have to be done by my husband, and with a lot of papers that we did not have available. As an Irish national born abroad, I would not be able to apply for an Irish passport for the baby without paperwork including my father's birth certificate (in Ireland), my mother's birth certificate, and my parent's marriage certificate (in the Netherlands), their naturalization of marriage form (in Ireland), and my own registration of foreign birth (in Ireland). None of these are items I would have been able to gather in any sort of timely manner prior to our move. Like all expats I keep both scanned and spare copies of our own documentation, but I was not even aware that I had a foreign birth registration, as I have never needed it before, and my father and I lost my mother's birth certificate shortly after her death. This meant that the new baby and I would be stuck in the UK until my husband could join us in the October break, denying the older children the chance to bond with their new sister and likely to be feeling, I was sure, abandoned by me in a strange country and replaced in my affections by a sibling they had never met. If this was not bad enough, we would also have to face the financial costs of running two households and the multiple long-haul flights between Malaysia and the UK.

I am normally quite stoic, but this development reduced me to tears. The idea that our much-wanted baby could fracture our family dynamic so badly was horrendous. After taking a little time to let the call sink in, I became angry. Malaysia is a health tourism destination and has some of the best hospitals in the world. This woman was not only very badly wrong, but her point of view was insulting both to non-European health care systems and our decision to have a third child (one which had, after all, been made in the context of expert medical advice). I called our insurers' Malaysian office directly and explained the situation regarding the move. They were able to identify a suitable consultant OB in a hospital in our new hometown. He was highly qualified and extremely experienced in surgical deliveries, and the hospital, while small, was fully equipped for almost all emergencies, not just obstetric. The only thing it did not have was a neonatal emergency incubator, but there was one in another hospital in town which, together with an ambulance, could be put on standby with a quick call from the operating room should it become necessary during the delivery, which would be attended by a qualified pediatrician. I put a complaint in about the nurse from Dubai, and I hope that she has received suitable training to prevent something like this happening to another person.

Knowing that the details of the delivery would be sorted out without the need to travel halfway across the world was a big weight off our shoulders. However, as soon as that obstacle was cleared, another hurdle popped up. Malaysia, we read on a website, denies entry to any foreigner more than six months pregnant, and as luck would have it I would be just six months along when we flew. I had nightmares of being denied entry to the country and, with my Kazakh visa expired, stuck in Kuala Lumpur International Airport's no-man's land, like Tom Hanks in the film *Terminal*. Our new employers had never heard of this rule and thought we would be fine. We checked with the Malaysian embassy in Astana, and they said it would be fine, but a friend there gave us his number to get immigration to call just in case we did have a problem on arrival. Of course at six months the baby should hardly be showing and indeed was very neat and tucked away until the day before the flight when, inevitably, she decided to turn around and have a stretch! I went through the airport wearing a poncho with my large travel handbag held in front of my body, and luckily I was not questioned once. I heaved a sigh of relief when we finally cleared immigration in Miri, Borneo.

When our older daughter was born, our son was only 22 months old. We introduced the idea of a little sister about a month before she was born, and he accepted her straight away. These days he cannot remember what life was like as an only child. This time around, the children were much older and of course had strong memories of life with just the two of them, so we told them when I was about five months pregnant, and they were overjoyed! I don't think I have ever seen them as happy as that day. They came along to the scans and were fascinated to see the baby. They spent ages debating whether it would be a boy or a girl, with our son having a preference for a little brother and our daughter for a sister, and they helped us choose a name for each eventuality. Unfortunately the baby was positioned cross-legged at the first scan they came to, but we found out at the next one a few weeks later.

Our son's face fell momentarily when he heard he would be having another little sister, but he put on a brave face, and when we went for coffee after the appointment, he asked to go to the toy store to spend his pocket money. He came out not with the new piece of Lego he had wanted and been saving up for a long time but with a cuddly lamb for the baby. From that time on she was an integral part of the family. My stomach was introduced to strangers with the words, "This is my little sister; you can't see her yet, but she will be born soon."

They spoke to her all the time, telling her stories and describing everything they could see.

Moving is fraught at the best of times, but moving internationally is even worse. It took us about a month to find a shipping agent that could handle the transport to Malaysia. Kazakhstan is landlocked, so all moves are very complicated and expensive. Sadly freight to Malaysia is even more expensive because there is no possible land route—our entire shipment had to go by air cargo.

Our agents seemed to have a shaky understanding of geography and confused Borneo with Java and Malaysia with Indonesia. We were told our shipment would fly to Kuala Lumpur and would then be sent to Jakarta to clear customs before being shipped on to Borneo. They were rather surprised when we pointed out that Jakarta was not in Malaysia and that it would be better to send it straight to Miri from Kuala Lumpur. We were relieved we checked as not only did this save us time, but the redirection also saved us $2,500 from the already eye-watering quote.

The packing went surprisingly well—we had only taken a small shipment to Kazakhstan in the first place and had not accumulated much while we were there. We put everything in one room and left the packers to it. Traveling on the day, however, was less simple. We had a small amount of extra luggage, five suitcases between the four of us, one piece of hand luggage each and of course the two dogs in their crates. Getting everything into the terminal was relatively stress-free in Astana as the children knew the airport, and we could leave them with the bags while we ferried the trollies here, there, and everywhere.

Once we got to Malaysia, however, it became something of a nightmare. Because the state of Sarawak, our final destination, has different pet import rules to Peninsular Malaysia, we had to handle the transfer from one flight to the other ourselves. The children were too young for us to leave on their own with bags or dogs in a strange airport, so we ended up getting them to struggle with the hand luggage while my husband and I manhandled two trollies each. My favorite quote, when the children are asking me to do multiple things at once is that "I am not an octopus"—I could have done with eight arms that day! Apparently there is a porter service in Kuala Lumpur's airport, but predictably, we could not find it when we needed it.

Once we got to Miri in Borneo we were relieved of the dog crates as the veterinary assistants whisked them onto a truck and into quarantine while we went straight to the hotel for our first sleep in 36 hours. My husband was able to rest his foot that he had, rather unfortunately, broken the day before our flight. Within two weeks we had found a house, unpacked (one benefit of air freight is that it arrives promptly), and rescued a dog from quarantine. It took us a few more weeks to secure the release of the second dog but, with just five days to go before our daughter's delivery, we were completely settled in our new home.

One of the problems with any new posting, as every expat understands, is knowing what is available and where to buy it. Before we arrived in Miri I had no idea what baby things could be found in the shops and what we would struggle with. Buying in Astana was not an option, as the import taxes make foreign goods expensive. Add that to the costs of shipping on to Malaysia, and we would have been paying at least double the normal retail price for our goods—so we just had to wing it. People have babies everywhere, after all, and so at the least a car seat, bottles, and clothes would be easy to source. It turned out, luckily, that Miri had a few shops that stocked (in albeit limited ranges) everything we needed and more. We may not have got the stroller we wanted, but we did get something perfectly serviceable.

Our expensive, big-ticket items such as the high chair and crib were sent out separately from our storage in the UK. When my husband had gone to the UK to sort out our storage and get the baby things out, we did not know whether we were having a boy or a girl, so there was little point in bringing out old clothes. Our older two were newborns in the colder months in any event, so nothing would have really been suitable. He did, however, bring back the clothing that both our son and other daughter had been dressed in during their first days. These were sleepers with *Nijntie* (Miffy) the rabbit, my favorite childhood character, on the front. My mother had bought these especially for me when I was pregnant with our son. Very sadly she died, age 55, just six months after he was born, and those newborn clothes were the only tangible gift I have been able to give the girls from their Oma who would have loved to shower them with cuddles, clothes, and gifts. They were hidden at the back of our gigantic storage container, and my wonderful husband pulled everything out to ensure that our new baby could wear these precious clothes. They were the only things I absolutely "had to have" for the new baby, and I cried bittersweet tears when he brought them home to me. All three of our children have now worn them as their first clothes, and they remain one of the most treasured things I own.

I cannot describe the relief when, a few days after landing in Miri, we were finally able to have a prenatal appointment with an English-speaking OB. Initially he asked me to talk him through a translation of the Russian notes from Kazakhstan, but it took forever, and he decided it would be easier to just do as much of the full anatomy and health scans as he could over again. Like the Kazakh doctors, he seemed overly interested in my weight gain and was, like the British doctors, very intrigued by my (always very low) blood pressure. We did get a full scan at every appointment and, much to our and the children's delight, we were able to take printed pictures home with us. He was also able to set up a date for delivery. Our daughter was desperate for her sister to be born on her birthday, September 1, but we thought that in the long run, it would be better for them to have separate days, and so we pushed the delivery date to September 2.

The tour of the hospital left us gobsmacked. The rooms were excellent, spacious, beautifully clean, and with a good bathroom and plenty of seating for guests. What surprised us, however, were the discussions concerning the extra beds. Would my husband be staying overnight? No, he would be at home with the older children. Oh no problem, we were told, they could stay at the hospital with us; sadly they would not be permitted in the operating room for hygiene reasons, but they could sit in the waiting room, and a nurse would keep an eye on them.

This was one of those moments of weird cultural disconnect. I could understand that people might want their children to stay overnight, particularly if they could not find alternative childcare for them. Indeed, we had asked whether this was possible in the UK when our older daughter was born and were greeted with incredulous looks. What we could not understand was that enough people had asked for their children to be present in the operating room that the manager felt that she needed to dismiss this option and apologize for it being company policy. As it happened, my sister traveled out for the delivery so that she could bring the children from school straight to visit their new sister and then home to sleep. This meant that my husband could stay as late as possible on the first day before going back to work again the next. The attitude of family and children being welcome at the hospital was nevertheless a truly welcome change from the hospital where we had our other children. The staff at the previous hospital had tried to turn our family away when they arrived to meet our son. It was all very frustrating and upsetting to have had my sister turned away, as it followed an unexpected and frightening emergency operation after a textbook pregnancy. We had wanted to show off our living, breathing, healthy son, and share him with our family and friends.

This time, on the day of the delivery the preparations progressed pretty much the same way as they had with the planned C-section delivery of our older daughter. We arrived early to the hospital, and following some tests, the nurses took me into the operating room for a spinal and a baby. In the UK, my husband was allowed to be with me throughout, but in Malaysia he was only allowed in the operating room for a limited amount of time. He was brought in only when the surgeon was ready to cut and ejected as soon as the baby was born. I was wheeled in on my own, and a very friendly anesthetist gave me the spinal while the OR nurses prepared the drapes and equipment.

There was a rather surreal moment when a popular song came on the radio, and they all started singing along—I felt like I was in a musical and half expected the surgeon (who bore a comical and unfortunate resemblance to a cartoon character from my childhood) to turn up singing too! As soon as he arrived (thankfully silent and not singing), my husband was ushered into the OR, and the operation got underway. A quick 20 minutes later and with a sigh of relief that parents from around the world are familiar with, we heard our little girl's rather indignant cry. She was checked and cleaned up before the anesthetist took a few photographs of my husband showing her to me, and then she was whisked off to the nursery.

This threw me a little. We knew it would happen, but in the UK our two previous babies and my husband had been allowed to stay with me. We had agreed that my husband would go with the baby so that she had a parent with her at all times, and I stayed, obviously, on the table in the OR getting ever more bored by the minute. I wanted desperately to see our new baby, but all I could look at were the five photographs on the camera and the surgical drapes. If we ever have another baby, I will ask to bring my Kindle into the OR because the long stitch-up phase is just plain dull without the grand prize to coo over. I was wheeled into recovery, where I had a quick chat with one of my husband's colleagues who had delivered in the adjoining OR at exactly the same time. She left after a few minutes, and I had to spend another half hour languishing on my own before being brought up to my room, where my husband was waiting with breakfast, having delegated baby watching duties to my sister.

I finally saw the baby two hours after she was born and when the newborn wakeful stage had passed. Annoyingly enough, she slept soundly for the next four hours while I had to resist the urge to wake her up!

More frustrations arose, as different cultural expectations reared their heads. We had been told that although the hospital recommended nursing, they were happy to provide formula for the baby, if requested. When our daughter woke up, my husband went to ask for a bottle, only to be told that hospital formula had to be spoon-fed by a nurse in the nursery. There had been no mention of that restriction on the tour, so my husband had to take the baby all the way to the nursery (a floor down) while my sister rushed home to get the bottles, travel sterilizer, and formula. I was stuck all alone in my room without the baby, but at least this time I had my Kindle for company. I never felt bullied into nursing the baby, which was an improvement over my experience in the UK where they did everything possible to try to force me to nurse, but the hospital certainly did not make it easy for us to feed her. The nurses also kept on trying to take the baby away to run checks, which, instead of being done in our room, were performed in the central nursery.

They could not understand why my husband or sister followed them around at all times and why, once they went home, I refused all permission for the baby to be removed from my side. Unlike the UK where I had been allowed to get up 12 hours after each operation I was kept bed-bound for a full (frustrating) 24 hours. As soon as I was mobile and had had my shower (with the baby in the bathroom so she could not be snuck away for temperature readings), I insisted on following the baby every time she was taken away to the great surprise of the nurses; I think they reduced the frequency of the tests as they were concerned I was being too active. I was surprised to see the other babies asleep in their cots in the nursery without any parent or family member, just in the care of a nurse. I am by no means an attachment parent and have happily left all babies with family and close friends from the moment of their birth, but I just could not leave a brand new baby in the care of a stranger, no matter how kind and competent.

I had hoped to go home the day after the delivery but unfortunately, just like in the UK, I was kept in for two days. I was anxious to start my life with my entire family and wanted to escape the hospital environment. Unlike in the UK where the car insurers forbid driving for between two to six weeks following a C-section, I was told I was clear to drive as soon as I felt able to do so. This was a real blessing as after a few days at home the baby and I were able to get out and about and avoid cabin fever. This led to a few more cultural surprises. It is normal here for Malaysian women from all cultures (Malay, Chinese, and Indian) to have at least a month of confinement following delivery. As a result it is very unusual for people to see tiny babies out and about. I don't think I could have managed to stay home for a whole month; I barely managed two days, and I think I would have gone quietly mad. In any event it would have been completely impractical as my husband had to travel for work, the older children needed to be picked up from school, and I had a stream of visiting family members to feed and entertain. Local people thought I was a little eccentric but wrote it off as another cultural quirk.

Exactly one month after delivery we were invited to the home of my husband's colleague (the one I had met in the recovery room), to celebrate her daughter's "full moon" and the end of the confinement period. Everyone brought gifts for the baby (red *Ang-Pow* envelopes of cash and toys to play with), and the parents put on a full spread. It was not unlike a christening, a chance for extended family and friends to meet and get to know the baby.

One of the things I love about Malaysia is that everyone from old grannies to young men loves babies, so sitting in a coffee shop and reading my book was a thoroughly pleasant experience. People popped their heads in the pram to tell me how beautiful she was. Everyone likes to hear how his or her baby is stunning. Our baby seemed to generate extra attention because of her very pale skin.

When our baby was very small, people would just take a peek, but as she has grew bigger people asked for the chance to have cuddles. When we are in a restaurant or a café she will often be entertained by a waitress while we enjoy our meal; everyone wants to meet her, and it is not unusual for the chef to come out of the kitchen to make a fuss. Add into the mix her adoring fan club of older brother and sister making up a trio of children who look very like each other and completely different from local families, and they are made a fuss of wherever we go. As a result of all this admiration, our little baby has turned into the most delightfully gregarious girl. Our other two children were friendly and neither was ever shy, but this baby truly relishes the attention. As long as she knows we are close by, she is happy to be picked up and snuggled by just about anyone.

The immunization schedule is slightly different here, and the baby received shots that the others did not get and have had to have as supplementary jabs later in life. Taking the baby in for immunizations was a bit of a mission, though, as she has to have a full developmental pediatric check-ups at the same time. I don't recall ever having any check-ups after about eight weeks with our older children. There have been some other differences as well; our nanny/housekeeper kept on wanting to put pillows, blankets, and stuffed toys in the baby's crib and was quite surprised that we would not allow it. Malaysian babies sleep either in a hammock or in a crib that is so padded with bumpers, duvets, pillows, and toys that it is a wonder the poor things can sleep at all. We almost gave up getting her to babysit, as no matter how much we tried to persuade her that the baby can sleep with lights and TV on, we would come back to find her sitting completely silent in the dark for fear of disturbing the baby. People out and about seem genuinely surprised at the variety of foods the baby will eat, and a number of friends have children who, at a year old, have not progressed further than rice porridge. I always get the impression people think I am being deeply irresponsible feeding raisins and peas while simultaneously thinking I am overcautious for strapping her into the high chair and using a car seat! What is wonderful, however, and a breath of fresh air for us is that the baby is welcome everywhere, from a decent restaurant to the cinema.

Having our first two children in the UK was a steep learning curve for me. Probably because the only reference I had was my mother's (by then completely out-of-date) experience in the Netherlands and Norway 30 years earlier. The two of us were bewildered by the (very non-medicalized) British system. Having found a doctor to trust in Britain, my husband and I had to completely relearn the system and adjust our expectations in Kazakhstan and Malaysia.

We found some aspects better, some completely confusing, and some downright weird, but I can honestly say that on balance it was no better (and no worse) than having babies in the UK. As we watch her grow, we are thankful, every day, for our beautiful Borneo baby and the Kazakh and Malaysian doctors who made sure she arrived safely.

The Ersatz Expat is a 30-something global soul, a perpetual expat with no permanent home base. Born in the Netherlands to a Dutch/Irish family, she has since lived in Norway, Nigeria, Turkey, Venezuela, the UK, Kazakhstan, and now Malaysia. She blogs about the ever-changing challenges of expat life at http://ersatzexpat.blogspot.com.

CHAPTER 8

BEAUTIFUL

Penelope Stanley
Nationality: Australia
Birthed in: Australia, New Zealand, and France

"Nathan, I'm pregnant," I whispered exhaustedly. We were sitting in a small, dim hotel room in the middle of Orléans, France. Light snow fell softly through the night onto the beautiful city I had only briefly glimpsed through exhausted eyes. Kody, our one-year-old, snuggled in the pillows on our bed. Miles and Tiggy slept soundly in the next room. The children and I had spent the previous 27 hours traveling halfway across the world from Australia to France to meet my research scientist husband who had done the same trip two weeks earlier to prepare for an almost two-year stay in France.

"Pregnant?" he hoarsely whispered back and I was glad I had waited till we were together again before telling him.

We didn't have to say any more. We felt so unprepared and overwhelmed by the unknown before us that there wasn't anything else to say. At that stage we were unaware how much God had prepared us already by our experiences with our midwife in New Zealand. Claire had not only helped us, she had empowered us.

I imagined what she would have said: *"Oh a French baby! Congratulations! Of course you can do this, you're a pro. You'll see, it will be beautiful."*

My previous three births had been almost identical, so much so that I knew how it should work out—from the birth date of the baby, to how long my labor would be, and how much pain I could expect. Pregnancy, birth, and newborn babies I knew well, but the French system—that was an entirely different matter.

Many weeks later, I lay under a tree outside the apartment we had rented. The children played among the dandelions and wild poppies. Tossing a stack of papers aside I slowly, deliberately breathed in the sweet smell of spring, persuading my mind to relax. I'd been struggling to understand the notes that my new friend had given me explaining the appointments I'd need, the endless amount of forms that had to be completed, and the people I'd have to contact. It wasn't that her notes weren't clear it was just that even with all her assistance there was so much to do. I was starting to see why French bureaucracy has the reputation it does. I lay my head back in defeat. The dappled sunlight flickered through the leaves, warming my now significantly bulging tummy.

You have a beautiful puku.

I smiled remembering the first time I'd heard Claire use the Māori word for "tummy" in New Zealand. My hand rested on my bump as I searched the branches above. The previous night a summer storm had blown violently through the tree where a *maman* bird had her nest as I had snuggled under my blankets on the other side of the window. I'd worried for her. And I'd worried for me. I was yet to have blood tests, scans, and midwife appointments. I didn't know the language and was really struggling to learn it. There was so much to do. I didn't even know if I knew all the things I had to do.

Yes you do. What you have to do is birth a baby. And you do know how to do that. Feel your ppi (baby) moving under your hand. Your baby needs its whnau (family) and you can give it that.

I sighed. My friend had told me that the French system was complicated and rigid. My hospital had an 82% epidural rate. She'd said they automatically give oxytocin once a woman is in labor. Mothers birth on their backs with their feet in stirrups. And that's not to mention newborn care and breastfeeding. I knew it was just a different culture, but at that moment I didn't like it. I was terrified that their way wouldn't work for me. But how much right did I have to go against the system when I was living in their country and benefiting from their "services"?

I suppose the only boobs they're comfortable seeing are ones in bikinis. Listen, the birth is yours. Regardless of what system you're in, you are still the mother giving birth to your baby. You'll do great.

I watched as the *maman* bird confidently left her eggs under the warmth of the summer sun to snack on the crumbs left by my children. She wasn't worried. She just did her job.

The first step: Speak with a general practitioner. It was a warm Sunday morning, quietly friendly and lazily busy in the way only French Sundays can be. My friend introduced me to a doctor who attended our church and spoke perfect English. He directed me to check that my toxoplasmosis immunization was still effective. Having had three other children I knew about toxoplasmosis being a dangerous bacterial infection for pregnancy but was unaware that there was an immunization against it. In my confusion I informed him that I'd never been immunized against toxoplasmosis but that I knew all about pregnancy recommendations.

So, you know the deal, avoid soft cheese, deli meats, and all that.

He looked at me in disbelief, and as I inhaled the wonderful scent of Sunday lunch coming from the church's kitchen I remembered that this was France. Soft cheese and rare meat are staples. How could I not eat them?

An English-born friend of mine contributed to our discussion confirming that in Australia, pregnant women are advised against eating foods that have the potential to cause toxoplasmosis.

"It *is* possible, you know," I grinned.

I want to know how mothers in France survive pregnancy without the wine.

He smiled, a bit skeptically at me, then gave me a referral to receive a blood test to check, among other things, my toxoplasmosis immunity and organized for me to receive my 20-week ultrasound.

Car lights flashed purposefully along the well-lit street where I waited in the evening breeze for the bus to take me to my 10 p.m. ultrasound appointment. For a moment I gave up the struggle against my weary, more-than-20-weeks-pregnant body and stared through the busy lights of the street into the unknown darkness of Jardin des Plantes where in the day my children liked to play. My eyes gave up trying to focus on the beautiful places I knew were behind the stone wall and closed metal gates of the garden. I could see nothing. The gates were closed, the path was dark, the road was busy, and the only hope in reaching the beautiful place was with the morning light. But the night was early, the darkness was long, and I was tired.

The bus came and made the short trip to the hospital in very little time. Inside, the fairly typical-looking hospital was, not surprisingly for 10 p.m., reasonably empty, giving me the freedom to look completely lost and confused. I was thankful to be able to stare for an embarrassingly long time at the directions board in the entrance without making a fool of myself. I finally deciphered where I was meant to be and headed down a dimly lit empty corridor till I found a narrow waiting area. After a short while a sonographer came out from behind a door, saw me, and invited me into her examination room. Very quickly she realized my lack of French language skills and, to my great relief, informed me that she'd worked in Australia several years ago and spoke English well.

I sat on the edge of the hard examination table, silently waiting while she studied my personal information. The room was well equipped but obviously old, and the boarded-up window blocked any expression of elegance in the ancient structure. The sonographer then looked up at me curiously and pointed out that my file was lacking the first 10-week dating scan required in the French system. I hurried to explain that we'd arrived in France, navigated the French bureaucracy, and registered my pregnancy too late to receive that scan. In the Australian system the early dating scan was only required if the mother was unsure of her personal calculations of her baby's due date. I explained that I hadn't had a dating scan with any of my other children but that my personal calculations of the due date had been very reliable for each of them.

"No," she responded, "This is not good; you can't know when your due date is without the scan. I'll have to do a dating today, but it won't be accurate."

Silently assenting, I lay down and looked around the room while she readied her equipment. As she touched the warm transducer to my stomach, I stretched my neck to get my first magical glimpse of our little baby on her screen.

Awww, look, I can see your baby's little fingers, just perfect.

I stretched some more just as the sonographer adjusted her screen so she could see it better—and consequently, I couldn't see it at all. My baby moved under the pressure, and I smiled. I didn't need to see an image on a screen to know my baby. Feeling more comfortable, I closed my eyes and relaxed, but the sonographer wanted to talk.

"The first scan is important," she said as she studied my baby on her screen, "It shows us if there are problems. Many problems are very serious, like maybe the baby has no bones in his head, or maybe there is a problem with the pregnancy, or maybe his heart is not working well."

My expression remained neutral, but inwardly I imagined what Claire's response would be: *Who is this woman? You'd think with her career she'd have some idea of what it's like to be pregnant.*

I opened my eyes and tried once more to see my baby on her screen.

She continued, "If we see these problems in an early scan it is easier for the doctor to tell the mother, because the baby is still very little. But if we don't have an early scan, we don't see these problems until 20 weeks. The baby is bigger, and it is very difficult for everyone."

I looked at her in veiled astonishment and asked her how my baby looked.

"*Très bien!*" she said, "*Parfait!*" I decided that an attempt to change the subject might be a good idea for both of us and asked her about the visit to Australia she'd mentioned.

"I was part of a team in Sydney teaching a more effective system of maternity care," she began to explain.

Pft, I'll bet!

"I spent some time teaching in New Zealand, too. The maternity care there is very inconsistent. The way we were teaching, everyone receives good care."

Hey! The system in New Zealand provides a very individual treatment of maternity care. It allows every woman to consistently choose to have whichever type of carer she prefers throughout her entire pregnancy.

Curious and somewhat puzzled, I asked her how she viewed consistent maternity care.

"For example," she answered, "You did not get an early scan. Some hospitals do the right checks, others do not. In Australia, not every mother has the same facilities. Some are monitored a lot, and some not much at all; there is a big variation. In France, all care is complete, and every woman is treated the same."

But every woman is different. Some women need more monitoring, others need very little. Sometimes medical intervention helps a pregnancy, and sometimes it leads to problems. Some women feel more comfortable surrounded by medical facilities; others feel more comfortable in the familiarity of their homes. Our job is to place you in the most ideal situation to allow you to give birth, so that you and your baby are healthy.

I gasped slightly as my baby kicked me suddenly in my ribs, and the sonographer continued to explain to me that the practice of women contributing to decisions regarding their own care and the failure of the government to provide consistency was much worse in New Zealand than Australia

Worse? Why, because they give the care that is based on the woman's needs instead of the government's?

Our conversation had gone from slightly awkward to almost humorous, but I had started to feel a bit defensive. My experiences in New Zealand had been wonderful and invaluable, especially when reflecting upon them during the past few months of struggling through the French system. Nathan and I had been so thankful that under the New Zealand system, and with the help of Claire, our midwife, we'd unquestionably been allowed to experience a wonderful home birth.

"Home birth?!" the sonographer shook her head but then kept her mouth shut.

Really? I do still shave my armpits you know!

I was 30 weeks pregnant, and I'd had an ultrasound, some blood tests, and a couple of appointments at my general practitioner. Yet, because of the timing of our arrival in France, I was only now at my first midwife appointment. After settling Kody on the chair with a stern warning to stay still, I climbed onto the examination table.

"*Je vais d'abord mesurer l'hauteur utérine,*" my midwife said and pushed the length of measuring tape against my bone.

We didn't try to communicate, so I let my experience with Claire lead the way.

Feel the edge of this bone, this is where we measure from right over your belly to the top.

The French midwife put her hand on my tummy and gently poked and prodded around. As the baby moved under her touch, my breath caught in my throat. At already 30 weeks of pregnancy, this was the first professional to feel my baby, and I was surprised at how comforting it was to know that someone else was now caring for it.

Feel here, this is your baby's head.

The baby moved under her touch, and my midwife smiled.

Baby doesn't like being poked.

I concentrated as the midwife moved her hand lower over my tummy.

Oh, another little bump, here's your baby's little bottom.

The baby moved, kicking hard against the hands. A heel, a knee, an elbow.

"*Et voici, un pied.*" She smiled.

Seems like your baby has long limbs like its mommy.

"*Maintenant je vais vérifier le rythme cardiaque de votre bébé.*"

The midwife continued her examination by squirting cold blue gel onto my stomach, then gently pressed a Doppler through my skin against where she knew my baby's heart would be, and I heard the steady rhythmic sound of my baby's heartbeat for the first time. I smiled at the midwife, unable to convey the extent of my appreciation. At this stage a simple "*merci beaucoup*" seemed so inadequate. I wished I knew the words to express what was in my heart. My midwife concentrated as she held the Doppler steady while my baby squirmed underneath, and we both silently and carefully listened to the miracle of life within me.

Listen, there it is. It's steady and strong. Just the right timing. Beautiful.

"*Très bien! Parfait!*"

"*Très bien! Fini. Venez vous asseoir.*" It was only a month before my baby was due, and the midwife had just finished checking my baby's heartbeat again. I awkwardly pushed myself upright and climbed off the high bed in the midwifery clinic. As I sat, I scooped up my almost-two-year-old and arranged him around the ever-growing bump on my front.

"*Comment vous sentez-vous? Vous avez des problèmes?*"

How are your hips and back? Any pain or discomfort? Not long now!

I confirmed as I always did that physically everything was wonderful. I had no problems and felt my baby moving strongly every day. I'd been well aware and very thankful that this pregnancy had been by far my easiest physically. Even the normal discomforts of pregnancy had been very minimal.

"*D'accord. Très bien. Pouvez-vous s'il vous plaît confirmer la date de votre bébé est dû,*" she requested as she turned the screen of her computer toward me and pointed to a series of dates under my personal details. I studied them in detail. After some moments I found the due date: October 18. In France, the due date is officially at 41 weeks pregnancy, which I calculated to be November 1, however after my 20-week scan the sonographer had adjusted the date to October 25. The 18th was over a week earlier than that. Regardless of what the official date was, I knew it was very likely that my baby would be born very close to October 27, but if my due date was recorded as the 18th, I would be under pressure to induce before my original due date had even been reached.

Inductions can be necessary, but if possible it is much better to avoid it. Often intervention leads to further intervention. This looks like a problem that needs to be fixed.

With a mixture of confusion, dread, and determination, I pointed out the inaccuracy of the date to the midwife. The midwife reached over, took my scans, and studied them while I sat holding my little boy closely, watching and waiting.

"*Ce ne sont pas votre fichier.*" This name is not your name.

Somehow I had come to the appointment with another person's scan. Slowly the full import of what she'd said sank in. If the name on the scans were not mine, and the adjusted due date was different, how much of the other information was incorrect? What if our baby had a problem and no one knew? And what could I do to get that date changed back again? I thought about the situation but was completely perplexed as to how the mistake could have occurred, and totally unaware of how it could be resolved. My body began to shake in fearful anticipation of the consequences.

Don't worry about the system. You focus on you and your baby. That's the important part.

I took a deep breath and attempted to focus. It was true. I was present during the scan, and although that was an adventure all of its own, I knew that everything was fine with the baby. This was just a paper problem and despite the confusing French bureaucracy, or perhaps because of it, the French are almost magically adept at resolving bureaucratic problems. I hoped this would be the case again.

"*C'est un problème. Je ne peux pas utiliser ces scans. Vous aurez à prendre ces analyses au bureau de l'échographie demain. D'accord? Vous devez expliquer au bureau de l'hôpital. Il y à une confusion avec la numérisation. Ils vont résoudre le problème.*"

I was confused.

"This is *problème*. I cannot use this. You go *to bureau de l'hôpital demain*, tomorrow."

Dubiously, I looked at the midwife and finally realized that this was a problem I would have to resolve by myself with the hospital staff. The sonographer knew English well, and the midwife and I managed to communicate, but the hospital staff—none of them knew English at all nor would they be able to understand my attempts at French. There was no way I could explain a problem like this to the hospital staff. No way.

She grabbed a piece of paper and pen. "I write. You take. Tomorrow."

I looked doubtfully at the hastily scribbled single sentence on the back of the paper she held out to me, took it, nodded reluctantly, and held Kody's hand as we made the thoughtful trip home.

The next day I took the incorrect scans, my note, and Nathan to the hospital. As we approached the hospital I looked at the beautiful Loire River flowing alongside the stunning old town of Orléans. Despite the seemingly endless difficulties, Orléans' beauty and atmosphere never failed to take my breath away.

"It's just as well you're so beautiful," I mumbled to the ancient buildings and stepped through the daunting hospital doors.

"*Un problème*," I offered lamely to the lady at the desk by way of explanation.

She took my scan and the short note and studied them, while Nathan and I stood together waiting uselessly. My faith in the confusing French bureaucracy, or rather in the amazing efficiency the French have in dealing with the bureaucracy grew, as with no hesitation or confusion, one of the staff called the sonographer who had taken my scans. Nathan and I didn't even attempt French when we saw her but rather explained as best we could in English that there was somehow a problem with my scan and that the one I had now wasn't mine.

"Yes," she said looking at it, "It is yours. The details are yours, but just the name is different." With the ability to use English my confidence had grown, and I looked at her skeptically.

"No." I said, "The date is incorrect."

And I tried to convince her to correct it. After only a short moment she took my scan, sighed, and asked me which date I wanted. I smiled. Maybe I would learn how to deal with the French bureaucracy by the end of my pregnancy too.

By the evening of October 27, the date on which I'd always thought our baby would be born, we'd rung my friend to babysit, explained to the children that mommy was in labor, and organized a rushed lift to the hospital. As I pushed myself out of the car, a strong contraction pulsed through me, and I knew that it wouldn't be a long wait at the hospital before we'd meet our baby. Fear of what might be required of me and of not being able to understand or explain, sat with presumptive familiarity alongside the excitement and confidence of birthing our baby.

Nathan carried my bag and a copy of our birth plan in French as we walked bravely through the emergency entrance to the hospital. The desk was empty, and immediately I felt an amazing sensation of my body pausing from the inside out.

After some searching Nathan found a midwife to help us. In contrast to the urgency I felt was warranted by our arrival at the hospital, she calmly looked at me, handed me a jar to collect a urine sample, and pointed to a door with *"Toilette"* written above it. I stared at her incredulously as I felt the niggling approach of another contraction, and without thought of our language barrier I burst out in rapid Australian English, attempting to convince her that my baby was very ready to be born, and that if she wanted me to provide her a urine sample it was very likely that she'd be dealing with a birth in the waiting room.

The midwife pointed, shaking her head, to the toilet door. And with a deep breath I remembered to focus on my body

Relax. Your body has slowed right down. It's waiting till you're in a safe place. I know you're nearly there, but this labor is not going to progress till you and the baby are comfortable. And for now that's a good thing.

"*D'accord,*" I said and took the jar.

When I was ready, she showed us into another room, bright, but too empty. I looked around in frustration realizing that she'd led us into an assessment room and not the place where they wanted me to give birth.

Nathan was studying me, his face shrouded in worry. He remembered how fast the other babies had come. He knew that I was almost there when we'd left our apartment.

"It's ok," I assured him, "It's stopped. My body knows we're not ready. Hopefully, it'll start up again nicely once they finally show us where we're meant to have this baby."

After monitoring my conveniently stalled labor and discussing and making compromises on our birth plan for some time, another midwife had eventually led us into a different room, organized us, and left us with instructions to press the button when we needed her. Thankful for the time alone, I slowly scanned the birthing room from my central position atop of the narrow foldable bed. Trolleys of towels and sheets crowded against the cornflower blue walls, a threatening jumble of monitors and machines behind me, tubes and a few surgical instruments laid out on the bench in front of me anticipating complications. A yellow glow from the corridor spilled under the slightly open door. As a contraction began to build up, I shifted slightly in my kneeling position on the thin mattress, carefully rearranging the drip taped to my hand. I closed my eyes as the contraction intensified, and I realized that my body was once again ready to birth our baby. The monitors beeped at me. Fear built in my mind and pulsed through my whole body with every wave of the contraction.

"I can't do this."

You're doing great. It's all perfect.

Breathe. After another short break, I shifted again. Nathan perched on the edge of the bed behind me, his hands gently caressing the small of my back. I moved my hand between the tight monitoring bands over my bulging tummy, careful not to disturb the drip. Everything loomed over me waiting, ready for me to fail.

"I really don't think I can do this. It's not going to work."

Of course you can do this. Our bodies are made to give birth. You've done it before. Remember it. Feel it. Take control of this, Penny, it's your birth. You do it. Everything else is only here to help if you need it.

Another contraction built up, pushing the fear away. As the contraction strengthened I felt the peace of trust and confidence flow through my body, stronger and stronger. My hand rested on my belly. I could feel the baby moving lower.

Can you feel the baby moving? See, it's coming.

Our baby was coming. Amidst the required concentration, I struggled to tell Nathan that the baby was almost here and to press the button.

The movement and pressure intensified simultaneously. It kept coming; wave after wave flowed over me from my center all through my body. I couldn't breathe. The pressure increased as I struggled to regain control till a burst of fluid gave me just enough reprieve to pause mid-contraction.

Wait, breathe, just wait a second, slowly. Slowly.

Nathan pressed the button.

Reach here and feel this, your baby's head is just there, can you feel baby's hair? See, you're doing it.

I reached down, my fingers fluttered over the surface of my baby's head. I closed my eyes, picturing what was happening.

The space I was in had narrowed. The ominous machines blurred out of view till all my focus and energy was centered on our baby and the job we were doing. I vaguely heard the midwife come into the room, and then heard a muffled yell in French out the door. Another midwife rushed into the room.

Are you ready to finish now?

I look down at my belly then over at the midwives, one eye on me, talking rapidly in French to each other as they rushed to pull their gloves on and organize their tools. I was ready, but they were not.

You're doing fine without them, they're ready enough if you need them, but you don't need them yet, and your baby wants to come now. Slowly, gently, and go. That's it.

I let the pressure go and slowly our baby's head moved lower and lower into my waiting hands till suddenly his whole body was out, and I held him gently just under my belly. I slowly took careful grip on his slippery little body and brought him up to my chest. One midwife draped towels and blankets over both of us, the other midwife clamped the cord and helped Nathan cut it. He hugged me close as we both looked into the squinting eyes of our new little baby snuggled in my arms.

I laughed. "Thank you God! Nathan, we did it. Look! It's a boy!"

I told you it would be beautiful.

Ezra Jérémie (meaning help, sent by God) was born to Nathan and Penelope in October 2013 in Orléans, France, joining his siblings Miles, Antigone, and Dakota (Kody) in their adventures around the world. Penelope's husband is a research scientist (organic chemist). It is a career that has so far led their family on a life of spontaneity, change, uncertainty, excitement, and adventure as they travel two years at a time between countries. Over the last five years they have lived in New Zealand, France, and Australia. Penelope and her family are currently living in Adelaide, Australia where she and her husband were born and raised.

They are enjoying the opportunity to reintroduce their young family to Australian life but also look forward with anticipation to future adventures from further travel. Penelope likes to read, write, take photographs, absorb local culture, and explore the streets of whichever city she is in with her family and camera.

CHAPTER 9

GLOWING IN GLAMOROUS DUBAI

Michelle Estekantchi
Nationality: Canada and Iran
Birthed in: Dubai

I entered this world with a unique background and often used it in awkward social situations when I was fumbling for a topic for discussion. It made me seem much more interesting than I actually felt and usually lifted eyebrows. It made me more memorable. It also provided barriers, created challenges, and gave my life a path that I couldn't help but follow—it comprised my destiny.

I was born in 1978 in Tehran, Iran. Yes, the Iran we all have heard about in the news. At that moment in time, Iran was a hot spot for travelers and expats. It was a very rich country with an amazing nightlife, great skiing, wonderful seaside, and large gardens. Iranians had all of the same freedoms that most people enjoy in the western world today. My mom, a young Canadian girl, moved to Tehran after graduating with a business degree from a university in California and started work as a computer programmer despite having no experience in the field. During her university years she had met some Iranian students who had piqued her interest in the country and, combined with the extravagant expat job opportunities offered by numerous companies, she jumped at the opportunity. She always proclaimed her four years in

Iran were the best years of her life. Keep in mind, my mother has lived an extraordinary life, so the statement is a bold one.

I grew up hearing stories of glamorous surroundings, parties with movie stars and singers, gardens that go on for miles, and a general life of leisure and love. It was a carefree life in a carefree country. All of that disappeared in 1979 when the revolution changed the face of Iran forever. Like many Iranians, we abandoned our lives there and were forced to begin again in California. I was two years old when we immigrated and never saw the Iran my mom reminisced about. However, the love she had for the country affected my childhood, and I grew up knowing every detail of Iran in its glory days from the constant stories, books, conversations, and movies my mom insisted I absorb. Perhaps she felt she could replicate the cultural immersion she experienced. She flooded me with love for a country I knew so little about. My dad, a gentle, kind, quiet soul never had that passion for his own country. He was truly Iranian and proud of who he was but not passionate about instilling patriotism in me. He was always very happy we had an opportunity to move to the United States and always felt there were far better opportunities for us in a country not governed by religion. And that is the introduction to my life and my common icebreaker for awkward conversations.

We remained in the San Francisco Bay area until I was 11 years old. The Bay Area is a diverse, busy, urban, forward-thinking heart of California. At age 11, I moved back to my mom's hometown in Canada. It was a rural town with a population of approximately 2,000 people. I was the only person who had tan-colored skin for towns, literally towns. My black hair and deep brown eyes stood in contrast to the blond-haired, blue-eyed classmates that surrounded me. I remained there for the remainder of junior high and high school. I was both interesting and different, and I learned to stand with confidence or crumble with my natural insecurities. It was an idyllic place to grow up in many respects. The intimate environment provided me love, safety, security, and a strong education. However, it was not a place rich with opportunities to learn more about my Iranian heritage.

By the time I had turned 33, I graduated with a master's degree in education and worked as a school counselor and private counselor for about eight years on the east coast of Canada. I was promoted to diversity management consultant for a school board, and I loved my career. The problem was, I had hit a wall in my career and my personal life. I wasn't married and had no possible candidate. Despite a full social calendar and juggling a few hobbies, I was mostly bored. No matter how full my life was—and it was super full and amazingly great in so many ways—I felt like something was missing, but I couldn't pinpoint what exactly what it was. In the summer of 2010 during a road trip to Montreal, a friend asked me what I was passionate about, and I automatically answered, "Iran."

I always wanted to spend more time there. I wanted my Iranian summer vacations to last longer. I cried endlessly every August when it was time to leave. When my father passed away four years earlier, my passion and longing to stay in Iran intensified, though I never seriously considered staying. I had other goals to follow. But now, in the middle of this road trip's introspective conversation, I realized that Iran was the missing piece in my life. All I wanted to do was to live there. The best memories of my life were in Iran. My large loving family and the best food I had ever tasted was in Iran. Beyond all else, I wanted to live there, the place the rest of the Western world was forbidden to enter.

In February 2011, I requested and was granted unpaid leave at the school board. I will be forever grateful to my supervisor who supported my dream and made it possible. I packed up my nicely furnished one-bedroom apartment and placed all my belongings into storage, save for two suitcases. I began the rounds of goodbye dinners, drinks, and heartfelt conversations. Many people didn't understand why I was leaving. Most just chalked it up to being crazy and reckless. Many cautioned that I was destroying my career, and they worried about my financial stability. Perhaps they considered moving to Iran as immature, a gap year way too late in life. Overall, I got a sense that most people either were either confused by my decision or felt bad for me in some strange way. However, I had my little crew of people who cheered me on, supported my dreams and understood what fueled my desire to go to Iran. February 14, 2011 was the date that one chapter ended, and my Iranian chapter began.

My time in Iran was everything I had imagined. It fulfilled my expectations and then some. The people were friendly, the family time was soul-soothing, and the food was delicious. The parties were extreme. My Farsi improved slightly despite intensive daily classes and being immersed in the language. The longer I stayed, the more I considered living there long-term. However, I missed the modern conveniences of a developed country. I missed conversing and doing daily things with ease, in English, and I wanted to work again. While in Iran, I had traveled to Dubai for two short trips and loved the city from the time I put my feet on the ground.

Dubai was warm, sunny, luxurious, modern, and shiny. Everything seemed to glitter in the constant sunlight. It felt like a depiction of paradise that you cut out of a magazine. There were so many different activities offered all day and all night. No matter who you are or what your interest are, Dubai has something to offer you. I loved the beach, nice restaurants, modern surroundings, luxury shopping, and all of the parties. Dubai was my oasis in the desert.

At one of those parties I attended during my first trip to Dubai, I met the man who would later become my husband. We met through a mutual friend and we kept in touch through emails and chats until he could visit me in Iran. I didn't move to Dubai just for him, but he definitely made my introduction to Dubai much sweeter. He took me to parties and clubs, and we spent our weekends on the beach. He introduced me to many people who would later become my friends. During the mornings I would look for jobs, but during the remainder of the time I lived a casual life and often walked along the beachside road lined with cafés, spent many hours browsing through the beautiful clothes at the malls, and spent lazy days at the pool. Despite this seemingly laid-back approach to job hunting, I landed a job as a school counselor a month later, though it took three more months to get my visa organized. I learned that certain things in this glittery city don't always move as quickly as you would like. Not everything is as organized or as well planned as the street structure. There were more than a few challenges to getting the logistics of the job and apartment sorted, but in every other way Dubai was an exceptionally easy place to navigate and settle.

My social life had taken off quickly and easily. My life in Dubai reminded me of what my mother's life in Iran had been. I was invited to parties with movie stars, golf stars, soccer stars, and singers. There were countless events and invitations—fashion shows, fashion week, club openings, restaurant openings, New Year's balls, and birthdays to attend. Everything was in full swing, and my personal life was feeling very idyllic. My then-boyfriend and I were having a lot of fun together, and I wanted to marry this fun, handsome, generous, kind, intelligent man. We decided to tie the knot. It was a magical wedding in Iran, and friends and family cheered us on as we were ushered into our lives as one unit. It was just the two of us—our little family.

Shortly after, I discovered that our little family was about to expand. It was truly a miracle for we didn't think we could have children. I didn't really want children at that stage in our lives. I took the pregnancy test to reassure myself I wasn't pregnant, despite feeling really nauseous and extremely tired. Rather than continuing to stress over whether I was pregnant, I bought a pregnancy test on the way to work. For some reason I took the test on a morning break in the staff bathroom. What kind of idiot does that? In retrospect, I can say that I was adamantly positive that I wasn't pregnant. In fact, I was so positive that after I saw the positive result I went to the school nurse and did three more tests that were still showing the wrong result!

When the information finally did make its way past the denial, I was devastated. I was nowhere near being ready to behave like a responsible adult. You know, the kind who actually cares for another human being and make sacrifices for their benefit. I was too young and fun. Okay, maybe not so young anymore, but I was definitely fun. My mind was full of self-doubt and clouded with questions. It took me sitting on the other end of a counselor's chair to figure out that I did want this little human. I was scared and a little confused; it took time to process all the change that had happened in my life in such a short period of time. Mostly, I was physically sick and exhausted, which made it difficult to be excited about anything. I was a bundle of crazy emotions but at the end of the day, I still wanted this little human who would be my baby.

I spent the first few months alternating between sleeping and puking. I would stumble home from work and lie on our couch for a "quick" nap. My husband would come in and eat his dinner and watch TV next to me on the couch. I would wake every so often and make a feeble attempt to lift my head but would fall right back asleep. My body was making someone special, and it felt so cozy and so content during those moments. I felt so in love.

The days were less idyllic. Between battling nausea and worrying about what was to come, I could hardly concentrate at work. Students and parents alike were speaking to me, but my mind was garbled and I was distracted. Gladly, I had given my resignation just months earlier, so I only had to endure one more month of working before I was off. I had planned to start with a new company a week after my school job had ended; however, when I told them of my pregnancy they were no longer interested in going forward with the planned employment. Serendipitously, I was off work for the remainder of my pregnancy, which was such a blessing. Without work to distract me, I became fixated on how fat I was becoming. Yes, logically I know being pregnant is different than being fat, but I kept telling the midwife that my bum bump was becoming larger than my belly bump. In fact, it was much larger. I enjoyed being home, making meals and taking care of the house. Once again, I returned to the daily beach routine and prepared the nursery very early. My husband and I tried to learn how to navigate our active social life while still accommodating my pregnancy. We still went out and about but not as much as before. We ended up spending lots of time on our own, going to different places to eat or watching movies at home.

The last few months, when I was in full waddle mode, I felt like a happy fat woman smiling at the world while the world smiled back. Reflecting on my pregnancy, I realize it was very strange for me to have enjoyed those last couple of months with such glee. I was big, very big. It was a blistering hot 113–122 °F (45–50 °C) outside, and it was Ramadan! During Ramadan in Dubai nobody is allowed to eat or drink in public. Keep in mind, my large baby bump meant that I was constantly hungry and thirsty. I would take short trips to the pool and float in the water before the noon sun appeared. I was not allowed to drink in public, and this included poolside. Before I turned into a dehydrated husk, I would waddle home and lie on the couch and drink loads of ice water. It was so refreshing and felt like drops from heaven.

The mall was air-conditioned, so it was a great place to escape the heat, but no food establishment in the mall was allowed to serve food during Ramadan. I would head out on the road and hunt down the few cafés or restaurants that were allowed to serve food. Once I found one, I would waddle past the long black sheets that covered the windows to throw myself at a blueberry muffin and chai latte. It felt like I was doing something highly illegal and somehow living on the edge. I guess the excitement of that experience made that laid-back time of my life a little more exhilarating.

We enjoyed going to Ramadan "tents" after 7 p.m. to celebrate the breaking of the fast. In my opinion, the best part of Ramadan in Dubai is these tents. Most hotels have them—they are more like lavish open spaces that are filled with modern Middle Eastern decorations, ladies dressed in beautiful but conservative clothing, and large spreads of food. Most people spend hours eating, chatting, and smoking *shisha*. It's a wonderful place for a pregnant lady (except for the *shisha* bit) during a hot summer in Dubai.

Another positive point throughout my pregnancy was my doctor. She was a Turkish doctor who grew up and trained in Germany and was recommended by a work colleague. She was detail driven, very efficient, and straight to the point. She always made time to answer my questions and was available if I had any questions after leaving the appointments. She addressed any concern no matter how small. For the first seven months, I saw the doctor every month and then every two weeks after that. I felt very confident in her abilities, and she always took into consideration my wants and needs. The staff at the hospital—everyone from the secretaries and the nurses to other doctors—was welcoming and friendly. In fact, I started to look forward to my appointments and chatting with everyone there. I had a lot of laughs teasing myself about the weight I gained or my eagerness to finally have this baby after what felt like a never-ending pregnancy.

My husband and I originally planned to have the delivery in Canada because despite me being Canadian, my baby, if born outside of Canada, was not eligible for citizenship, and Canadian citizenship was very important for us. However, the logistics of me going back to Canada to have the baby weren't looking very appealing. My mom lived in a very rural part of Canada, and the one-hour drive to the closest hospital made me feel uneasy about the situation. Therefore, I had planned to go back to the east coast of Canada, where I had formerly lived, and stay at a friend's house for two months before delivery. After delivery, I secured another friend's basement apartment that wasn't being used. The idea of couch surfing was not particularly appealing, especially while pregnant, and I wasn't eager to embark on this delicate arrangement while giving birth and living with a newborn for the first time in my life.

Given the odd Canadian housing situation we had arranged for the birth and time directly thereafter, my husband and I had many discussions about securing Canadian citizenship for our baby. He felt that he had personally suffered and had been denied many opportunities by holding only an Iranian passport. I reluctantly agreed but worried tremendously about how it was all going to play out. Those last few weeks of pregnancy are stressful enough, and now I had to worry about flying halfway around the world and sleeping in temporary apartments with a newborn.

At 36 weeks, I went to my last appointment before hopping on a plane to Canada, and my doctor informed me that it looked like baby boy would be coming early. She simply could not recommend with a good conscience that I fly to Canada. That was her professional opinion, and she ultimately left the decision up to us. Honestly, I can't remember how I felt. I know I spent the entire day between the appointment and my departure flight time fretting about what we should do. Finally, we decided to stay and deliver the baby in Dubai. After the decision was made, I felt a tremendous amount of relief. Perhaps it would have been better if I had left earlier and had Little Mr. in Canada, but I'm selfishly happy it happened the way it did. I'm not sure my baby would have gotten the care he needed to enter this world if we would have decided to deliver in Canada.

Feeling relieved and comfortable in our Dubai oasis, Little Mr., the trickster, didn't come early. For the past few prenatal appointments, I would bring my husband along to see the baby on the scan so we would both get to hear what the doctor was saying. My last appointment was so close to my due date—just four days prior—that I thought it was fine if my husband stayed at work. He would have to take some time off soon, and I wanted all of that time for us to bond as a family after the baby arrived.

I arrived at the doctor's office early and leafed through some magazines and joked with the staff while I waited. I wanted to write in detail about how my emergency C-section took place. I wanted to share with you, the reader, the blow-by-blow details and have you feel each moment as I did. Truth is, I can't. I can't remember the details, the sequence. I remember going into the check-up feeling fine. Feeling big. Feeling like I wanted this baby to come out. I was pretty jolly and happy. I remember feeling worried as the routine check-up seemed to be less and less routine. They kept asking me to move around from side to side. Nurses coming in and out. The laugher and joking seemed strained on their part.

I remember the doctor coming downstairs and telling me we were going to the hospital to deliver the baby. That's where it all becomes very blurry. I don't know if she told me then or later that they couldn't find the baby's heartbeat. I remember wanting to call Amir, my husband, to tell him to meet us at the hospital but not being able to and asking the nurse to do that. That was the moment I broke down in tears and fear flooded me, but not for long. I remember the car ride to the hospital in the doctor's car. It was so weird. The doctor was calm, so I tried to remain calm. We talked about car safety of all things. I remember feeling more panicked as the ride went on but also having the urge to appear calm. She was calm after all; I should be calm—this was my train of thought that seems so absurd now.

I remember Amir and the doctor disappearing and leaving me in the hospital room; paper work and billing had to be organized. I called my aunt, no answer. I called my cousin, no answer. I called my other cousin, the one who never ever picks up his phone, he answered. He laughed and cheered and told me it was great news I was going to have the baby. I wondered if he heard what I said. It was an emergency; for sure he understood the word emergency, he's a dentist after all! He kept telling me it was really good news. His calm, happy voice soothed me. I wished he were there. I was so happy he picked up.

Then I don't know what happened. I remember going to the operating room and Amir not being allowed to follow me there. I felt alone and scared, and maybe brave or confused, I'm not sure which. The C-section was painful. They had to give me more anesthetic partway through. Sadly, I passed out after that and only remember a glimpse of my baby boy on my chest. I remember holding my little *jojo* in my arms. He was alive and healthy and my little precious baby. Yes, it was all the things people talk about, all the love, all the joy, all that and more.

I was taken to a recovery room where a nurse sat by my bed. I was in a lot of pain, and she was happy to give me more painkillers; I was thankful for her. She talked to me, although I can't remember much of what she said. I do remember she told me that once I got home I would be in pain, but she said, "Keep moving and never feel sorry for yourself," and that's just what I did. Any time I would start to feel sorry for myself I kept those words in mind, and they kept me moving. Hours later, friends flooded the room with flowers and balloons. I never expected any visitors that night. It was a nice surprise. The next five days I always had friends who came to visit. It seemed baby and I were never alone. It was such a great demonstration of friendship. All these ladies whom I barely knew, not more than a couple of years, stuck by me. Four friends came every day. They brought me gifts and food and made me laugh. They washed my back and helped with breastfeeding as much as they could. They cheered me on and showed me love. I'm always grateful for the outstanding care of my doctor and the outpouring of friendship during those days.

I know it wasn't until I left the hospital that I felt truly sad for not being able to have a natural birth and mostly for not having that skin-to-skin time immediately after the birth. That was the only part that really mattered to me, and it didn't happen. I still feel sad when I think of that, and a part of me wonders if my boy didn't bond with me as much as he should have in those moments. It may sound silly, but I'm sure if you're a mom and reading this you can share those concerns. I think only mothers truly understand all the irrational fears of being a mom.

I'm glad for the health care system of Dubai. Canada doesn't offer those types of scans as frequently. I think it was another little miracle that we had to stay in Dubai and have our boy there.

When I was finally released from the hospital after five full days, it felt good to be home. It also felt empty and terrifying. It would be three days before my aunt arrived from Iran, and I was frightened. *What do I do now?* Baby Shayan seemed so small in our house. I didn't know where to put him. The basket I had bought from a friend seemed a weird place as it was on the floor. The couch seemed too big. His crib was in his room, and I couldn't just leave him there by himself. We ended up having Shayan spend a lot of time on the center of our L-shaped white couch. He wasn't a baby who liked to be put down a lot, so he also found a comfortable resting place on my chest most of the time. The rest seems very much like every new mom's story: a cycle of sleeplessness, anxiety, happiness, love, exhaustion, and amazement.

Things may have been different if I had birthed Shayan in Canada or Iran. I would have had family members or long-time friends who were like family coming to visit us on a daily basis. I would have had my mom or my aunt to fall back on when I really needed a conversation or some advice. In Dubai I was very much alone. All my friends were single and living the fun social life I had just left. With the exception of my good friends, Megan and Jenny, a few friends came around for a coffee at night to say congratulations during that first week, but from then on we were very much on our own. I wasn't used to being on my own for that amount of time. I wasn't sure what I was doing with Shayan. I struggled a lot with our new life.

I spent a lot of time on the walking track below our apartment. Shayan had colic, and he wouldn't stop crying or fall sleep unless he was being walked attached to my body, in a carrier. Sadly, I didn't realize this until two months into his life, poor little lad. I spent no less than four hours a day walking around that track. Two hours in the morning, and two or more in the afternoon/evening. It was a track lined with palm trees and playgrounds with children and nannies playing every 500 yards. There were small fountains and a cute little pond. It was soothing for Shayan and me. That is where we spent most of the first six months of his life—walking around the tree-lined path, and on our balcony. I still love thinking about how I sat on my balcony while he slept in his bassinet with his little legs tucked under his stomach. He was so small. He was so sweet. He was my little boy.

Looking back, that was such a monumental time in my life. I feel so lucky. I experienced great joy, learned, laughed, cried, and loved so much. I never could have dreamed of the wonderful life experiences I have had. Sometimes it's difficult to embrace change—like moving to a new country or having a baby—but when you do, it leads to great things. I'm thankful for all those who have been a part of my journey. I'm so lucky to have these people, my family and friends to walk this path with. I'm especially happy to have my husband by my side day by day. I couldn't be more grateful for his support, love, kindness, and fun spirit through it all. I have seen the Iran of my mother's dreams, and it is here, in Dubai.

Michelle Estekantchi worships her son, loves her husband immensely, values family, and cherishes her friends. She is currently a stay-at-home mom who used to have a fabulous career that she misses sometimes. She enjoys fashion and all things glossy, as well as heart-to-heart, soul-searching conversations. She prefers to live by the ocean in a warm climate but can adjust to a variety of settings. Is she a citizen of the world? Maybe. She is definitely a local in many cities around the globe.

CHAPTER 10

THE LAND OF BIRTH

Jannecke Balys
Nationality: Norway
Birthed in: Norway and USA

As long as I can remember I have always wanted to travel to unknown places and foreign lands. So no wonder two of my three children were born while I was living abroad. Just like travel, pregnancy and birth is much like a journey to a foreign land: The land of birth has its own language, culture, and even its own dress code. A passport is needed to get the provider you want, sometimes in the form of the right health insurance, other times by living close to the right hospital. There are many destinations, and there are as many travelers' stories of these experiences as there are women having babies. But most importantly there are many roads you can take in the land of birth, and unless you have a good map, compass, and travel companions, there are many people who will try their best to lead you down roads you never ever wished to travel. The first time I got pregnant I knew nothing of this, but throughout my pregnancies I would sure find out.

I was 22 years old and living in my native country of Norway the first time I got pregnant. I had recently returned from studying social anthropology abroad in Mexico and was back in Norway with its snow, ice, wind, rain, cold weather, and fjords. The town I was living in was a university town filled with students and cafés on every corner. The pregnancy was a surprise, both to me, my boyfriend at that time, and my fellow student friends—none of whom had any children. As they continued to go out and party, I would stay home more and more as it is only so much fun to be sober around a bunch of drunk people.

The pregnancy was amazing, and I enjoyed every part of it. Luckily I also had friends who were happy to spend sober time with me and my growing stomach. I did not feel isolated, but I did feel like I was entering a new stage of life compared to everyone else. The first time I had heard the baby's heartbeat I immediately went to a friend's house after my appointment. As I excitedly told her the news of the beating heart, she was more interested in sharing her latest boyfriend drama. Around that time I reflected a lot over not letting motherhood change me too much. After all, I didn't want to lose my friends. But it was difficult sometimes not to feel strange around my non-pregnant peers. I definitely felt that I was entering motherhood at a relatively young age. At one birth class I showed up alone in a short black dress and my usual blue combat boots. I felt pretty out of place as I was surrounded by couples who already looked the traditional picture of mommy and daddy. To me they were straight as arrows with their proper parenting clothes, stable jobs, homeownerships, and at least 10 more years on this planet than I had. Ten years was a lifetime back then.

Everyone told me I was absolutely going to go past my due date, since this was my first child. Did they know something I didn't? They obviously had access to some magical book of knowledge that I did not know of. Imagine my surprise when my water broke early in the morning, 11 days before my due date. My boyfriend and I left for the main hospital in town. I was very happy to give birth at that hospital, since I knew they always had an anesthesiologist on hand. Other, more rural hospitals did not, and I had been told that it was not uncommon for women not to be able to get an epidural in those places. I wanted to have as natural a birth as possible, but since I had no experience I had a very "take it as it comes" attitude. I would leave the medical stuff to the professionals; after all, what did I know?

After some fetal monitoring I was led to a large room with six beds. There was one other woman laboring there, and we were both mostly left alone by the staff. I had contractions, but they didn't hurt too much, so I waited and waited and waited. While waiting, I stuffed my face with the many meals that were served to me by the hospital staff. The food was traditional Norwegian cuisine, mostly bread and potatoes. It was no culinary experience but definitely good enough to keep my energy and strength at a high level. I waited so long that the midwife who had admitted me had gone off duty, slept, and returned for another shift.

I was in the shower when she peeked in and with surprise said, "Oh, you are still here. Let's make that baby come out."

I was transferred to a single room and given Pitocin. After the Pitocin came laughing gas, an epidural, two hours pushing, many tries with vacuum, forceps, and finally the baby.

His head was blue when I first saw him.
I had not known he was a boy.
He was limp and did not cry.
I thought he was dead.

The doctors were worried about him so they immediately whisked him away to make sure he was fine. After about five minutes I finally got to hold him—my son was here! The birth had been hard on him too, so he mostly slept through the week we spent at the hospital. The doctors wanted to keep an eye on us both due to my massive blood loss and his jaundice. My recovery room was hardly restful as I shared it with three other women and their newborns. I couldn't wait to leave the chaotic din of that room and hated having to wait in line to use the shared bathrooms in the hall.

As a result of my first birth, I was naturally nervous when my next birth rolled around six years later. I was unable to put all of the lessons from my first birth to good use, because this time I was a fish out of water and had to navigate a completely different health care system in a foreign country.

Life had changed a lot for my son and me in those six years. His dad and I had broken up. As a single mom, I began my master's studies in social anthropology. Together my son and I moved to Hawaii just before he turned two. I must have a restless gene in my DNA. We were living in the surfing mecca of the North Shore of Oahu. I was writing my master's thesis in social anthropology about masculinity, surfing, and surfers. That is where I met my husband—he was originally one of my informants for my thesis. We fell in love surrounded by pink, red, and orange sunsets, white sand beaches, and lazy palm trees. He was a surfer from California and was so exotic to me. His upbringing and childhood had been the polar opposite of mine. He had grown up with a single mom who worked two jobs to support him and his sister. He had spent years living in Europe and had worked in Africa, Polynesia, and South America. I shared his interest for adventure and seeing new, exciting places. I would spend hours just looking at his tanned skin, sun-bleached blond hair, and green eyes. But what I loved the most about him was his confidence, sense of humor, and carefree attitude. He would make a joke about most things and was one of those people that get along great with almost everyone. Similarly, he found my accent and me to be equally exotic. Growing up in a small Norwegian farming village was hardly exotic. No one had ever before called me exotic, but to him I was.

Well into our romance and engagement I had to move back to Norway so I could finish my studies there. My husband and I kept in contact for those two years via email, weekly phone calls, and the occasional visit. I would later perhaps over-communicate our long history, as some people seem to think that foreign brides in the US are mostly ordered online and delivered in a crate to the doorsteps of their future husbands. Sort of like a Green Card-hungry foreign bride mail service. What a strange idea that I married my husband out of love and a connection of our souls and not as a pass for entry into America.

After I graduated from my Norwegian university, my son and I moved back to Hawaii for a second time. My husband and I married, and our family of three resided at the edge of Waikiki, close to the hustle and bustle of thousands of visiting tourists. With the surfers, aloha, palm trees, tourists, and a string of beaches, I was once again thrilled to be living in such a beautiful place. The air was always filled with the sound of cars, waves, wind, people, occasional ambulances, and the fragrant smell of plumeria trees. Someone once described the air in Hawaii to me as "velvet," and it is so true. That is exactly what the air there feels like.

As my son started kindergarten, I started planning to be a mother of two. After an early miscarriage, everything looked like it would be fine during the pregnancy that followed. Walking my son the two blocks to school from our small apartment was a breeze in the warm, comfortable weather. It was so nice not to have to bundle him up in winter suits, boots, and scarves. I enjoyed small talk with the Asian grandmothers who were there to pick up their grandchildren as I waited for my son every afternoon at his school. My son was enrolled in ESL (English as a Second Language) classes at his school, even if he did not really need them. The school he went to had children of numerous nationalities, mostly from other

Polynesian islands and Asia. My son stood out everywhere among the other children. People would often comment on his blond, almost white hair, with his very tan skin and tall build. He was a Viking in Hawaii.

At the first ESL meeting the parents were paired up with the translator who was right for them.

I was standing there alone, finally asking jokingly, "Does anyone speak English?"

My English was pretty fluent at this time, but I did have an accent making me feel partly like an "invisible" foreigner. After all, I did look like I could be from there. Hawaii has such a mixed ethnic population that most people can look like they are from there. Only dress codes expose the typical tourists, combined with shades of white and red skin. I had both figured out. My skin was light brown from hours in the sun every day, and the dress code was not a problem for me: flip-flops, board shorts, and a tank top. But it was funny how every time I opened my mouth I would always get questions about where I was from. No one was ever able to pinpoint my accent. When I told them, most people had either never heard of Norway or thought it was the capital of Sweden.

As my stomach grew, I stopped surfing but still enjoyed walking around in flip-flops. Walking down to the ocean for a swim or simply just floating around felt like having a private spa in my backyard. Almost every evening my husband, my son, and I went for walks around the park by our apartment, always strategically planning to pass by the public restrooms as my pregnancy progressed. We would discuss how lucky we were that we got to live in paradise as we looked at the tourists who would shortly have to leave.

From our tiny balcony, we saw straight into the Diamond Head volcano. As the clouds floated over the sky, it would sometimes look like they were white and gray shapes of cotton animals and mystical creatures, making their way across the volcano's crater. The house next to our apartment building had a huge aviary that made the air in our apartment vibrate with the birds' song. Mixed with the sounds of the birds was the on and off smell of pot emitting from our next-door neighbor. He was a nurse and obviously loved the relaxing good life in his time off work.

Our apartment building had more characters than some stage plays: There was the gay guy with the little dog who lived on the first floor, and he encouragingly said that I looked "faaaabulous" as my stomach grew larger.

There was a strange tall and thin lady with the cats on the floor below us who would yell, "Did you go sheeshee?" every time I accidentally overwatered my balcony plants.

"No, no, it's just water. I'm so sorry!" I would yell back down as I thought, *No, I am not taking a leak off the balcony in broad daylight. I am not that pregnant—yet.*

After she learned that I was Norwegian, she would on occasion speak French to me. Luckily I did know a little French, so she might think French really is the native tongue of Norway. An old Japanese man lived in the penthouse. He sported a lean figure and a long white beard. Every day he would walk around Diamond Head with a carved, brown, exotic-looking walking stick that made him look like a Japanese warrior. He loved that there were children living in the building. He even cried the first time he saw our newborn baby.

My husband being in the US military meant that I was covered under the US Tricare health care system. I quickly came to realize that the prenatal care would be different this time, and that pregnancy and birth is highly influenced by the surrounding culture. Compared to Norway's socialized health care system where health outcomes are closely tied with risk and cost, the American privatized health care system is too concerned with liability, with medical tests for everything under the sun and what seemed like excessive fear-mongering—never mind any holistic approach. I was terrified of an unnecessary C-section for what would have been a routine vaginal birth in Norway. The increased fear of liability and bizarre fascination with everything having to fall into certain medical parameters seemed so foreign to me.

Statistically, birth has a healthier outcome for both mother and child in Norway, so we can't be that wrong, I thought.

But okay, I tried my hardest to think "when in Rome." After all, I was the odd one in their system. I was the one who had to adjust.

At the time I got pregnant, there was only one option for me and that was to give birth at the local Army hospital. The hospital was a large, pink building located in the hills on the outskirts of Honolulu. That is where I had all my prenatal appointments and my son's doctor's appointments. It was very strange for me to see so many people in uniform; even some of the doctors and nurses were in uniform. It felt even stranger that the TV in the pediatric waiting room sometimes showed graphic news stories from war zones. I felt very lucky when I found out that the hospital had a midwife program. Between the three midwives, I would be in good hands, and I had nothing to worry about. Imagine my panicked surprise when I found out that all the midwives were going away to a seminar the weeks before my due date. I complained a little about it but was told that I probably would not give birth when they were all gone. These midwives obviously had magical access to the same book of knowledge about when I would go into labor as the people in Norway. At this time there were thousands of soldiers sent to fight in Iraq and Afghanistan. On the hospital tour, most of the women were there without their husbands, and due to deployments they most likely would not see them for another year. So in the big picture I felt it was then a little unseemly to make a big fuss about the midwives possibly not making it to my birth; after all, I would still have my husband there.

As a result of me feeling so out of place in a foreign medical system, I sometimes left my prenatal appointments and cried in my car. I was the prisoner of hormones, I know. My husband did after all refer to me in this period as a "Molotov cocktail of hormones." During my preparation for the birth and trying to allay the fear of a C-section, I read about doulas and how their presence decreased the likelihood of a C-section. I had never heard of doulas before. Doulas are uncommon in Norway, because midwives deliver all babies who are born without identified complications. So I hired a doula for what felt to me as added safety and peace of mind.

As if the pregnancy, my husband's deployments, and the adjustment to a new culture weren't enough, I also had to deal with the INS (Immigration and Naturalization Service). Since it is best to live in a country legally, I was in the process of getting a Green Card. A stressful part of that is going through the big INS interview. I had seen the movie *Green Card* with Gerard Depardieu, and I thought, if my husband has to remember all the facts about my favorite color and what brand face cream I use, we are screwed. I was heavily pregnant at the time of the interview, and my big belly gave us away, I think. We were legitimately in love, unless of course we had gone to the great length of making a baby to make sure I got my Green Card.

My water broke early in the morning two weeks before my due date. Perfectly timed with all the midwives being gone for their seminar! So instead of a statistically more natural, midwife-accompanied birth, random doctors and nurses on duty would oversee my birth and help with labor. Someone really needs to get rid of that magical labor-predicting book, because it is obviously wrong!

After the discovery that my water broke, we called the doula. She suggested we stay home and have a nice breakfast. My husband and I then walked up and down the road leading up to the volcano behind our house to try and get labor going. My normally calm husband started getting a little nervous, so we headed to the hospital. The hospital had recently remodeled two of its rooms into huge birthing suites. They would put some fancy hotel suites to shame, that is how grand they were. As we arrived at the hospital my husband was mostly interested in getting "the big room," and we did. He was ecstatic and spent much of the time taking videos of this amazing large ocean view suite and its amenities. There is also some video of me laboring.

Since my water had broken and the baby's head was not completely down, the doctor told me I could not walk around. I was very surprised, since I had the same medical situation in Norway where they let me walk around no problem. After several hours the doctor decided it was time for Pitocin. I didn't feel I had a choice and saw this going down the same path as the last birth with all the complications, and I was very scared. But worse than the fear was the fact that I was hungry; very, very hungry. I was not prepared for the fact that in the US all births are treated as possibly ending in a C-section, and I was totally unprepared for the not eating part. I mean I am a person who cannot function on a normal day without food every few hours, and here I was in the middle of my biggest physical endeavor, and they were going to starve me?

After begging for food for hours, I was finally provided some broth. It was one of the best meals I have ever had to this date, but it still left me hungry. The pain got worse, and the doctor suggested a pain reliever that I had not heard of before. I was worried about the effects it would have on me—after all I wanted a clear head during labor. The doctor assured me it would just help me relax. Well, it did not.

My husband was laughing as he said, "Honey, you are stoned."

His laboring wife was now not just hungry but also high; I was rambling. But the worst was that it did not take away the pain of the peaks of labor. As the story often goes with Pitocin, there was only a matter of time until an epidural was on the way. I remember feeling most grateful to the anesthesiologist that gave it to me. I would have given him all my earthly belongings at that point in time. As the anesthesiologist put the needle in my back, I made my husband promise to "never ever do this to me again." He promised he would not.

Our daughter finally came into the world without any further complications. I ripped the hospital gown off in the pushing stage as I felt an intense need to be nude just like the baby would be when we first met. It startled one doctor who saw my naked laboring body as he entered the room. Later I thought, *do most women keep their clothes on when giving birth in America?* I got to hold my daughter right away. At this point I was mostly interested in getting my hands on some food. My husband went looking for some, and came back with a tray he told me he had found in the hallway. I thought it was someone else's leftovers but did not care as refueling was the only thing on my mind.

My husband is not very good at keeping promises, and I found myself knocked up and still living abroad eight years later. After another miscarriage I was pregnant, and everything was looking good. No longer living in Hawaii, we had relocated twice with the military. After a four-year tour living on an Air Force base in the middle of Cape Cod, Massachusetts, we had moved to Florida. I was happy to leave Cape Cod and its green forests and cold weather. I was also somewhat happy to leave all the playgroups I had joined with my daughter. After years of going to those groups, I felt my brain was slowly melting and seeping out through my ears, having sung "Itsy Bitsy Spider" and talked about the fact that "yes, Pampers definitely is the best brand" a million times. I was ecstatic to once again get the opportunity to live in a warm climate and was excited to find out what Florida had to offer. I loved having the ocean so close again. Our condo had an amazing view over the intercostal waterway. There were dolphins playing in the cerulean blue waters. Dolphins!

My daughter had grown from the baby born in Hawaii to a young girl attending elementary school. She was into all adrenaline-filled things, just like her father. My son was no longer the small towheaded child but a teenager attending high school. His hair was still blond, but it was now carefully crafted into a Mohawk every morning, accompanied by an all-black wardrobe. I had transformed into the typical soccer mom, at least in looks. I blended in perfectly in the terrain of moms with my ponytail and yoga pants. The only thing missing was the minivan.

I kept driving both of the children to school, friends, and activities while I was also enduring the pregnancy and my husband's deployments. I was sick as a dog for the first four months and could barely make it to the mailbox in the hot, humid weather. Florida is always miserably hot in the summer, but that year I swear it was warmer than ever, at least according to me. Having a 14- and an 8-year old, it was strange to think about waking up at night and entering the diapering stages again. I felt especially odd when volunteering at my son's school with my big belly, as most of the other moms had more than a few grey hairs and had been past the baby stage for ages. In addition to volunteering at both of my children's schools, I would keep going to the gym throughout my pregnancy. Together with other housewives and some of Florida's many retirees I would do classes like body pump and yoga. Sometimes I gave it my all, other days I would, after a few downward dogs, collapse into child pose and stay there. Rest and relaxation is important too right? Namaste.

I had now lived in the US for almost a decade and had learned that in America you do have options. You do have choices when having a baby. But you have to carefully choose the people you surround yourself with. With my Tricare health insurance I was now able to pick between different hospitals and did not have to go with a military provider or hospital. In my search for the best birth team I settled with a provider who had been recommended to me. They had three midwives on the team, and they never went on vacation or seminars at the same time. The biggest selling point was that they were the only provider in the area that offered water birth. Water birth—imagine my baby coming into the world in the water. What an amazing start to her life. What an amazing pain reliever. I was in good hands.

I had thought that the prenatal care in Hawaii was rushed and non-holistic, but it turned out I had seen nothing yet. For most of my appointments the midwives were late; often I waited an hour, even for the morning appointment. There were times when I wondered if they had fallen into their morning cup of coffee. I had my usual many questions that there was sometimes no time for. No one asked how I was, how I really was feeling. I was once again summed up as my medical measurements. But I was, as usual, asked about my funny-sounding foreign name and strange accent. There was definitely time for that. Halfway through my pregnancy I tried to change providers and found a birth center that looked and felt amazing. Unfortunately my insurance would not cover the cost, and together with my husband we decided to stay where we were. They did after all have a good reputation. Since I did not know which of the midwives would be at my birth, I once again decided on a doula, since she would for sure make it to my birth. The doula my husband and I chose seemed like she would be able to withstand the winds of medical advice trying to blow us to unwanted places.

Now having experienced two births that were in one way similar and in another so very different, I set out on a mission: I would do everything in my power to have this baby as naturally as possible, and I was going to be as prepared as possible. I wanted a completely natural birth, with no drugs, since I firmly believed this would be the best thing for me and my baby. I now knew that in American culture it is common to interfere with the natural pattern of a birth, and once interfered with this often leads you down a path of a lot more interventions.

So in my quest for a natural hospital birth I read every book I could get my hands on. I read magazines, watched TV shows, documentaries, and learned a lot of statistics. I researched different strategies on how to increase your chances of getting a natural birth while in the hospital. The strategy I found most interesting is that you can always ask for more time. There are choices, and sometimes you do not have to follow the rules. Since I knew this time that they would not let me eat, I decided that I would sneak food. So I packed a lot of different power bars in my bag. Better to ask for forgiveness than permission, I thought. My husband and I did several classes where I learned that techniques like squats can help in labor. I learned about aromatherapy and which oils helped with what. I wrote it all down and put notes with the oils I bought, since it was my husband who would be in charge of administering the oils.

I spent countless hours shopping for a birth skirt. My thinking was: The better I feel and the more relaxed I am, the better my chances are of making it through a natural birth. Few things make me feel more at ease than wearing clothes that look nice and are comfortable. Hospital gowns with a slit down the back are not my idea of either comfort or a sense of fashion. I even bought the right socks for the event: anti-slide for safety, soft for comfort. Perfect for the birth. I had tennis balls for my husband to rub my back with, breath mints for him, and a birth ball, and I would bring my own pillow. The pillow was blue with a pattern that made me think of water and the ocean. I wrote memory cards for myself. I wrote a birth plan. I made a focus board. I downloaded music. I packed it all in my bag. I had it all. I was prepared—a bit of a neurotic mess, but definitely prepared.

Since my two births came earlier than my expected due date with my water breaking, I was very surprised as the days came closer to my due date and still we had no baby. I was hoping my water would not break since I now knew that in the US that means you are on the clock. You more or less have 24 hours to get the baby out or you have yourself a C-section. I had no such luck, since early in the morning the day before my due date my water broke. A third birth starting with my water breaking—what are the odds?

My husband called the doula and my mother-in-law who was going to watch the children. To increase my chances of a natural birth, we waited an hour to call the midwives, giving me a little more time. My husband and I stayed in bed a long time; he was holding me, and I felt so safe. Then we walked across the road to the white sand Florida beach, taking in the sights of the calm water and birds flying overhead. We talked about how the next time we would go there, it would be with the kids and the new baby. We then drove to the hospital and got checked in.

My doula entered the room, with her she brought a calm presence to the entire room. She was like a warm, nice blanket of understanding, love, and protection. Like the big sister I never had. From the hospital room we could see all the way to the beach and the hotels lining it. When I wanted to walk around, I was in my new birth skirt, anti-slip socks, and a long top. Since I had the top pushed up under my breasts when I was on the monitor, I was told by one of the nurses that I had to cover up when walking the halls. *What?* I thought. *A naked belly in the birth wing of the hospital. Shocking.* I covered up, and my husband, the doula, and I walked the halls, and I did squats. My husband administered aromatherapy. All the nurses complimented us on having the best smelling room in the hospital. I ate my power bars in the bathroom so no one would catch me being naughty. But in all my efforts I was not laboring fast enough for the doctor who oversaw my birth, so Pitocin was mentioned. This time I was prepared and asked for more time. And I got it! I was amazed.

The midwife suggested I should try a breast pump, and I pumped and pumped. I was listening to calm Zen music, but quickly changed it to Depeche Mode and INXS as the Zen just felt a little too Zen for the occasion. But it was not until I put on Rage Against the Machine that I got really relaxed, and labor hit me like a freight train. Labor went from a calm walk over fields of wheat in the summer with your fingertips touching the tops of the straws and soft wind in your hair to downhill skiing off the highest mountain hearing your skis cutting into the snow below you. It was so fast, and my head and body was like a white noise of pain. I felt the baby coming; she was ready to enter the world.

My husband had wanted to catch the baby, and with some help from the midwife he did and handed her to me. She was pink, swollen, and so very warm. And she was screaming! She was 21 inches and 9 lb. 10 oz. (4,366 g). We named her Alva. She was here, and she was healthy. I had done it! All natural, no drugs! I was up and walking right after the birth. The sheer fact I was doing this felt amazing. Also, my head was clear of drugs. But I did feel high on endorphins and love for my baby girl. A nurse came in the middle of the night to bathe the baby. I shuffled down the hall with her and watched as Alva was being washed. She looked enormous compared to the other babies in the nursery; I was so proud. She was so big and strong. The next day she lifted her head inches off my chest that she was lying on. I was filled with such joy. My family was complete.

I felt so amazed and empowered afterward that my body had done that. That no one had intervened and forced me to go down other paths. When they had tried, they did not succeed, because I had learned the terrain and how to read the map this time, and I knew how to operate the compass. I had learned the language so I could communicate my wishes. I knew the culture that I was operating in well. I felt an enormous gratitude to my husband and the doula; they were the best travel companions. When I lost my voice and sanity in waves of pain, the two of them led me exactly where I wanted to go. I fully trusted them, and together the three of us made the perfect little travel group on my last trip to *my* land of birth.

It has been 17 years since this journey began. In those years I have lived in many different apartments and houses, gone through countless cars, bought several one-way tickets, gotten married, had three children, enrolled those children in several different schools, gained many new friends, and said countless goodbyes.

I don't know what the next 17 years has to offer for my family and me. I do hope for more years abroad. But there is one thing I know for sure, and that is that I will never ever find myself knocked up abroad again.

Jannecke Balys is a Norwegian citizen who grew up in a small farming community in eastern Norway. After moving away to start university, she would never live landlocked again. For 12 years of her life she called the United States of America home. All those years she spent residing on different islands: Honolulu, Hawaii, Cape Cod, Massachusetts, and Indian Shores, Florida. Last year she returned to her native country and is currently calling the coastal town of Stavanger home. Over a decade of living abroad as a military spouse and resettling her family time and again has made her feel that "home" is a fluid state of mind more than a physical place.

Together with her American husband, Jannecke is raising their three bicultural children, ages 3, 11, and 17. Between giving birth and raising the children, she obtained a master's degree in social anthropology and has taught sociology and anthropology at the University of Massachusetts.

Jannecke loves exploring new places, cultures, and people. One of her biggest fascinations in life is observing contradictions both in humans and cultures. She is a yogi, sometimes more avidly than others; as with most things in life, she prefers the Middle Way.

CHAPTER 11

LUCY'S BIRTH PLAN

Lisa Ferland
Nationality: USA
Birthed in: USA and Sweden

Climbing onto the Swedish ambulance's gurney outside of our house with no underwear or pants on was hardly embarrassing or awkward. It was necessary because the ambulance medical technicians left an obscene amount of umbilical cord hanging between my legs, presumably so the midwives would have something to grab onto when we arrived at the hospital. My newborn daughter was still on my chest, covered in an aluminum foil-like space blanket. She looked like a little astronaut burrito, only much cuter. My husband climbed into the front seat of the ambulance as the medical technician strapped a blood pressure cuff onto my arm.

"We should call our parents to let them know we had the baby," my husband suggested as the ambulance doors closed around us.

"Eh, it's only 5 a.m. where they are. Let's just wait until we get settled at the hospital and we can call at a reasonable time and explain everything," I replied.

How to explain what had happened, I still wasn't sure. My vision tunneled onto our daughter's lips as they found their way to my breast and she began to nurse. The sharp bite of the first nursing session reminded me that even though I had done this before, this was definitely not the same experience. Our daughter surprised us in the most memorable way possible—by arriving on her own terms.

My first birth was very typically American, and I delivered our son in a hospital nicknamed "Atlanta's Baby Factory," as it was known for having the highest birth rate in the state of Georgia. The hospital ran like a well-oiled machine with midwives attending uncomplicated births, and they could accommodate any type of emergency.

The initial labor backaches began after a typical workday on a Friday afternoon because, of course, I worked until the day I went into labor. The backaches radiated around to the front and transitioned into belly contractions—just like all of the pregnancy books had described. My first labor was of a textbook quality. After seven hours of laboring at home, we drove to the "Baby Factory" at 2 a.m., and they started me on Pitocin to help keep the contractions moving smoothly. Around 5 a.m., I requested an epidural. It felt like a million bees were stinging my spinal cord before it quickly numbed.

"I can still move my toes," I anxiously told the nurse as she walked by my bed. I wasn't convinced the epidural was effective if I could wiggle around.

"You can still move your lower limbs. The epidural only takes away the pain," she explained.

What a miracle drug! I fell into a very much needed two-hour nap after silently praising the scientist(s) who had invented this wondrous thing called an epidural.

I awoke to a loud beeping noise of the machine next to my bed. The annoying beeping indicated that the epidural was empty. Like a beacon, a midwife appeared to turn off the noise. She told me that I was completely dilated. Apparently my naptime and the drug and hormone cocktail had been quite productive. It was time to push.

At 10:02 a.m., our son, Calvin, was born after three leisurely pushes. His entire labor and delivery was 11 hours long. Not bad for a first-time mom, I was told. I attributed his very uneventful and easy arrival all to the relaxation provided by the epidural. It was only after my daughter's birth that I was to truly comprehend that I come from "good peasant breeding stock," as my mother described.

"The women in our family have wide hips, easy labors, and never hit menopause. We were born to make lots of babies," my mother explained to me later on.

Apparently we descend from a long line of birthing warriors. My maternal grandmother delivered one of her five children in the breech position—without any pain medication or C-section. Huzzah! My mother also birthed both my brother and me without any drugs, as epidurals were new in the 1980s, and she didn't trust their safety ratings or lack thereof. Consequently, I never heard any terrifying birthing stories from my own mother. She only reported feeling a mild discomfort. But she wasn't exactly boasting a painless childbirth experience either, so I always credited her stoicism to her personal strength—one that she still displays to this day—rather than possessing a body that was quite literally designed to birth effortlessly. Even still, my own inability to handle the minor pain of a stubbed toe was enough to convince me that an epidural was absolutely necessary for me to have a good birthing experience. I was terrified of the unknown levels of pain, and the promise of an epidural numbed that anxiety.

Besides, the epidural was glorious. Why anyone would toil and writhe in pain during labor was beyond my comprehension. Everyone deserves a comfortable birthing experience.

The leaves were falling onto the cold wet October ground. Their faded yellow colors were an indication that the sunlight was rapidly decreasing every day as we plummeted into the darkness of fall, soon-to-be winter. Seasons in Sweden are distinct, with strong beginnings and enjoyable middles. With winters that never end soon enough and summers that never last long enough. The damp cold fall air required a sweater under a jacket, hat, and light gloves. This is the season for multiple layers, thicker socks, and waterproof boots.

"Should we go for a walk? It looks nice outside," my husband, Jonathan, asked as we drank our morning coffees on a Sunday morning.

"I don't know. My back is aching. I think I'm going to take a shower and try to relax," I replied, heading up the stairs.

The 40 weeks of my second pregnancy were busy. There was a full life to juggle around my large belly. Calvin seemed to demand more and more energy from me, but I just had none left to give. The belly was sapping my reserves. Another finite resource, attention, was divided and didn't allow me to daydream about the source of these strong kicks. Her movements within my womb were sharp and a painful reminder that space was limited within.

"Time to come out if you're so uncomfortable in there," I encouraged her. My due date came and went, and life continued.

Sleeping as a 40-plus-week pregnant woman was uncomfortable. I couldn't breathe, turn, or find a suitable position. Constant waves of backaches became my new normal, and I couldn't wait to return to my old normal. The moment in pregnancy where you are convinced you will sleep better when the baby is on the outside is when you know you have reached your limit. It is a fool's dream, but you believe it anyway. You can't imagine your stomach stretching beyond its current capacity, and yet it does—week after week. Just. Be. Over. Already. That's life when you have passed your due date.

We always knew that we wanted to have a family of four. Both my husband and I hail from a family of two siblings with one boy and one girl. When our lives took us to Sweden, we knew that it was highly likely that I would become pregnant again and give birth to another child while living abroad. That is, if everything went according to plan.

Sweden's low rate of C-sections, 17%, is attributed to their holistic approach during labor and delivery. After speaking with my friends who delivered their babies in Sweden, it became clear that pain relief options, including my own beloved choice of an epidural, were fairly limited, with preference toward a more "natural" approach. Midwives encouraged breathing exercises, and mothers could utilize nitrous oxide gas. The mothers who had used gas, in my unofficial discussions with friends, reported feeling light-headed, loopy, and nauseous during labor. Epidurals were technically available, but your Swedish midwife that day may "do you a favor" and take her time finding the anesthesiologist. She may return and state that the doctor is busy placing an epidural for a woman having a C-section, thereby guilting you into pushing naturally. Gee, that sounds swell.

Prior to arriving at the hospital, laboring mothers must first call the phone number of their first-choice hospital to see if they have availability. If all of their beds are full, as Swedes often birth in predictable clusters in the warm summer months, then the laboring mother is redirected to another hospital that may have space. Often, this results in a last-minute scramble to a new hospital—on a route that may have never been driven before, especially for non-native Swedes like us. Having a printed birth plan is essential in Sweden, because the midwives who work in the hospitals have never met the mothers before. They read the birth plan and try to follow it within reason.

Since I couldn't trust a midwife I didn't know to provide an epidural, I researched self-hypnosis, specifically Hypnobabies®, as an alternate means of reducing anxiety during pregnancy and, hopefully, pain during birth. I felt comforted by knowing that this was something completely within my control. I would be in charge of providing my own birthing pain relief. However, if it didn't work, I would only have myself to blame. I prepared myself for a natural birth by reading *Childbirth without Fear* by Grantly Dick-Read and *Confessions of a Scary Mommy* by Jill Smokler to provide some laughter and to keep things in perspective.

The customer reviews for Hypnobabies® were exceedingly positive and encouraging, and it seemed like an avenue worth exploring. I religiously followed the program and practiced every day simply by listening to the tracks and napping. The MP3 tracks were so relaxing that I found myself sleeping through each and every session. Mandatory naps every day? Now this was a pain relief program I could get behind.

I asked my midwife friend if sleeping through the hypnosis tracks would sabotage my birthing experience. After all, if I was sleeping through everything, how would I know what to do when the time came to birth the baby?

She reassured me: "If you're sleeping through the sessions then it means that you are totally relaxed. You are going to have an amazing birth!"

Her confidence bolstered my confidence. Luckily, you don't have to know what to do during the birthing process, as your body takes care of everything. The hypnosis tracks replace the words "labor" with "birthing," and "contractions" with "waves" in an effort to change your mental approach to childbirth from something that is scary and painful to something that is natural, normal, and comfortable. My job was to keep any fears and anxieties out of my subconscious during birth. With my head out of the way, the theory was that my body would take the reins, and all would run smoothly and comfortably.

Frankly, it all sounded like a bunch of mumbo-jumbo hocus-pocus, but I was all alone on this birthing island. An epidural was more than likely out of the question, and the nitrous oxide gas was going to make me feel sick. I had two choices: I could either firmly believe in the anesthetic ability of the self-hypnosis or crumple into a pile of despair and succumb to my worst birthing fears. I chose the former and fully bought into the hocus-pocus.

This would work.

It had to.

I would have a quick, safe, and comfortable birthing.

The backaches didn't stop while I was in the shower. Instead, they started rolling with increased frequency. I waited for the backaches to slowly radiate to the front and turn into belly contractions, as they had with Calvin, but they stayed in my back. The self-hypnosis birthing playlist was playing on my phone's speaker, and the steam from the shower clouded my vision. I drifted in and out of relaxation as I stood there, letting the hot water cascade down my back.

"When you are having your wonderful birthing waves, you easily and naturally remain calm, relaxed, confident, and in control at all times. No matter what is happening around you, no matter what anyone is saying, you naturally remain completely relaxed, calm, confident, and focused," the familiar hypnotic voice radiated over the sound of the shower.

Standing upright in the shower was no longer comfortable. I stepped out of the shower and grabbed a fluffy purple towel. It barely covered my large 41-week belly. I had to change positions. I moved onto my hands and knees and started rocking back and forth on my bed, only partially dressed. There wasn't time to put pants on in between the back waves, and it seemed needless anyway. I told my husband that this was more than likely the early stage of labor, and I sent a quick text to our Swedish friend to invoke her babysitting offer later in the day.

I wandered my way downstairs into the living room, plugged my phone into the wall charger and continued listening to my hypnotic playlist. The morning sun was streaming in through the large windows as I listened to the calming cues while draped over a blue yoga ball. I kept rocking back and forth gently on my knees. The aches in my back weren't dissipating, but surely I wasn't far into labor—nothing had progressed beyond a mild discomfort. I hadn't felt one contraction. In fact, there was no belly movement whatsoever. Usually Lucy was a bit more active in the morning. This was still the beginning.

I moved frequently from the yoga ball rocking position to the downstairs bathroom. Sitting down felt like a relief. I was able to relax completely and let go as my mind stayed in the foggy haze of hypnosis. Constantly moving and changing positions provided and maintained comfort. The backaches were intensifying, and during one wave I reached behind and pressed into my back to apply counter pressure. I didn't think I could continue much longer if I was still only in the beginning stages of labor. Things were becoming intense.

Two minutes later, I sat down in the bathroom and felt a shudder and a gush of liquid into the toilet. Did my water just break? It was convenient that I was in the bathroom at the time. I looked down, and there was blood. That was my bloody show. Calvin was born within 15 minutes of my bloody show. Perhaps I'm farther along than I thought.

"Jonathan! Call the hospital and see if they have room for us. It's time to go!" I called up from the bottom of the stairs. Actually, it was past our time to go to the hospital.

Jonathan came downstairs, saw me on the yoga ball, and dialed the labor and delivery phone number. The hospital operator asked to speak to me to gauge how far along I was.

"What is your *personnumer*?" she asked calmly.

"83...05...30...ahh, I can't right now," I zoomed past Jonathan and briskly walked into the bathroom again. I placed the phone down on a shelf in the hallway on speaker mode.

I reached between my legs. I felt her head. Her head was fully crowned, and I still hadn't felt any pain. My thoughts came to me slowly, as if wading through thick mud. My brain was turned off to focus entirely on keeping my body relaxed.

Insanely, for a split second, I contemplated holding her in until professional help could arrive.

Very calmly, still very deep in relaxed hypnosis, I informed my husband, "I can feel her head."

This information sent him into a panic, and he shouted at his phone, still on speaker mode, "Call 911 or 112 or whatever emergency phone number! We are delivering this baby now!"

I stepped out onto the tiled hallway and instinctively lowered into the squatting position. It just felt right. I felt a shudder and saw her head emerge and then Jonathan lifted under her arms and pulled her out on the next shudder. Our daughter was born within five seconds and without any deliberate pushing on my part. He passed her over and handed me a towel, and then he disappeared from my vision.

This not-as-slippery-as-I-had-imagined baby girl in my arms was quite large. Her size surprised me considering I hadn't felt any pain during her birth. It wouldn't be until hours later, when she was finally weighed at the hospital, that I would learn that I had effortlessly birthed a 9 lb. 1 oz. (4,100 g) and 20 inches (50.8 cm) long baby. She was making a gurgling noise, and I yelled at my husband to get the nose-sucker thingy. He returned with pacifiers, towels, flip-flops, and toys but no nose sucker. She was dribbling fluid out of her mouth, but I didn't trust myself to gauge her health. I wasn't a nurse! I sat down on the floor and held her against my chest with the long umbilical cord draped over my legs.

All of a sudden a calm, disembodied voice came from Jonathan's phone that was sitting on the shelf.

"Is the baby breathing? Are you okay?"

It was the anonymous midwife operator from the hospital. She had stayed on the phone during the brief delivery and the chaos that followed. A silent witness listening to the birth. An event that, from my perspective, slowed through a time warp, though in actuality it took place within the course of just a few seconds.

"I think so. She isn't blue, but she isn't crying. Isn't she supposed to cry?" I asked in the phone's direction.

"No, she doesn't need to cry if she's okay. I can hear her gurgling. She is breathing. Just wait there until help arrives."

My brain wasn't capable of complex thoughts, and I was grateful for her short directions.

She's breathing. She isn't crying. She is okay. I am okay.

I sensed a presence and looked up to see Calvin standing silently in the doorway, watching me with his new sister. My maternal instincts took over, and my internal dialogue shifted from the swirling thoughts repeating in my head to the familiar role of mom-of-toddler. Put on a brave face. Pull it together.

"Oh hi, buddy. Want to meet your new sister, Lucy?" I said in a warmed tone.

"Hi Lucy!" he shouted and he turned and ran outside to play with his cars.

What had just happened? We weren't prepared for a home birth. We were supposed to be at the hospital for all of this. Why had the labor gone so quickly? It was only about two and a half hours long in total. It had progressed so quickly because everything was healthy and there were no complications. My labor "pains" were reasonably indistinguishable from all of the other end-of-pregnancy aches I had felt in the weeks prior. My printed birth plan remained useless in our overnight bag. It went straight into the trash, as Lucy had followed her own birth plan.

In between rocking on all fours and constantly walking around the house, I had been waiting to feel some type of pain or contraction before escalating the lets-go-to-the-hospital request. I had experienced neither. I had had no idea that I was calmly walking around fully dilated. There was no heavy breathing, no screaming, no sweating—nothing. Truly, the hypnosis had kept my fears and anxieties from creating tension in my body. I had only felt a mild discomfort—similar to what my mother had described during her births. No fear, no tension, no pain. Only relaxation, calm, and comfort.

"You didn't feel any pain? None whatsoever? Weren't you scared?"

I held an impressive ring of Swedish midwives encircled around my bed at the hospital. They had gathered around me as if I was a famous storyteller. A pain-free unassisted home birth by an American woman was most likely legendary in their holistic birthing worlds. It certainly was in mine. It was the Holy Grail of natural birthing—no drugs, no pain, and no complications.

"No, no pain whatsoever, and no, I wasn't scared at all. It all happened so quickly; we just did what we had to do."

My midwife confirmed that I had experienced no uterine contractions after she tugged on the umbilical cord to find a firmly attached placenta. It is possible to birth a baby without contractions—I am walking proof. They left me alone to nurse Lucy in hopes that the combination of breastfeeding and a shot of Pitocin in my thigh would stimulate the detachment of the afterbirth over time.

It had been hours since we had arrived at the hospital, and the midwives seemed to be in no rush. Occasionally they would peek in on Lucy, nestled under her warm down blanket as she lay sleeping on my chest, her little head tucked into the hollow of my neck under my chin. Everything looked fine.

"Do you need to take her away to get her height and weight measurements? Or will you do that here in the room with me?" I asked out of curiosity.

"No. No need for that yet. She is fine on her mother's chest. She is exactly where she needs to be."

Lisa Ferland, her totally unqualified midwife-husband, and their two children live in Sweden where they enjoy a lifestyle of picking blueberries and mushrooms in the woods, exploring new playgrounds, and making frequent trips to the beach in any weather. Lisa's unique birth story is always a crowd pleaser at dinner parties. Despite a pain-free child birthing experience, she still winces when she stubs her toe. You can follow her adventures as an American family living in Sweden at http://lifeisgoodferland.blogspot.com.

CHAPTER 12

ISLAND-HOPPING IN THE SEYCHELLES

Chantelle Howell
Nationality: United Kingdom
Birthed in: The Seychelles

Laboring under the hot sun, I had spent the day out on a boat as part of a volunteer project, which involved transplanting coral to try and rebuild a section of coral reef that had been destroyed. I felt sick as a dog. The water was pretty rough, and the small boat was tossed around violently. I had some previous experience with seasickness so I didn't really think too much of it. Then for the next few days I was tired—really beyond tired. Again, I attributed my exhaustion to a full day of throwing up on a boat in the boiling hot sun.

After a few more days of extreme tiredness, I began to wonder if I was pregnant. My husband, Mark, convinced me to buy a pregnancy test. Okay, so where was I going to go to buy a pregnancy test!? There aren't exactly pharmacies on every corner like there are in most countries. We did have a little pharmacy— hmm, the term pharmacy might be giving it a bit too much credit— a tiny store that deals in a few pharmaceutical items. It does sell really basic pregnancy tests. The kind that looks like a strip of paper that you might use to measure the pH level in your pool or drinking water. I didn't see any on display, so I had to ask the lady for it specifically. For some reason this made me feel very nervous, like a teenager trying to illegally buy alcohol. I'm not really sure why I felt this way. So anyway, I bought a test, took it home, and then waited for the next morning to take it.

I dipped the strip in my morning pee, and there it was. Two lines. Or were there? The test line was very faint. A digital test result of Yes or No would have been much easier to interpret and much more reassuring than a very faint line. We didn't know whether to get excited or what to do next. As it happened, we were going out on an island-hopping boat trip with friends later that day. It should have been a bit of a boozy day, but I made weak at best excuses all day and then pretended to drink a cocktail as we watched the sun set.

It was a beautiful day, one of those days when you love living in the Seychelles. We had only been living there for about two months at that point, so we were definitely still in the honeymoon phase of expat life, but I spent the day wondering what I should and shouldn't be doing.

Is it safe for me to go swimming? Should I be eating this fish? Was I supposed to have seen a doctor as soon as I took a test?

In hindsight, I realize how naive and unprepared I really was. The next week I went to a private doctor and took another pregnancy test there. The lady at the reception desk, who apparently also doubled as the doctor's assistant, looked at my little jar of pee and said, "Yes you are pregnant," before even conducting the test on the urine sample. Apparently she could tell just by looking at the color? I was fairly impressed. She dipped her own stick into the jar, which also yielded another positive result. I was really pregnant! It was officially confirmed. She asked me if it was a planned pregnancy and seemed surprised when I said yes. Apparently there are a lot of unplanned pregnancies here in the Seychelles. At this point the lady then took me through to the doctor who then charged me money for the visit and told me that we should have gone to the government health center—he was just a general practitioner, and I needed a midwife.

Mark and I then went to the health center with excitement to meet the midwife. She was a dinosaur. She had to be in her sixties; she was very short, built like a brick wall, and very stern. Her face displayed no emotion and apparently our happiness and excitement were not contagious.

We sat down with her and determined my estimated due date. At that point she told me that there was no way I could have had a positive pregnancy urine test already. She took my blood to get an "official" confirmation and then booked me in for a scan to determine my due date. She told me I must be at least two weeks further along than I thought in order to have had a positive pregnancy test.

In this short meeting she told us several times that we would have to pay as expats for the "antenatal package." She couldn't tell us how much that was though at this point; I would have to wait until my next appointment for those details. I think she was very surprised that we were okay with paying for this package. In all honesty, I think she was more surprised that I was planning on staying here during pregnancy and to have the baby!

It turns out, the antenatal package, which along with all medical care is free for locals cost 5,000 Seychellois rupee (SCR)—about $380.

The package included:

All of my antenatal check-ups—these are monthly from 12 to 26 weeks; they then become biweekly from then until the last few weeks when they are weekly. This includes all blood tests and the always-lovely glucose test where you have to chug a sugary drink to see how your body copes with the onslaught of sugar to test for gestational diabetes.

All scans*: At 12, 20, and 32 weeks they were standard, but no extra cost if more scans are needed for any reason.

Dental check-up: Usually expats pay for the dentist too

*A little tip from me: If you don't want to know the sex of your baby during your scans, be sure to let the sonographer know that before every scan. It is much more common in Seychelles for people to find out the sex of their baby. We had been "um-ing and ah-ing" over whether to find out or not, but the sonographer made the decision for us by just telling us during one of our scans. Oops!

We excitedly shared the news with our family. The expat's best friend, Skype, was how we told our parents. It was the weirdest thing to share such a huge moment in our lives in that way. We couldn't exchange hugs and kisses; we had no cute little Pinterest-inspired colored balloons or the like to share the news. It was essentially just a phone call; we couldn't even turn video on to see each other because at the time our Internet was intermittent and allowance heavily capped, not allowing for a video streaming connection. Nevertheless, I am very grateful that we have that technology available. At least it was an instant and free way to share the news.

My first scan showed that I was actually not as far along in my pregnancy as I had originally thought, let alone the two weeks further that the midwife was certain of. It also showed a separation from the placenta, and I was told that I must do absolutely nothing and come back for a scan two weeks later.

This was a really difficult time as we were very scared, and for the first time we felt very isolated. As luck would have it though, that day my parents were traveling out to come and see us. It meant I couldn't talk to them that very day but that they would be there the next day for support.

That Christmas we were housesitting for a friend. It ended up being the ideal way for me to get lots of rest. We stayed in the main house, which had two hired cleaners, so I didn't lift a finger the entire time we were there. The view of the ocean wasn't bad either. One of the perks of living on a beautiful island in the middle of the Indian Ocean is that the aquamarine water lapping against the white sandy beaches is a view you can never tire of. The next scan showed us that everything was now fine, panic over. We were growing a healthy little baby.

I had a pretty eventful scan at 32 weeks. We walked into the room, and the sonographer immediately asked if I had been eating enough. This being my first pregnancy, and my midwife appointments not being all that informative, I did a classic first-time mom thing and panicked, "Ummmm, I think so." I was then told that my bump was nowhere near big enough and that essentially I was starving my unborn baby. He then said that the chances of baby's survival were very low since he was so small. Cue insane panic and fear from Mark and me.

The sonographer then went on to say, "I have to deliver this baby in two weeks, and he is too small."

"But I'm only 32 weeks pregnant. Why would the baby need to be born so early?" I asked the sonographer.

We then realized that my clinic notes had the wrong due date on them—remember the dates I mentioned earlier? The midwife had never adjusted her incorrect due date prediction in my chart! It turned out that everything was absolutely fine, and the baby was very healthy and the right size for my actual dates. He was breach though, so I would almost certainly be having a Cesarean section, so he booked me in for another scan a couple weeks later to confirm. We left the room and I burst into tears, feeling a mixture of relief, anger at the midwife, and annoyance at the way I'd been accused of being a bad mother before my baby had even arrived.

The weather in the Seychelles is really hot and very humid. That can be hard some days when you are sporting extra baby weight. It's especially bad being pregnant in March/April, which is the hottest time of the year. Both of my pregnancies spanned this time, so I definitely have it on good authority that it is best to be avoided if at all possible.

"Oh but there's air-conditioning," I hear you say. Well, we have air-con in our bedrooms, and that is pretty fancy, but the bulk of the day is spent trying to position yourself under the nearest ceiling fan that does a pathetic job of circulating air in your direction. My other favorite solution was to take multiple cold showers to cool down. Of course we do have the advantage of having access to lots of lovely hotel pools and beautiful beaches, so I'm sure none of you are feeling too sorry for me.

The Seychelles is made up of 115 islands located in the Indian Ocean, off the east coast of Africa. Only a handful of these islands are inhabited, and the total population is only around 90,000. The majority of people live on the island of Mahe, around 80,000, and just 6,500 live on the island of Praslin where we live. It is a dream destination with white sands and clear waters. My husband's teaching career had brought us here as he had successfully landed a job at the International School on Praslin.

Wearing appropriate clothing is another hardship as there aren't really any maternity clothes available in the Seychelles. Shopping here in general is really limited. Most things seem to come in a variety of neon colors in the sweatiest polyester material available. Although I do think that you can get some maternity wear in Victoria on Mahe, there's not a lot of choice like you would expect elsewhere in the world, so I was delighted when family shipped me a few things to wear from the UK. For the most part, I lived in a mix between sarongs, those massive tent-y beach dresses, and my husband's shorts and T-shirts by the end of both of my pregnancies. The good thing is that no one bats an eyelid at how you dress here, so I've definitely never felt any pressure to look stylish while hugely pregnant.

Being told that I was "glowing" always made me laugh; it was definitely a lot more sweat than any kind of pregnancy glow!

Many aspects of being pregnant are pretty much the same wherever you are in the world. Everyone can experience morning sickness, tiredness, weird cravings, and all of those lovely, glamorous things. In the Seychelles, if you are craving a McDonald's, some delicious fresh strawberries, or a yummy

Chinese takeaway, which I do at the best of times let alone being pregnant...just forget it. There are no fast food chains here. We do have takeaway pizza, but it's mediocre at best, and fresh strawberries are the things dreams are made of. I can't tell you how often I would have loved to take a quick McDonald's trip during both my pregnancies. What was particularly cruel in my first pregnancy was that all the shops here were importing their cans of Coke from Dubai where they had one of those ring pull promotions. I kid you not; every time I had a can of Coke I won a free McDonald's meal that I of course could not claim! It was torture to endure unsatisfied pregnancy cravings and to have all of those free meals left unclaimed. I think if I had been pregnant in the UK, I would have ended up the size of a house indulging in my every craving.

The people of the Seychelles tended to be very friendly and smiley while I was pregnant. People will always ask if you're having a boy or a girl. There is an unbelievably strong gender preference for girls here! During my first pregnancy, every time I told people I was having a boy, I got comments such as, "Don't worry, the next one will be a girl!" The second time around I was told on several occasions that I was very "unlucky" for having another boy. I also heard, "Ooh congratulations, well, no, commiserations, oh another boy!" All of these comments are always accompanied by a sympathetic look.

Barely two weeks after my second son arrived, we were told that we would soon be trying for another baby so we can have a girl. Um, okay? I have been involved in many debates about how I should feel lucky that I am in a country where women are so celebrated, and how I shouldn't complain because there are places in the world where people do all they can to have boys. Yes I agree with all of that; however, it was not making me feel any better when I was basically told that I cannot be happy with two boys or that our family is incomplete without a little girl. The general belief here is that boys are lazy, evidence to the proportion of boys to girls in the international school where my husband teaches. The vast majority of children who attend the school where parents must pay fees are girls. Those "lazy" boys must attend local schools; I don't know.

Like anyone having their first baby in the Seychelles, expat or otherwise, I had to go to the big island of Mahe to have my baby. I live on an island, Praslin, which only has a small hospital that is not capable of performing Cesarean sections. It is not standard here to do a hospital tour like it is in other places around the world. We did arrange one though, as we had never seen the hospital on Mahe, and we wanted to see where we would be going before the big delivery. To be quite honest, our first impressions of the hospital were not great. It didn't help that there was a large amount of construction going on, but it looked sort of like something from a World War II movie. The paint was peeling off the walls, there was mildew on the walls, and the condition of the hospital was not what I was used to in the UK. We left in a bit of a haze after a conversation with one of the midwives. I had asked her whether epidurals were available.

"No."

I asked if nitrous oxide gas and air was available.

"No."

So I then asked if there was any pain relief available.

"Panadol"—that's Tylenol/paracetamol.

I spent the rest of the day trying to convince Mark, and therefore convince myself, that I would be totally fine! My poor parents immediately started looking at ways they could get some gas and air delivered to me from the UK when we told them about the condition of the hospital.

We later found out during a scan that all of those things were indeed available through a doctor just not the midwives themselves. By this point we didn't need to worry about that anyway, as our son was breach, so I was to have a planned Cesarean section. Maybe the midwife just enjoyed the look of terror she could put on this poor naive expat's face.

There's an opinion here among the expat community that expats are "encouraged" toward having a Cesarean section. I'm not 100% sure why this is the case, but I think it's to guarantee what doctor you will have. Cynics will also tell you that it's because you have to spend more money—the cost of the operation plus a longer stay in hospital means more money out of the unsuspecting expats.

The day before my Cesarean, I had to "check in" to the hospital. During my first pregnancy, I met the anesthetist who discussed the different options of pain relief. We settled on having an epidural as opposed to general anesthetic. He made me feel very positive and relaxed about the whole thing. I had never actually considered general anesthetic being an option, but it was weirdly reassuring to know that different options were actually available after the midwife had led me to believe that Panadol was the only form of pain relief.

During check-in at the hospital, I was asked a bunch of questions including some about my religious beliefs. I couldn't help but feel judged for saying that I didn't have any—the Seychelles is a predominantly Catholic country. During my second pregnancy, the questions were even more cringe-worthy as when I answered the awkward religion question the guy said, "But you do believe in God, right?" I replied no, and he looked shocked and disappointed. Cue awkward laugh from me and a "Sorry!" I don't know why I said sorry. Perhaps I wanted this guy on my side in case he was looking after my baby at some point.

I was taken to a bed in a large shared room, but there were no other people in there.

By around 2 p.m. I was left to my own devices. I was not allowed to leave the hospital, and there was no Wi-Fi, no air-conditioning, nothing. It was boring and of course sweaty to say the least.

The day of the operation I was allowed to have Mark and my parents with me before I went in. In the Seychelles no one is allowed in with you during the operation itself.

Getting wheeled into the operating room was the most surreal experience ever. On the outside it looked like I was going to enter into something from the 1970s, but once inside, the room was very clean and looked like it had all the right equipment—I say that as I have no idea what the right equipment would be.

Prior to the birth, I had read lots of Cesarean birth stories online to try and prepare myself for what it would be like. Being there by myself made the whole thing feel pretty clinical despite how nice everyone was to me in the room. I had a mask on, it was either gas and air or just oxygen, but I honestly couldn't tell you which—not because I can't remember, but I actually don't think I was told, and I was never asked which I preferred.

At 9:25 a.m. our little guy was born, and I burst into happy tears when I heard his little cry. I got to give him a kiss, and then he was quickly whisked away. I was assured my husband could at this point be with him; I couldn't bare the idea of him being on his own. I was given morphine and acetaminophen when I needed it afterward. The morphine ensured that the first day was covered in a haze.

I stayed in the hospital for a total of five nights, and in that time I had three different rooms. It was annoying to move so often, but I understood why. The first night I was in the "waiting room," the two days following the Cesarean was spent in a room directly opposite the midwives' station for easier monitoring, and for the last two nights I was moved down to the end of the hall.

When I had my first son, the nurses took him away during the evenings. I was absolutely mortified, and I assumed they thought that I wasn't capable of looking after my son. I was struggling to breastfeed, and I'm pretty sure that taking him away didn't help me much. Looking back on it now, I think they could see what a state I was in and that I needed the sleep. In the end I was given some tough love in terms of breastfeeding, with kind of a "man up and get on with it" approach. I think it was what I needed to snap me out of my stressed-out state.

During my second pregnancy, the midwives in the hospital treated me very differently. They were mostly kind, and they all remembered me. Most likely they remembered me as the hysterical white woman who had no idea what she was doing. I think they were impressed that we were still living in the Seychelles, let alone back having another baby.

There was one midwife, however, who earned her spot in the record books as being one of the worst midwives in the world. She was a nun who worked as a midwife in the hospital, and I didn't have much interaction with her during my first birth. She was reasonably helpful with my breastfeeding struggle but perhaps a little judgmental that I had no clue what I was doing with a baby. After my second birth, I received the full brunt of her difficult personality. Luckily, I had been told that if all went well with my second birth that I could go home the next day. This made me extremely happy, as I just wanted to return home and start our little family life of four. I was in a good mood. If I hadn't had that good news, I would have been less inclined to hold my tongue! In the space of a day, this fine specimen of a midwife told me that I had my children too close together. They are separated by two years and a month—that's not really that close, lady.

She also told me that I should be working and that "no man's salary can sustain a family," which I thought was a pretty unusual thing for a nun to say.

I told her that I would rather go without the extra money from whatever job I could do in the Seychelles in exchange for raising my children myself. She was surprised at my response and proceeded to give me ridiculously filthy looks when I told her I would be flying home to Praslin the day I was discharged from hospital. We didn't want to pay rent on a place on Mahe any longer than we had to, and it was only a 15-minute flight back home. In fact the place we were renting was further than 15 minutes away. I was also told by the lady with whom I was sharing a room that this nun had slapped her when she wasn't breastfeeding her baby "correctly" when she had had her daughter 11 years earlier. What a woman!

While being discharged from hospital, particularly the first time around, I was repeatedly told that I needed to register the baby as soon as I left hospital. Both times I told them that my husband had already done it, and they didn't believe me. They truly did not believe that a man would go and do that all on his own. Again, men are supposed to be "lazy," right? Not my man! After our first son was born, the midwife asked me if I had someone with me, aside from Mark.

When I said my mom would be there as well, she told me, "Good, otherwise I wouldn't let you leave."

Essentially she was saying that we couldn't be trusted on our own—how great for a new mom and dad's self-esteem! All I could think was that I was being judged as not good enough.

Upon discharge, we were given our bill that we had to pay. We couldn't pay it that day, because it was a public holiday and the office was closed. The bill was kind of hilarious, and we couldn't believe how literally everything during my five-day stay was individually itemized and charged for—right down to individual capsules of acetaminophen.

It ended up costing us a grand total of 15,000 SCR, or roughly around $1,150, for five nights' stay, my operation, and all aftercare including medication and food—the hospital is most certainly not high on my recommended places to eat, I must say.

So, I have had my two boys. They are safe, healthy, and happy. Would I do it again? Absolutely! Was the hospital perfect? No, but what hospital is? There are things I would like to change, naturally, but in the end we are proud that we had our babies here in the Seychelles.

Looking ahead, we are planning on staying in the Seychelles for at least another four years, but most likely we will stay even longer. For now, we will just enjoy watching our little island babies grow and continue to make the most of our beautiful surroundings. We are so happy to be raising our children in a place where we can spend so much time outdoors. Although we don't know where our next move will take us, if we move at all, we do know that we have no desire to return to the UK. There are many adventures that await us.

Chantelle Howell is a British expat who moved to the Seychelles with her husband in 2012. She is now living her dream of being a stay-at-home mom raising her two little island babies, two-year-old Arthur and two-month-old Freddie. You can find Chantelle blogging about her expat family life at http://www.seychellesmama.com.

CHAPTER 13

BABY IN BENIN

Sarah Murdock
Nationality: USA
Birthed in: USA, Togo and Benin, West Africa

"**I** want a little sister," declared my firstborn, then aged four. I suggested we pray about it, and he did, absolutely confident that a sister was now on the way—and actually, she already was. I was in my first trimester with my third child.

We were living in Benin, West Africa, where my husband, Matt, and I had been missionaries for nine years, ever since we were married. Prior to meeting me, he had spent a few years in Togo, just to the west of Benin, while I had been living in Washington, DC. Raised in Wyoming, living in rural Africa was a far cry from anything he had experienced before. I had lived in Africa as a child, so it was not quite as foreign to me, but I still had a lot to learn about the culture.

Benin is regularly toward the bottom in lists of Africa's poorest countries. It is largely an agrarian society, with cotton exports being one of its few commodities. The southern part of the country, along the coastline, is the most prosperous, and the further north you get, the bleaker it is. We lived in the northwest corner, in a town where even many southern Beninese were reluctant to come.

To them, we were in the uncivilized hinterland. To be honest, the first time I visited, I got pretty depressed thinking that I might move there. Most people there are subsistence farmers living in villages that have no electricity or running water, and most don't even have wells. Even in the larger towns, the majority of homes don't have latrines, the roads are dirt, and the homes made of mud brick. As far as food went, we didn't have much variety, but at least what we did have was organic and free-range.

What put our town of Tanguieta on the map is that it has one of the best hospitals in the country, and arguably in the region. Established in 1970 by the Catholic order of Saint Jean de Dieu, it is now an official government hospital, and people come there for treatment from as far away as Ivory Coast. An interesting feature of the place is that they use both conventional medicine and natural/indigenous treatments. Most of the staff is African, and many of the doctors trained in Europe. The staff is terribly overworked, the crowds can be huge, and many cases are very discouraging as the patients wait too long to seek help. In Benin alone, there are over 50 languages spoken, not to mention the ones spoken by people from nearby countries, so overcoming the language barriers is very frustrating for the staff, who have to find interpreters wherever they can for those who don't speak French.

The hospital is a collection of buildings, all with wide, covered verandas along their lengths serving as corridors. The surgery is air-conditioned, as are the administrative offices, but nothing else. When days can reach 120 °F (48.9 °C), and nights sometimes hover in the 90s °F (over 32 °C), it can be quite uncomfortable. The large waiting areas are all open-air, and there are large tree-shaded courtyards outside the patients' wings, where family members sleep and cook for the invalids who choose not to eat hospital fare. Wealthier families can afford the semi-private rooms that have attached bathrooms and a quieter atmosphere. The normal patients' rooms have eight beds and much coming and going. The attending family members (which a patient is required to have) are pressed into service to help keep the floors swept and communal toilets cleaned.

I chose to have my first child in the US (in 2002), partly because I wanted some sense of familiarity as I launched into this new experience, and partly because I wanted our parents to be able to be there. My mother had cancer, and this might be her last chance to be present for the birth of a grandchild (it was). It was a typical American hospital birth—I was not given much choice in how I gave birth, was induced shortly after the due date, had an epidural, and consequently felt robbed of the full experience.

My second was born two years later in a mission hospital in neighboring Togo. The medical staff in the Tanguieta hospital was convinced he was going to be born early, so I had put myself on bed rest for two months, and at my eighth month we went to this hospital, where they might be able to fly us to the nearest place that could deal with preemies, if necessary. I think that was the Ivory Coast, a few countries away. Defying expectations, he also ended up being induced, a week after his due date, and he made his way into this world rather dramatically in the bathroom of the guesthouse we were using. So when they began to warn me that my third child might be early, I discounted it. I began to get Braxton-Hicks contractions as early as my fifth month, much as I had with my second child, and I figured this was just the way I rolled.

Matt and I pondered our options about where we should have this baby. Should we go back to Togo, or stay in Tanguieta, or go to another hospital? I felt pretty comfortable staying in Tanguieta with this one, but I went and talked to the doctor about what sort of pain management they had available. I had to be stitched up after both my boys were born, and my worst nightmare was not having any anesthesia. He assured me they had it, and as we talked further I decided that this hospital was as good as any to give birth.

Along with my monthly prenatal exams, I had to sit in on the "lectures" given by the midwives to all of us expectant mothers. I was usually sitting in the open-air waiting room from 8 a.m. to noon along with the rest of the captive audience before I got the cursory exam. The lectures were invariably on AIDS and what to bring with you to the hospital for the birth—essentially everything, including a bucket with which to take home the placenta. Apparently they used to loan out cloth for diapers, but with the increased risk of AIDS infection, they began to require patients to bring their own. The exams did not consist of much, and the staff mysteriously seemed to change my due date each time I went. I have no idea why this was so, but one conversation I had some time earlier may shed light on this.

When telling the story of a woman in another part of Benin who gave birth after a supposed two-year pregnancy, a Beninese friend defended the claim by saying, "You whites—you take nine months to have a baby, but we Africans—it can be anywhere from a few months to two years." Apparently I had become more African than I realized in my nine years in Benin.

I had my first of two sonograms on October 25, and a due date of February 11 was fixed. This was pretty close to the date I had calculated on my own.

Then I had another check-up on November 28. Here's how that one went:

Doctor: "So, your due date is March 12."

Me (panicking): "What?! That's not possible! It's got to be February 11!"

Doctor: "Oh? Well, March, February—same difference."

I laugh somewhat hysterically, thinking only a man would say that to a pregnant woman.

Doctor: "Hmm. Maybe the other doctor miscalculated. Let's see...Ah yes, you should give birth sometime between January 17 and February 18. No sooner than January 18, okay?"

Me: "Okay, you got it."

On January 2 at another check-up the midwives calculated I was at 32 and a half weeks. That put me at February 23. Crikey, I was confused.

When I told her that some of my contractions were getting a little painful, she said, "Let's see if you are in labor."

"Ack, I can't be in labor," I gasped.

She just smiled at me patronizingly.

In the last few months, I got so big and felt so cumbersome they began to wonder if I had twins ("the sonogram doesn't always show twins..."), and the women in the open-air market where I shopped nicknamed me "Titan"—their name for semi-trucks. I felt quite self-conscious, especially because Beninese women were so compact in their pregnancies and fully mobile right up to and right after their births.

As the nebulous due date(s) approached, and I was thinking about how I was going to have this baby, I reread a book on natural childbirth and pondered my options. Apparently, as far as the hospital staff was concerned, I did not have options—I would lie on the table, with my legs in stirrups. I asked a Beninese friend about what the women used to do in the villages or still did if they could not get to the hospital. She said they often gave birth on all fours or squatted. However, several friends also told me that you had better do what the midwives said, or they would slap you! I heard not a few stories of women who were "bullied" by the midwives. I was counting on the fact that I was a foreigner to spare me some of this treatment. I discussed my thoughts with my wonderful midwife, Lydie, and she advised me to lie on the table because any accidental contact with the floor could be dangerous for my baby.

On Valentine's Day I had another check-up. I was kept on my back for a good hour as the doctor monitored the baby's heartbeat and did a sonogram. When I got up, my back was killing me so badly that I could not even step high enough to get into my car. I was grateful when an orange vendor I knew across the street saw me and came running over with a stool to help me up.

On the evening of February 15, I began getting contractions. They became painful around 9 p.m. I decided to try to sleep them off, as I had (successfully) with Number Two. By 3:30 a.m. or so I still had not slept much, and I figured the contractions would be more bearable if I were up and walking. It didn't help. Since neither of my two previous births had been without some kind of intervention, I wasn't sure where I was in the process this time. Uncertain, I woke Matt up about 15 minutes later, and asked him to send for Lydie. Although not on hospital staff, she knew all the midwives there and had agreed to accompany me. We sent our night guardian on his motorcycle to go fetch her. When she arrived about half an hour later, the contractions were a minute apart.

She examined me and exclaimed, "You are completely effaced— we need to go *now*!"

So we headed toward the car, and I had a contraction on the way. I stopped to lean on Matt, and Lydie urged, "Keep going—we need to hurry!"

I begged Matt to take the "long" way—only about a mile—to avoid the bumpy roads, and we drove through the hospital's main gate past the parking lot straight up to the maternity ward. I began walking down the veranda to the delivery room and had another contraction, so I stopped to lean on the wall.

"Hurry!" Lydie cried, coming to get me, and propelling me to the delivery room.

We entered the room—Matt ignored the "No men allowed, don't even ask" sign and stayed with me—and headed toward the birthing table. My back was still killing me, so I took one look at that table and I knew that if I were to lie down on it, there was no way I would be able to push, because the pain would just be too great. So, much to the consternation of the midwives, and admittedly taking shameless advantage of the fact that I was an American, I just crawled up on the table and stayed on all fours.

They were aghast, "Oh, you can't do that! You have to lie down! We are not used to this position! We don't know what to do if you take this position!"

How ironic, I thought, given that that is the way their mothers probably birthed them. Grimly, I did not budge despite their protests, and I did not take long—a couple of pushes, and out came Bridget at 4:33 a.m., just seven minutes after we arrived. The cord was around her neck, so she was blue-gray, but after a few minutes on oxygen, she turned a nice rosy pink. My first daughter—she was beautiful!

Matt occupied himself with her, while I got on my back so the midwives could examine me. Lo and behold, I had torn quite badly, about three centimeters. This, of course, was my fault, I was told, since I had "chosen a bad position." They then set to work stitching me up. It was bad enough getting poked with a needle about 10 times in various places with anesthesia—but just imagine how hellish it was to find out the anesthesia did not work!! And they just kept right on going.

When I screamed at the first stitch, the midwife doing the sewing upbraided me, "Oh, you're just a big sissy!"

The nurses chided me, "Come on, you were so brave during the birth, just like a hardy African woman, hardly making any sound, and now listen to you."

I have never screamed so loud, so often, or so long in my life. It was sheer agony, about 15 minutes' worth, but it seemed to last forever. I felt like Westley in *The Princess Bride* when he bellowed as the life was getting sucked out of him.

Matt was next to me, holding Bridget, and I was squeezing his fingers in a death grip. At one point, he told me he had to go—he was either going to vomit or pass out. He had to hand Bridget off to a nurse, and he left the room. My fingers were hard to pry off him, and stayed in a claw like position as I transferred the death grip to Lydie.

After Matt returned, the midwife said, "Last one"—then did another stitch. This happened a few times, and I cried, "You've *got* to tell me the truth! *Don't* lie to me!"

To top it off, every now and then as she stitched, the midwife would ask Matt to look at her handiwork and tell her if he approved.

"The husband has to be happy," she explained to me matter-of-factly. On one of the "last" stitches I just broke down and sobbed and sobbed. It felt really good to let out all the tension that way. Finally I was done, and we went to the bed prepared for me, which was in the labor room next door, thankfully vacant. This was a nicer arrangement for me than the normal recovery room with eight beds, and I was thankful for the special treatment, even though I felt a tad guilty.

The midwives praised my husband and his helpfulness—they apparently had had temporary amnesia about that "No men allowed" sign, thankfully. They all said that if Matt had not been such a huge help, they would have had to call the doctor, but as it was, they were able to manage without him.

A little later in the morning, Lydie came to check on me. She felt bad that I had been in such pain. I explained that the crying had helped me deal with it, and I apologized for yelling at the midwives.

One of Bridget's first visitors in the hospital was a woman who wanted to pierce her ears—something all newborn girls in Benin get done. I politely declined, and from then on all the Beninese thought she was a boy. It didn't matter how pink I dressed her, especially since in our town the men seemed to prefer pastel-colored clothing, while the women chose darker, striped motifs.

There was no shortage of other visitors that day—some I knew, many I did not. One was the orange vendor who had helped me into the car a few days earlier. There were plenty of curious onlookers who had never seen a white newborn baby before. They had probably also come to see the woman with the powerful lungs who had woken up the entire hospital earlier that morning.

About a week before I was due, Matt's aunt had arrived to help out, and I took her to see the hospital. When we got to the bathroom, I found a man working in there, and asked if the toilet he was working on was broken.

"The whole bathroom is broken," he replied nonchalantly.

Eh? I asked some of the women where we were supposed to go, and was casually told, "Go down the veranda stairs, through the courtyard, past the gate, across the road—and see those trees? There."

Gulp. The day I gave birth I decided to eat and drink nothing, to reduce my chances of needing a toilet as much as possible. The one time I needed it, my aunt-in-law held up a bedpan for me, as I used a length of cloth as a "curtain."

I barely saw the doctor the whole time—I saw him briefly at 10 a.m., and again around 6 p.m., when he sat at his desk in the adjoining consultation room. I was anxious to go home, so I wrapped a cloth around me and waddled over as best as I could muster to ask him if I could leave.

"How do you feel?" he asked.

"Great!" I answered enthusiastically.

"Okay, you can go."

Yippee! My wonderful husband had made dinner, and after devouring it, my first food of the day, I finally got to clean up. Taking a shower never felt so good.

Despite the "violence" I suffered immediately after her birth, I recovered very quickly—because she was my third? I rested on February 17, and by the next day, I was up and making pancake batter (but let my hubby cook it). By the 21st I was cooking, making granola and bread and yogurt, washing and ironing diapers, going shopping and to the post office. On the 26th Bridget had her first outing when we went out to lunch.

By the 28th she already had three offers of marriage…

Sarah Murdock is an American who has lived more out of the US than in, first as a dependent of her Foreign Service father, then with her husband, Matt, as a missionary in Benin, West Africa. Their three children, born in Virginia, Togo, and Benin have finally been convinced that they are Americans, after repatriating to the US in 2011. She enjoys the outdoors, traveling, and exploring new cultures, cooking and chocolate. While she is happy to be in Wyoming, she would love to live overseas again, and hopes to give her children the chance to experience life in another country.

CHAPTER 14

SURPRISES ACROSS THE POND

Erin Boeck Motum
Nationality: USA
Birthed in: England

I've always loved escaping to other worlds. But, usually, I did this through books. Containing sacred bits of knowledge, books were the answer to many of my life's problems. Whatever I was feeling, I knew I could find a book that would make it all feel okay or at least make it all make sense.

And then, I was pregnant.

In a foreign country.

Without my family around.

I couldn't find a single book that could answer all of my questions and make me feel at home. I was lost.

I was born and raised in Saint Louis, Missouri, and I didn't really get out of the area much. It wasn't until I was a senior in high school (aged 17) that I left the country for the first time. But once that happened, I was hooked. My dad always told me that it was a great big world out there, that there were so many things to see and do. (He now thoroughly regrets saying this, by the way.) And so, when I had the chance to study abroad while at university, I ran with it.

I found someone online who was my age and lived in England, where I was going to study abroad. I wanted to familiarize myself with the language, with the nuances of the culture. Sure, he and I both technically spoke English, but that did not mean we always understood one another. (The cliché "two countries separated by a common language" is cliché for a reason.) Although we didn't meet in person when I studied in England for the semester, we continued to write one another. In the end, we wrote back and forth for four years before we actually met up. And the rest, as they say, is history.

I've never been good at relationships. Awkward, shy, bookish, naive, a bit "intense"—those are all great adjectives to describe me. And yet, after meeting up for the first time on Saint Patrick's Day in 2008, I found myself in a relationship. And it was a great one. After just over nine months of dating, George and I were married. We had our wedding in the US, which meant the reception was a wedding/going away party all rolled into one.

Settling into our new life in London was challenging and exciting. We took in the sights, went to the shows, and explored the surrounding areas. I adjusted to the ups and downs of public transportation, and I did research (where I could) to figure out the translations and where to buy food I recognized. When the bank took three months just to add my name to George's account, I (reluctantly) played the 1950s housewife and asked him for money to go out or buy things (even though my paycheck was going into the account, too). And then, a couple of years later, baby fever took hold of me.

Everywhere I looked, there were babies! And adverts about babies! And the sounds of babies! Babies, babies, babies—oh, baby! Looking back now, I was mental. I had no idea what we were signing up for. George worked for the police in London. And the police life...well, it's hard. Crazy hours, unreliable finish times, potentially dangerous situations day in and day out. My job as an editor allowed more flexibility (and although the pen might be mightier than the sword, it's a heck of a lot safer), but we were still in London. New York may hold the title of the city that never sleeps, but London is still pretty busy.

After careful consideration and lots of discussions, we decided to try. It took my sister several years to conceive, and I had had some health issues in the past. I mean, it probably wouldn't even happen right away. Right?

But it did.

And oh, did it.

We were on holiday (vacation) in America, visiting my family and seeing the Grand Canyon. George had to leave to go back to England for work, and I stayed on for another week in America to see more family in Saint Louis. I felt a bit off, so I went and bought a pregnancy test that night. I told no one. Not even my sister. Ever the reader and rule-follower, I obeyed the box that said to wait till morning to take the test. First thing, I jumped out of bed. I went to the bathroom. I peed on a stick. And that's when everything changed.

I told my husband over Skype that we were going to have a baby. Not quite the big baby reveal you see on Pinterest these days, but it worked. And being able to tell my parents face to face was actually so much fun. It was George's birthday, and I made this big deal about how they had to Skype George for his birthday. They all thought I was crazy, particularly when I made them open baby-related presents, but then they realized why. George recorded their reactions, which I love re-watching.

When I got back to England, one of the first things I did was make an appointment for a scan. (It was so nice not to have the stress of trying to find someone who would take a certain insurance.) It was pretty much expected that George would go with me (whereas most of my American friends seemed to go to those types of appointments alone while their spouses were at work). Both together, both excited and nervous. Were the tests I took (yes, tests, plural) right? Was I actually pregnant? Would our baby be okay? And as they got me all set up on the table and put the cold gel on my belly, I looked at the screen for the answers. And I got them. Plural. Two. There were two blips on the screen.

"Are there two?!" I asked, definitely aware that I'm not a medical expert.

I thought maybe there were two different views on the screen. You know, so they could see it from multiple angles. Maybe that's just how things were done in England. (Denial.) The ultrasound technician grabbed a multiples specialist right away to confirm it all, and the first words out of my mouth were, "We're going to need more names."

You see, we had one name for a boy and one name for a girl. Now, we needed to plan for multiple scenarios.

We were having multiples.

In a daze, we went to our favorite pizza place, the place we went to on our first date, and ate. We exclaimed, "Two!" over and over again to one another. The receptionist at the hospital commented on how calm we were, having heard the news. I think we were just in shock.

In hindsight, I should have known. I had started showing early. My bump bumped out like nobody's business. (But since everyone could see it, it seemed it was everybody's business.) And, as I will never let them live it down, my parents joked about there being "two in there" when we told them about the pregnancy in the first place. How on earth they called it, I'll never know.

I didn't stop much to think about how the pregnant life might have been different in America. I was just focused on trying to get through each day, trying to make it to all of my appointments. (I saw both a midwife, as is customary in England, and a doctor, as deemed necessary by my "high-risk" status.) But there we were, thrust into the world of multiples. It was a world that was completely foreign to me. And to top it off, there I was, in a foreign country. The twins were our first, and I had no idea what to expect. A whole new slew of words (and worries) opened up to me. Amniocentesis. Singletons. Fraternal. Identical. Tandem nursing. Twin-to-twin transfusion syndrome. We went to all of the recommended classes, and then there were all of the scans and tests! I peed in a cup like the world was depending on it. Which, in a way, it was.

In between all of the appointments, I tried to carry on with my normal activities. Life in London is great for a lot of things. You have access to so much, all basically on your doorstep. And public transportation can take you pretty much anywhere. Using it at peak hours usually means having your personal space violated somewhat, which wasn't as big of an issue pre-pregnancy. I'm a relatively compact person, and listening to music does wonders when it comes to tuning out the outside world. But because I carried most of my weight to my front when I was pregnant, people behind me didn't necessarily know I was pregnant. When trying to get to work one morning, this fellow kept trying to shove his way onto the train carriage because it must have appeared as though there were space in front of me.

After a few shoves, I finally turned around and said, "Sorry, but I can't really move forward more."

He had the decency to look horrified by his behavior as he

backed away, muttering apologies. After that, I moved my "Baby on Board" badge (the one that's handed out to pregnant moms for free by the transport authority, TFL) to the back of my coat. Problem solved.

In my experience, England's National Health Service (NHS) was amazing. Coming from America, land of even-with-healthcare-coverage-you're-still-getting-a-big-bill, I was so thankful for the onslaught of midwives and other specialists who offered their time and expertise to us without the expectation of us owing them our firstborn. (Any idea of how that deal would work for someone having twins, by the way? Would it literally have been the first one to be born, or would the deal mean they got to keep both?)

The technician who gave me a 3-D scan one day when George couldn't go to the appointment with me, just to make me smile and let me watch the girls playing what appeared to be a baby version of karate in my belly, was so kind. The specialists who answered my long, long lists of questions were so patient. The midwives who amazed me with their skills and expertise were nowhere near the image of untrustworthiness you sometimes see them portrayed with in America. Then, when we moved two months before the girls were born, the team who took on our case and made sure there weren't any major gaps in my (our) care were brilliant. And the health visitor who came to see me at the house after the girls were born so I didn't have to trek into the clinic was perfect. All amazing. And really, most of these things would not have happened in America. Not on our budget, anyway.

America is great for a lot of things, but from what I've seen while living in the US for a year recently, health care is a nightmare. It's costly. Making money is so entwined with the system that you sometimes feel like you're just a number. Or sometimes you worry that they're running tests simply so they can charge you more money (through your insurance company, of course). And there was the gratitude (selfish gratitude) of knowing that, if like many twin mothers, my babies had to spend time in the NICU, at the very least we wouldn't even have to think, *Oh, but how are we going to pay that bill when it comes?* (My sister's friend had twins who were really premature. The bill was high. Like, really high.)

In England, if you have a "normal" pregnancy, you have lots of delivery options. You can deliver at home. You can have a water birth. You can deliver in a home-like setting at the hospital. You can do pretty much whatever you want—you generally don't have to be constantly monitored, and you're actually encouraged to move around while in labor. But in America, I probably would have been seen as quite strange for wanting to try for a vaginal birth with multiples. (I hate using the term "natural" there; it seems to try to diminish the alternative.) Even my family members thought I was crazy for not really considering an epidural, but the NHS mostly seemed to support that decision. Mostly.

Starting all over again after the move and trying to find a doctor who would let me have the birth I wanted was a bit emotional. (I was a bit emotional. Okay, really emotional.) Being pregnant with twins, I was classified as high-risk, so I knew the water labor I had imagined was pretty much out of the question. I still wanted to try to avoid the C-section. Surgeries and knives and whatnot scare me to death. I'm very squeamish. And I wanted to avoid the epidural. I had heard horrible stories from a friend, which put me off the idea instantly. And so, after a couple of conversations, I found a doctor who supported the "my body, my choice" mentality. With one caveat: He requested that I deliver in the operating room just in case. Because both of us just wanted to keep the babies safe, I agreed.

Although we were lucky enough not to have had to deal with any major complications during the pregnancy, that didn't mean it was all smooth sailing. I bled at one point in the pregnancy. Freaked me out enough to send me to A&E (the emergency room) for tests and scans. (My wonderful employer, who knew I had to go to A&E, insisted that I take the rest of the day off to rest. I'm almost certain that would not have happened back in the US). And I'm hypermobile, which basically means my joints rotate more than usual, so as the girls (and I) put on more and more weight, my hip bones rotated out from the pressure. You know the pregnant woman waddle? I could barely do that. I was eventually put on bed rest because I just couldn't walk.

(So Google, please take this opportunity to add a "heavily pregnant woman walking" speed. I Googled how long it would take me to walk from our house to my new doctor after we moved, and it said 10 minutes. Confident that I could walk for 10 minutes, I set out. It took me more than 30 minutes.)

One of the girls was breech for the last part of the pregnancy. So I worried and worried about how that would affect the delivery. But then, sitting on the sofa with my husband and one of our friends, having a chat, *wham*! She turned around. Just like that. It hurt like hell, by the way, even more than the damn delivery. But at least she was now facing the right direction.

At 4 a.m. on Sunday morning, I woke up to a sort of twinge in my belly. Unsure of what it was, I did the only thing I could think of doing: I called one of my friends back in the US to ask if I was in labor. Yes, I realize the humor of this now. I was in England, more than 4,000 miles away, and I called someone who wasn't even there to ask her about what my body was doing. George was doing the much more sensible thing: He had phoned the hospital. And so, after calling around to various family members to let them know where we were heading, we set off for the hospital, George nervous ("Do you need me to drive fast to get there, or take it slow?") and me feeling rather at ease. I don't know why, but I was so calm at that moment.

We parked at the hospital, strolled on in, and waited for them to get me all set up in a private room. It didn't take long, but when the midwives checked me, I was already five centimeters dilated. Then came all of the fun with the water breaking and the labor pains. They gave me gas and air (and George wisely saved the remarks about how I sounded like Darth Vader for another time), and a bit later my mother-in-law had arrived, just in time to see us off to the OR for delivery. (She brought Krispy Kreme donuts with her so I could have them after delivering. She's a good woman.)

To be honest, I don't remember a whole lot about the delivery. It all seems rather vague and fuzzy in my brain. But I do know that they had every possible person I might have medically needed there for me. Seriously, I think there were about 20 people standing around, ready to give me meds or to remind me that I didn't want meds or to help in an emergency. (To the woman who had to deal with the poop, I'm very, very sorry.) But even though I had so many people there to help me, I can't really recall any of their names. I had never met them before. From what I can tell, in the US, you have your doctor—and that is the person who will likely be with you for the delivery. For me, I had a room full of strangers. Well, strangers and my husband.

Push, push, push. Push, push, push. More than an hour later, and with the help of a suction (Kiwi) cup, baby Isabella was out! Healthy and relatively happy, I got to give her a quick cuddle before setting up for the second delivery. By this point, I wanted to quote Phoebe from *Friends*, "I already had a baby. Leave me alone!"—but I still tried. And tried. But things had stalled a bit here, too. Was I going to need that C-section after all? At this point, I would have done whatever they told me to do. But 29 minutes later, baby Adriana came out "on her own" as the doctor said. (Funny that. I seem to remember having something to do with it all, too.) But she had the cord around her neck. I have absolutely no memory of this part, but George told me about it weeks later. I'm not sure if I've just blocked it out or if I was just too exhausted by that point to notice anything. But like I said, everyone was there. Immediately, she was evaluated, and they said she was perfectly healthy.

My mother-in-law later told me that while she was eagerly awaiting news, the midwives, some of whom stayed late just to make sure they were with me till both babies came out, kept giving her tidbits of updates. So even though I don't remember their names, I know they went out of their way to help me. They did their jobs, they did them well and they treated me fabulously. I couldn't have asked for more.

I was wheeled back to my room, where I was allowed to take a shower (the blood...why does nobody warn you about the blood?!) and drink some water. It was just after 1 p.m. when all was said and done. I was hungry, and I finally got to eat one of those donuts (chocolate iced with sprinkles, in case you were wondering).

They put me in my room (which, although it wasn't a private room like I probably would have had—and paid for—in America, was curtained off and had plenty of space for me and the girls) in the transitional care unit, since the girls were technically premature. Basically, they let George and I get on with things with minimal interruptions. I remember pausing to bask in the beautiful sunshine, which seemed to be celebrating the success and joy of the day. It was a somewhat rare British treat.

It was assumed that I would attempt to breastfeed. (I wanted to try, at least.) The midwives were all there to offer support (most of the breastfeeding support team people were amazing, although there was one lady who was a bit...brusque) and reassurance (yes, the babies would be okay with her while I napped). They let George stay well past visiting hours. And when he did go home, he took care of updating everyone for me.

At night, because we were in a shared ward, I was really conscious of the girls crying. I never seemed to hear other babies cry (which, I later learned, was because most of the women on my floor had to visit their babies in the NICU because their babies were all struggling). The notion that my girls were well, well enough to be with me while their babies were not, left me feeling both grateful and guilty.

We were in the hospital until Wednesday, but it wasn't until a week after the girls were born that I sat down and wrote a blog post to update my family about how it all went down. And that's been one of the biggest tools in our arsenal to keep everyone updated: the blog.

I still missed seeing my parents, family and friends, and being able to show the girls off to them, but I had never experienced a pregnancy and birth that way before, so I didn't really know what that was like. I don't think I even thought to feel sorry for myself when I couldn't have my family there with me for the delivery. And I did get a chance to show the girls off. Just not right away. My dad, stepmom, and sister all came to visit me shortly after the girls were born. A few wonderful friends came to visit, too. And those who couldn't visit chatted with me on Skype or kept up with the blog or sent me wonderful care packages. We used the blog as a tool to connect, and I eventually bought a new phone, one that could easily allow me to post pictures and videos to the blog.

When they were just shy of two weeks, we took the girls to visit family in Somerset, a two-or-so-hour drive away. George's granny (and the rest of the family members) was all tickled to see the girls. When the girls were about five months old, we took them up to Scotland for a friend's wedding. (I'm so grateful we did, because recently those friends died in a plane crash. There are many wonderful things about being an international family, but it makes you even more aware of how much you need to treat each moment with someone as your last.) And when they were seven months old, we took them on their first international trip to see the American family members, including my mother and grandparents who couldn't travel to England. We put in the effort to bridge the gap between our families, our cultures, and our countries. Believe me, it is not always easy.

Having two babies at once—particularly without the comforts of home and the support of your own friends and family members who know how to deal with you when you're at your most tired/crabby—was so difficult. That first year...it nearly killed me. Particularly since my husband was caught up with work because of the London Olympics and the queen's Diamond Jubilee. But I still wouldn't change it (unless you count me wanting to convince a few key people to move to England, too). Our girls are now citizens of the world. They've been to more countries than quite a few people I know. They've seen so much and met so many people. They are already pretty open to interacting with new people and cultures.

And yes, I know they probably won't remember all of the things they've already seen in their first three (nearing four) years, but I'd be willing to bet that it will definitely shape the type of people they become. And isn't that the point of any life experience, no matter how old you are?

Erin Boeck Motum is a mother of twins who loves to read, edit, plan, travel, and help make the world a better place. Having been an editor in her pre-children days, she was pleased to realize that, after a couple of years of being a stay-at-home mom, she could still (kind of) form coherent sentences. Erin is currently juggling being a stay-at-home mom, writing children's books featuring twins (with her first, "Bella and Drew Go to the Zoo," being illustrated right now), editing for a communications agency, volunteering as a marketing professional for a new NGO that works with wounded soldiers in the country of Georgia, and writing about her experiences for blogs and books.

CHAPTER 15

THIRD TIME LUCKY

Olga Mecking
Nationality: Poland
Birthed in: Germany and the Netherlands

If there is a way to describe the Dutch approach to giving birth in one short sentence, it'd definitely be, "Pregnancy is not an illness."

I wholeheartedly disagree.

Pain and suffering? Check.

Vomiting? Check.

A parasite taking over your body? Check.

Copious amounts of bodily fluids? Check.

But the Dutch are undeterred in their belief that giving birth is one of the most natural and *gezellig* (one of these untranslatable words that means quaint, nice, comfy, social and nice) things a woman can do in her life.

When I was pregnant with my first, I was living in Germany. A friend, also pregnant at that time, told me that in the Netherlands things are done the natural way. So very natural, in fact, that the Netherlands has a home birth rate of approximately 25%—the highest in all industrialized countries.

Midwives preside over the majority of healthy births, while gynecologists are for risky cases (hint: you're only deemed at risk if your midwife says you are). No wonder I got scared. I decided I'd rather live with my parents-in-law in Germany for a few months than subject myself to a fully natural birth.

A few months later I was certain this was the worst idea of my life. It took 38 hours, including three hours of pushing, for my eldest to be born, and for a long time I was traumatized by this experience.

When my baby was six weeks old, we crammed everything (and I mean everything, including the crib, the stroller, and the changing table) into my in-laws' huge caravan car and drove to Delft, in the Netherlands. Finally, I was able to be with my husband, and for a while I felt my family was complete.

Except that it wasn't.

I was still traumatized, but then I remembered something I had learned when I was horseback riding: When you fall off the horse, get back in the saddle or you'll be scarred for life.

I decided to jump right back on the horse's back and when my eldest was not even a year old, I found myself pregnant again.

This time, I was excited about giving birth in the Netherlands. I was so terrified of the hospital that I decided to go full Dutch and have a home birth.

I looked forward to my midwife appointments. I felt sure I didn't need all these medical tests. I watched the documentary, *The Business of Being Born*, read all the right books. But deep down, I still had my doubts.

At every appointment, I was told that I was normal. The Dutch have a saying, *doe gewoon normaal, dan ben je al gek genoeg.* In other words, "just be normal, that's already crazy enough."

Horrible heartburn? Normal.
Low blood pressure? Normal.
Sciatic pain? Normal.

I was obviously suffering, but no one did anything to help me. I was considered normal until proven otherwise. And in a way they were right: Nothing bad was going on, but I felt neglected and ignored. On my due date, my husband got a call from his long-time friend. I think he wanted to congratulate me on my pregnancy, but instead of thanking him, I told him he was not allowed to talk to me. In hindsight, I must have known that something was on. I started having light contractions while my husband was still on the phone. We put our eldest to bed. I lied down and soon after my water broke. It was yellow, not clear and transparent like it should have been. I called the midwife and told her what happened. She told me to wait, and soon she arrived and confirmed what I had feared all along: I will not have the home birth of my dreams.

The midwife said that she needed to transfer me to the hospital. So we woke up our eldest—we didn't have any friends we could have called then—put her in her car seat, and went to the hospital.

The hospital staff was not at all surprised by the fact that we had a child with us. They even brought a bed for her. But of course, things were too exciting for her to fall asleep, so she ran around, tried to make sense of the beeping machines, and basically attempted to figure out what was going on.

At some point, I thought the contractions were getting too strong, so I beeped the midwife and asked her for an epidural. She said she'll get it and disappeared, to rematerialize only when I needed to push.

And then when my second daughter was finally out, my eldest looked at her, made a funny face, and said, "No!" She really didn't know what was going on.

After the birth, they weighed and checked the baby and said that because she had pooped into the amniotic fluid, she had to stay the night for observation. My husband and my eldest went home to get some rest, and I stayed at the hospital till the next day.

In the end, I didn't get a home birth but I got a healthy, beautiful baby girl. I only felt somewhat sad that the midwife lied to me about getting my epidural. She could have told me I was in transition, but instead she simply disappeared. I later heard it was actually common behavior here, right up there with telling women they don't need an epidural after all. Those tricky Dutch midwives!

When I became pregnant with my third child, we moved to a new house, and I needed to find new midwives. Luckily, there was a midwifery practice, right out there under my nose—on the opposite side of the street, actually.

The midwives were fine, but I didn't feel entirely safe with them. Since I found out I was having a boy, I had been petrified just thinking about another difficult birth, and was told—say it with me—everything is normal! The midwives said that the second and third babies are bigger than the first as they have more space to grow. They said I could expect to have a baby as big as 8 lb. 13 oz. (4,000 g). I told myself that I would not, under any circumstances, have a baby that big. You must understand that I am petite. My firstborn, who weighed 7 lb. 15 oz. (3,600 g) at birth, seemed huge to me—which would explain why it took her so long to get out and why it was so hard.

I was determined not to have a long, difficult birth and decided that I may be better off with a C-section. At the same time, I decided that I might give birth in a birth center in The Hague. I know these two options are mutually exclusive, but remember, I was pregnant, suffering from another bout of heartburn, and not entirely in my right mind. I was simply looking for a way to give birth without suffering and pain. I started entertaining the idea of a support partner. I decided I would have a doula.

During our appointment, she had me write a birth plan, and this is when the thought of getting pain relief actually occurred to me.

Maybe it's ironic that to get pain relief you need to voice it in writing and you had better be accompanied by someone who will actually advocate for you, but it's the Netherlands where you have to be very vocal in order to be treated with anything more than paracetamol. While I spoke Dutch fluently, I wanted to make sure I was understood and my wishes respected. Sophie had dual nationality and a Dutch husband. She could handle the language issues and would advocate for me in a loud, clear voice. In short, she was perfect for the job.

Together we toured the birth center. I took her to one of my midwifery appointments where we discussed what would happen if I was to go overdue. Of course nothing would happen until 42 weeks or so, when they would finally take action, like maybe induce me. But not much before that. That wouldn't be natural.

Luckily, it didn't come to this. Ten days before my due date, I had an appointment with my doula. She showed me some of her tricks of the trade, including a massage with a huge rectangle of textile called a *rebozo*. She was standing behind me, the wrap around my belly and she was gently moving it from left to right. And after a while I began feeling contractions so she stopped and went home.

The contractions didn't last long, but the next day, I woke up slightly uncomfortable. My husband was sure I wasn't in labor. He then went to work, leaving me alone with the two girls.

I started timing the contractions; they came at seven-to-eight minute intervals. I called my husband saying I had contractions, and he told me to call the midwife. I didn't want to bother her and secretly dreamed of being transported to the hospital so that I wouldn't need the midwife at all.

But then it was getting worse, and I didn't know what was going on, so I called the midwife anyway. She arrived 30 minutes later and checked me. She decided I was maybe two centimeters dilated and that we should wait, and then she left.

I brought the girls to daycare (they were going half days, from 1 to 6 p.m.), went back home, and called the midwife again. Things were not improving. On the contrary, the contractions were getting closer together and stronger.

Then several things happened simultaneously: My husband came home, my water broke, and it was a nasty green color. My midwife arrived, and I had to be transferred to the hospital. Well, maybe natural birth just isn't for me. When we arrived at the hospital around 2 p.m., Sophie was already there. I had called her on the way to the hospital.

I was wheeled into the nice and comfy-looking hospital room, and I decided that while I'm here—and this being my last birth—I will make use of my birth plan, and my doula, and ask for pain relief, damn it.

The doctor told me that she couldn't even tell I was in pain and that I was smiling (I am sure I wasn't), but she gave me a shot of pethidine and after the initial dizziness wore off, I realized that pain relief was the greatest invention of all times. After a while, they started preparing the clothes for the baby. Why are they doing that? It's not like he's coming right now? Oh, no, wait, he is.

My son was born at 4 p.m. in the nice and tidy hospital room with windows overlooking The Hague. We called friends to pick up the girls from daycare. The hospital staff brought us the customary *beschuit met muisjes*—a twice-baked round bread with white and blue aniseed sprinkles (it would have been pink for a girl and orange for a royal baby), and then we were left alone. I took a shower while my husband stayed with the baby, and we were very happy that it all went so well.

They asked us whether we wanted dinner, and I said yes because no one would make me dinner for a long time.

We were home around 7 p.m. The girls came back home at 8 p.m. and reveled in their new brother.

You're probably wondering why I was released from the hospital a mere few hours after birth? Let me tell you that the Dutch approach to birth isn't all scary, and the *kraamzorg* is proof of that.

A *kraamzorgster* is basically a guardian angel who comes to your house after birth. She does the usual: weighing, checking on you and baby, and teaching you to breastfeed, but her responsibilities don't end there. She cleans the bathrooms, vacuums, does the laundry and prepares light meals. She can also take care of older siblings and run errands.

One of her very important duties is to remind you to rest and shower, and she is also very good at keeping unwanted visitors at bay. Unfortunately, she only comes for eight hours for eight days, but I'll take that.

The Dutch approach to birth can be described as follows: pregnancy and birth are natural; deal with that. But after the birth you'll be pampered and fussed over—maybe it's a reward for your suffering or something. I don't know.

But I know this. Giving birth in the Netherlands requires plenty of preparation and advocacy on your part, especially if you don't want to go the natural route.

I should know. After all, it took me three attempts to get it right.

Olga Mecking is a writer, blogger, and translator living in the Netherlands. Olga's writings have been published on many websites, including The Huffington Post, Babble, Scary Mommy, and Mamalode. Olga is the editor and contributing author of Dutched Up, an anthology about living the expat life as an expat woman in the Netherlands. When not blogging or thinking about blogging, Olga can be found reading, drinking tea, and reading some more. She blogs at The European Mama about parenting, traveling, and her life abroad. Read more about Olga at http://www.europeanmama.com.

CHAPTER 16

BABY AND TEA WITH MR. T.

Cathy Ferland
Nationality: USA
Birthed in: England and USA

My "knocked up abroad" experience took place in England in the late 1980s. My husband, Peter, was in the US Air Force, flying A-10's out of the Royal Air Force station Bentwaters in Suffolk County, which is about 70 miles (113 km) northeast of London. We chose to live off base in a little village called Woodbridge, because we felt that living locally would allow us to fully experience many aspects of living abroad that living on base wouldn't provide. We were newly married and ready for some adventures. I first became pregnant in the summer of 1988, but sadly that pregnancy ended in a miscarriage at 12 weeks. It was on Halloween, and not a year goes by that I don't think about it on October 31. We needed time to grieve the loss, and we did not want to think about trying to conceive again right away. In March of 1989, we decided to try again, and I immediately became pregnant with our daughter Kate. (Obviously this time there was a happier ending!)

Because we lived off base, the nearest military hospital that offered emergency services was an hour and a half away. My due date was in the winter, and my health care was covered by

CHAMPUS (Civilian Health and Medical Program of the Uniformed Services), so we decided to find a local obstetrician nearby. That was fine by me, because my first experience at the base hospital after my miscarriage was very unpleasant and actually ended with someone being reprimanded. I was quite happy to have a different option for care with this pregnancy. The local off-base OB/GYN, named Mr. Thomas, was highly regarded by the Air Force wives. In England, for whatever reason, if a doctor is also a surgeon, they are known as Mister (female surgeons are Miss, Mrs. or Ms.). The Air Force wives' "stamp of approval" was good enough for me, and I felt very fortunate to have him as my doctor.

At the time, I was working part-time as a substitute teacher at the high school on base. Apparently, they took anyone with a college degree in, well, just about anything. I was much more confident substituting for an English class as opposed to subbing for the calculus teacher. I had no idea what I was copying onto the board or what it could possibly mean! I was a good substitute teacher—just please don't ask me any calculus questions. It was a great job to have as there were not many options for employment as a dependent wife—military term, not my own! The schedule was very flexible, which allowed for a lot of travel. We gladly took advantage of every chance we could to explore our world.

Peter was gone quite a bit, flying out of FOLs (Forward Operating Locations) in Germany, Italy, and Spain. One of the many perks we received was the ability to fly free of charge in the back of C-130 cargo airplanes up to four times a year. It wasn't luxurious, first class, or even comfortable riding on the net seats in among the cargo containers, but it was free. You can't beat free.

We took several trips while I was pregnant, because we knew that after the baby arrived, we would never be as spontaneous as we currently were or travel as lightly. We traveled to Crete for a two-week trip when I was four months along and enjoyed relaxing days on the beach, sometimes reading for pleasure and other times reading my one pregnancy book, *What to Expect When You're Expecting* and getting really nervous! When I was seven months pregnant, we also took a two-week trip to Germany, Switzerland, Austria, and Italy. Back in those days you could rent a Q room on a base for $6 a night, which was fabulous for struggling young couples on a tight budget. We flew into Ramstein Air Base in Germany, rented a car, and then determined our itinerary depending on what food cravings I was having at the time. We raced to Italy for pasta and gelato; Germany for delicious salty pretzels, cheese, and most of all meat—

which I just could not get enough of. We also drove around and took trains all over England to pack in as much travel as we could before our lives changed in a profound and wonderful way.

With our husbands off flying around Europe, the wives in the squadron really had to depend on each other for companionship and support during this time in our lives. Many of us were in the 25 to 35 age range, and at any given time several of us were pregnant or had recently given birth, so there was a lot of sharing of information going on. Of course way back then, there were no computers, cell phones, Skype, etc., so it could feel pretty isolating. We did not have our mothers or sisters nearby to pass along knowledge or share our experiences with, so these women in the squadron were very important to the young, first-time mothers living overseas that a lot of us were. Our social network wasn't on Facebook or Twitter but was made up of friends who met together on a regular basis. We couldn't Google anything, so how we ever survived is truly a mystery!

My doctor, Mr. Thomas, practiced out of a lovely Victorian house in the city of Ipswich—a mid-sized city about 20 minutes from where we were living. From the outside, it looked like a very nice residence on a tree-lined street. The waiting room was in the downstairs area, which was decorated in a traditional English way, with flower-patterned rugs, plush couches, and heavy velvet curtains. His receptionist would greet you downstairs, offer a cup of tea, and ask you to wait on one side of the room. When it was your turn to be seen, there were a few areas that had exam tables surrounded by velvet curtains for privacy. Mr. Thomas worked alone, and I don't recall there being a nurse or any other sort of medical assistant. It was a very warm and welcoming environment—not the least bit clinical or sterile. The environment matched his demeanor. I saw Mr. Thomas for exams, but had my lab work done at the base clinic.

Because my pregnancy was progressing normally, my care was very basic and non-invasive. There were no ultrasounds or additional testing—just listening to the heartbeat, feeling the position of the baby, monitoring my weight gain, and letting things proceed naturally. Because I was young and there was no Internet, and I did not go to nursing school and do my preceptorship in labor and delivery until many years later, I was somewhat sheltered from even imagining all the things that could go wrong.

I recently looked up the paternity leave policy for the Air Force, and it is 10 days. I don't recall if Peter was able to take the full 10 days, but to be honest I don't remember much of anything from the first few weeks after giving birth. My husband is a pretty efficient guy and had mentioned that it would work best with the flying schedule if I could have the baby after 5 p.m. on a Friday, but before Monday morning. I'm assuming he had this time frame in mind as a result of the time off he was allowed for our wedding three years earlier. He was given Friday through Sunday off and had to report back first thing Monday morning, which wouldn't have been so bad except that he was based in New Mexico at the time, and we got married in California! Peter got out of the Air Force over 20 years ago, so I do not know if getting leave time for important family events has gotten any easier since then.

Anyway, my due date was December 2, and Peter's birthday is the 3rd, so I decided to throw a surprise party on Friday, December 1 just to make sure to fit everything in before the baby arrived. My last day substitute teaching was on Wednesday, so that gave me a couple days off to get ready for the party. I was still feeling great, so I walked all around our village gathering my party supplies. I cooked, cleaned, and vacuumed on Friday. I wanted to have the place looking good, and who knew when I would have a chance to do those things again after the baby arrived. As the day progressed, every now and then I would feel a twinge or an aching in my lower back, but I had things to do and pressed on. After dinner, at the appointed time—surprise! I could tell Peter had no idea about the party, because he had already changed into his pajamas. A lot of our friends from the squadron came and spent the evening. It was a fun party, but by now my back was really starting to hurt. Around midnight people started to leave, but a few stayed to help me clean up.

I remember one guy in the squadron asking, "When is the baby due?"

I looked at the clock and noted the time and said, "Today!"

We finally crawled into bed around 1 a.m., and I got up a few hours later to go to the bathroom when all of a sudden my water broke. I immediately started shaking and felt cold, and I woke Peter up to tell him it was time. My husband, who had really enjoyed his party, thought that perhaps we should just go back to sleep and think about this again in the morning. However, I started having contractions and realized this could not wait, and by then Peter was wide awake and had gone into full operational mode, and we were out the door.

When we arrived at the hospital, I was brought to a private room because of my private military insurance. I felt a little pang of guilt that I got to stay in a more comfortable room, while most citizens had to be in rooms with multiple beds. England has a National Health Service, and since I was a US citizen with private insurance, I had more options. I remember changing into my gown and feeling really cold and shaky, and also so excited but nervous that this was really happening (and on a weekend, no less). I tried to get a little sleep, but the contractions were really starting to intensify. I was able to breathe through them for the most part and had the advantage of being a young, first-time mother blessed with ignorance as to what was to come. After a short while, Mr. Thomas arrived. He was wearing his usual suit and tie and mentioned that he had been to the theater (say "theatre" in a posh English accent) with his wife earlier that evening. He had been called to the hospital to deliver another baby and was getting ready to go home when we showed up. He was very lovely about the whole thing, even though it was in the wee hours of the morning.

He took off his jacket, rolled up his sleeves, flipped his tie over his shoulder and got to work. He did a quick exam and discovered that I was almost completely dilated. Some nurses came to help, and I was moved onto a gurney and wheeled down the hall. I can remember hearing other birthing women moaning, screaming, and crying as we went past their rooms and thinking, "What on earth have I gotten myself into?" Peter asked very nervously one last time if perhaps I would want him to wait outside and someone could just come get him when it was all over. I answered with a look that made it clear that we were in this together without verbally answering his request, and we proceeded on to the delivery room.

Once in the room, I was transferred onto a table. I don't remember too much else about this particular space other than it had really bright lights and a bathtub in it. I had been asked earlier if I wanted something for pain, but since I was young, naive, and epidurals were not routinely used or covered by our insurance, I had said no. Women have been doing this since the beginning of time. I was tough, and I could take it. However, after a few hours, I wished that I had answered differently. I was fully dilated, and that ship had sailed! I could not find a position that was tolerable. I tried all the positions—on my back, all fours, on my side, on my other side, standing up, sitting down—but nothing seemed to ease the pain.

At one point, Peter said, "What do you want? What can I do?"

And I replied in all seriousness that I had changed my mind, and I did not want to do this anymore, and I just wanted to go home. He very calmly reminded me that actually I was the only one who could not go home right now. Okay, fine. I will have the baby.

I was afraid. Despite reading my book and taking a Lamaze class, I still didn't know what to do when the time came to give birth. However, something primal took over, and I pushed like there was no tomorrow. Mr. Thomas told me to ease up and remember to breathe.

I think he had taken off his tie by this point, but was still in his civilian clothes. His calming tone and reassurance helped to keep me focused on the task at hand. Peter was hanging tough near my head—far away from all the action. Mr. Thomas massaged the perineum (episiotomies were not routinely performed) and safely guided the baby out with one final push at 7:13 a.m. We did not know the sex of the baby, and it was a wonderful surprise to discover we were the new parents of a baby girl. I will never forget the experience of looking into Kate's eyes for the first time. Instant, overwhelming love. She was so alert and was looking all around the room. Peter held her after she spent some time on my chest, and then I was offered a bath in the tub that I had noticed earlier. I was also offered a cup of tea, as we were in England after all.

Eventually, we made it back to our room, where I felt the rush of adrenaline from giving birth and the energy of meeting our new baby girl. I felt as if I was floating on air—a true hormonal, adrenaline high—but Peter was exhausted and had to take a nap. One of my favorite pictures is of Kate sleeping on his chest in the hospital bed. We could have stayed in the hospital for several days, but we opted to leave the next day. They were doing some remodeling right outside our window, and we really could not get any sleep. The hospital food, in all honesty, was not our favorite, and baked beans on toast were the most popular item on the menu. In addition, it is tradition in the squadron to provide dinners for the new family for several days, so we packed up our baby and headed home. Peter went to work for a little while on Monday, just like he had oh-so-jokingly said he needed to do.

We had a lot of trial and error during the first few months, but eventually figured it out. My mom flew over to meet Kate Elizabeth (yes, she is named after the queen) when she was six weeks old, but no one else met her until we flew back for our next assignment a few months later. We flew to Tucson via Boston so she could meet her East Coast family for a few days before continuing on. We only saw Mr. Thomas one more time, and that was right before we moved back to the States when Kate was four months old. I took a picture of them together that I still have to this day. I will always remember him and the care he provided to me and to several of the other young mothers in our squadron. He was truly a gifted practitioner who cared deeply for his patients and allowed them to realize that they had it within themselves to do what they needed to do to birth their babies naturally.

When we left for England, our families saw us as a newly married couple heading off for an overseas assignment. The next time they saw us, we were returning with a baby in our arms. We moved back to the US in 1990, and our next assignment was in Tucson, Arizona. Peter was now working as an A-10 instructor pilot at Davis-Monthan Air Force Base. Again, we were in a squadron with a wonderful group of people, mostly in their childbearing years, so there was no shortage of pregnant women and babies. When Kate was a year old, we started entertaining the idea of having one more child. A couple months later, that dream was realized when I discovered I was pregnant. I had vowed I would never have another child right before Christmas, but wouldn't you just know it, the new due date was December 10.

This time around, I received all my prenatal care at the base clinic. I saw a different doctor each time and missed the personalized care I had received with Mr. Thomas. Our circumstances were a bit different for this pregnancy, and this all occurred during Operation Desert Storm. I volunteered at the base clinic as a small way to help out and do my part. As a result, I was able to have a couple ultrasounds done when patients missed their appointments. Not a bad perk for volunteering at the clinic. I had a scan done at 12 weeks and again around 15 weeks, and I was very relieved to see that the baby had a strong heartbeat and was developing normally. I underwent routine blood work around 18 weeks and didn't think about it again until I got a call letting me know that some of my lab values were elevated. They wanted to schedule an ultrasound just to take a look. They didn't mention that it was the hCG level ("pregnancy test" hormone) that was very high.

The ultrasound tech was almost done doing measurements, looking for abnormalities, etc., when he repositioned me and suddenly another circle appeared on the screen. I said, "I see the baby's head, but what's that other circle on the screen?" He said that it was another head.

"Oh no! A two-headed baby!" I was in a complete state of shock!

I was measuring right on target, my weight gain was within normal limits, and twins do not run in my family. I was planning for one more baby—two babies was not my plan! Cue anxious tears.

Somehow, I made it through the ultrasound appointment and in a probably unsafe-for-driving daze drove over to the squadron to give Peter the news. By the time I got there, I had really worked myself into a hysterical state and lost my ability to speak. Perhaps the only thing to make a room full of fighter pilots nervous is a woman who is bawling her eyes out. Peter had just finished a flight and was on a van coming back to the squadron.

I went out to meet him, sobbing. Later he told me that someone had said, "Captain Ferland, look it's your wife! Oh no, and she's crying."

Peter knew I had just had the ultrasound done and ran over with full concern on his face. I could barely get the words out but I managed somehow to mumble out the news, and he was overjoyed.

"Twins! That's fantastic!" he said.

I think I realized at that moment that—even though this was not at all what I had envisioned—it was going to be okay.

This pregnancy, like my first one abroad, was very uneventful and progressed as expected. Despite being completely normal, it was labeled "high-risk" simply because it was multiples. Because of that label, once again we used CHAMPUS, and I received my routine care on base with an OB/GYN who was also affiliated with the University of Arizona Medical Center in downtown Tucson. Dr. Samuelson was another phenomenal doctor who just happened to wear scrubs and did not practice out of a cozy, velvety English house. Since we were having twins, this time we decided to find out the sex of the babies. It's hard enough to come up with two names, let alone four! I also wanted to be as prepared as possible for the babies' arrival, as I knew there would be no time for that afterward. My husband is the youngest of five boys, and now he was going to be the father of three little girls!

I felt pretty good until about week 30. The heat in Tucson was really unbearable, and Kate and I did a lot of indoor activities to escape the high temperatures. Our days were usually quite busy, with lots of errands and activities. On one particular day, I remember getting up early to take her for a walk and setting off to run our errands. We walked around the mall and then went off to a water aerobics class. Later in the day, I started having contractions and ended up at the base clinic hooked up to the fetal monitoring machines. When my doctor arrived to assess the situation, he asked what I had been doing before the contractions began. I replied, "Oh, nothing much," but when I told him about our day he reminded me I was 30 weeks pregnant with twins, and that I needed to take it easy from here on out. I then reminded him that I had a 20-month-old daughter at home, and that wasn't really possible! Thankfully, my sister and then my mom were able to fly out for a few weeks to help out during this time. Peter also rearranged his schedule as best as he could to allow for more time at home. That was a little easier to do with his current assignment. With all the extra help from family, I felt pretty good right up until the end when people would exclaim, "Oh. My. God. You're huge!" Actually, I really was huge, but come on, people. Those comments were extremely rude, and I think I would now respond quite differently, but at the time I was just too exhausted.

I went into labor with the twins at 37 weeks on November 20, 1991. Because it was a high-risk pregnancy, we needed to deliver at the medical center downtown. The base clinic was just not equipped to handle any sort of emergency complications. We arrived around midnight, checked in, and were brought up several floors to the labor and delivery ward. Comparatively, Ipswich Hospital was a very small local facility. This hospital was very large, very modern, and had lots of activity even in the middle of the night. Once again, I had a private room but did not stay in it for long. Once I was hooked up to the fetal monitors, it was discovered that Baby A was tolerating the contractions, but Baby B was having late decelerations, which is not what you want to see. An ultrasound showed that one baby was head down and the other baby was transverse breach. It was explained to us that I could go ahead and try to deliver the first baby vaginally, but most likely I would need to have a C-section with the second baby. I felt like I had experienced natural childbirth with my first baby and had a wonderful experience. I did not feel like I would be missing out on anything this time around. I was also exhausted and was very nervous about the baby's fluctuating heart rate. Honestly, I could not imagine delivering two babies in two different ways. Talk about a rough recovery on all sides! After discussing our concerns with Dr. Samuelson, we decided to go with the Cesarean option.

The Medical Center is a teaching hospital, and we were asked if we minded if some medical students were in the operating room to observe. We agreed to that, and between the two teams of doctors, nurses, and OR technicians plus several students, it was pretty crowded in there. As you can imagine, it was very sterile, very bright and very busy. No suit and ties or bathtubs anywhere. After the initial preparation, Dr. Samuelson very skillfully delivered Baby A (Melissa) and Baby B (Nicole). Different country, different doctor, different methods of delivery, but the same instant and overwhelming love for our babies. Cue joyful tears! Peter was a champ and got to hold each of them first and show them to me before they were whisked away for all those measurements that simply must be taken right after birth. I was so filled with emotion and relief that both babies were strong and healthy that I just cried as the rest of the surgery was completed. I was then wheeled into a different room to wait for the spinal block to wear off and stabilize following the surgery. During the C-section, I thought for a moment, "Wow, this is great! I can't feel anything! I don't even have to do anything!" It wasn't until the anesthesia was wearing off and certainly the first time I had to stand up, that I came to my senses and remembered why this would not be my first choice for delivery under normal circumstances. It was the safest choice for the babies, though, and I would do it all again in a heartbeat.

We stayed in the hospital for four days. Luckily, my mom was able to come out to stay with Kate during this time and then extended her trip through Christmas when my dad was able to join us. They were very helpful, mostly taking care of Kate and cooking so I could nurse the babies and sneak in quick naps every now and then. Peter's mom also came out after my parents returned home, which was also a big help. We did not get to experience that level of family involvement or assistance from others when we were living abroad, even though we had the support of our Air Force friends. To be honest, that was just a sweet time of bonding for the three of us over in England. I will always be thankful for that time—everything was new and uncharted, and we just had to figure it out. That said, I'm also thankful that we had our twins after we moved back to the United States, because we had more support, and it allowed our families to be much more involved at a time in our lives when we absolutely needed it.

Our birthing experiences were very unique in each country—one very natural and one very clinical. It was a very different time and place, and I would think that giving birth abroad now would be a completely different experience with technology, communication, social media, etc. However, at the end of the day, we have our three beautiful adult daughters, and I wouldn't change a thing.

Cathy Ferland and her husband Peter live in Sebastopol, CA. She is a registered nurse, and also works as a credentialed school nurse. She and Peter are now empty nesters and still enjoy traveling the world (but no longer on cargo airplanes), bicycling, hiking, and spending time with Kate, Melissa, and Nicole.

CHAPTER 17

AUSSIE MOMMA

Demi Jones
Nationality: USA
Birthed in: North Queensland, Australia

I am a mom of three gorgeous Aussie-Americans. My shy seven-year-old, Lego-loving, Minecraft-obsessed big boy likes to play cricket, ride BMX, and spend time with his friends. My five-year-old daughter managed to acquire some extra-girlie genes that seem to have skipped me entirely. She would gladly change her outfit and accessories all day, much to the dismay of my washing machine. Her collection of sunnies (sunglasses), nail polish, and shoes could give a fashion model a run for her money. My free-spirited (okay, wild) child is my three-year-old boy, the baby of the family. His arrival added an entirely new dimension to our family and proved to be a lesson in humility. Before he came along, I thought I was completely and utterly in control of this parenting thing. I had it down pat. I had two beautiful, well-mannered children who were quiet and respectful. They listened to me and ate everything on their plates. Clearly, they were shining examples of my exceptional parenting skills. The moment Jackson was born though, I realized that in actuality I knew nothing about parenting, and it was mostly by coincidence that my first two children were so easy in comparison. Essentially, Jackson has resisted every parenting lesson

I had ever learned from my first two children, and he has taught me so much more than I ever thought possible. My husband and I have spent the past three years negotiating with this tiny human about absolutely everything under the hot Australian sun.

My family of five lives happily in North Queensland, Australia. We live on the coast of the Coral Sea in the northeastern part of Australia, about a two-and-a-half-hour flight away from Sydney. When we are not avoiding all of the deadly predators lurking around each corner, we spend our time at beaches, parks, gorgeous nearby islands, or with friends, socializing at backyard barbies (barbecues). The weather here could be described as summer all year long. It may sound appealing if you don't like seasons and are comfortable at boiling-point temperatures on a daily basis. All jokes aside, it is a beautiful place to live, and it often feels like we are on a vacation whenever we slow down enough to reflect and soak in our surroundings.

My husband and I met while I was on a one-year study abroad program during my third year of college at the University of Tampa in Florida. We met through "mates," and hit it off immediately. His big blue eyes and Aussie accent had me at "G'day." Leaving my home in the US as a naive and inexperienced 20-year-old, I did not have much first-hand experience of adult living in the US. My entire adult life—you know, the one where you have to find a career, pay bills, call the tax office, find home insurance, decide on a health plan, navigate the health care system, choose a bank, research and then purchase a car, grow small humans inside of you and then attempt to raise them properly—all happened in Australia.

I didn't always plan on living overseas, but I had always planned on becoming a mother. It was the one thing I knew I could do well. So when I was blessed with my third and biggest little miracle, my heart was happy and full. The small bundle that would complete our little family was on his way. Although it did not take much "practice" to conceive him (much to my husband's disappointment), the road to his delivery was slightly more involved and less straightforward than I had experienced in my previous two births.

Conceiving Jackson was both a decision and a blessing. I use the word decision because, although he and his siblings were all "planned" by my husband and me, I was advised prior to conceiving him that I should strongly consider not having any more children. After my first child was born, my body was struggling with rheumatoid arthritis (RA), an autoimmune disease that causes my body to attack itself relentlessly. My condition worsened from the time I gave birth to my second child, our baby girl, Jane, until I was officially diagnosed over a year later. Current protocol, as I understand it, stipulates aggressive treatment as soon as possible as the best way to achieve the most positive outcome. This aggressive treatment involves low-dose chemotherapy drugs that are not compatible with pregnancy. Therefore, I ultimately had to choose between completing my family or treating my disease. Left untreated, the RA would eventually result in deformity and disability. However, as I had always wanted at least three children (and to be honest, if my husband had agreed and my body supported me, I would have had 10), we decided to try for a third before commencing this aggressive treatment plan.

Fortunately, Jackson was conceived quickly, and I broke the news to my rheumatologist on my next visit. We set a basic plan, which included the medications I could utilize when necessary to safely get through the pregnancy, taking into account the pain and discomfort brought on by my flaring RA.

One of the medications that aided me through my third pregnancy was a steroid. Steroids drastically reduced the unbearable pain caused by the frequent flare-ups. A flare-up could be described as pain, swelling, and/or inflammation in and around various joints. The pain would range from bearable to excruciating and could increase in a matter of hours, especially evenings and early mornings. RA is unpredictable, but my flares, being so constant, were always active.

Though steroids are thought to be quite safe for a growing fetus, I was advised that there was a slightly increased risk that Jackson could have a cleft palate. This was something that weighed on my mind throughout the pregnancy and added to my anxiety.

Having experienced two previous pregnancies, I already knew what to expect and how my body would cope. However, for my final pregnancy, I changed my choice of medical care. With Austin and Jane, I had gone through the private health care system. I was happy with the level of care, as my births were very straightforward and I liked leaving the hospital as soon as possible following the birth. Given that my rheumatologist was in the public system, I switched from private medical care to public. I had the option to choose to deliver my son at the birth center, a medical center located adjacent to our public hospital. Throughout the pregnancy, I met with my allocated midwife for check-ups. She would be present during my child's birth, and there would be no doctor to intervene unless there was an emergency. All of the costs associated with having our baby through the public system were covered by the Australian universal health care scheme Medicare, so the out-of-pocket expenses were substantially reduced. The midwife visits were free, as were the ultrasounds, standard tests, and general prenatal care.

Around three months into my pregnancy, I got to watch my baby kick and roll in my belly via ultrasound. The technician specifically looked for his palate to put my concerns to rest that the steroids could be harming him. After an hour and a half, it was too difficult, and the technician was unable to get a good look at his palate. My mind was not eased, but I greatly appreciated the time watching my baby, and of course it was wonderful to gaze at his tiny growing body. Further along into my pregnancy, I was told that Jackson had dilated kidneys. Apparently, this is not anything to panic over and can be relatively common. It could also be a red flag for Down syndrome, but having a cleft palate was also an indicator. There were no definite answers, only new questions. My midwife was excellent in explaining the various abnormalities to me and stressing the fact that his kidneys would most likely correct themselves. He would need to have an ultrasound once he was born to ensure that everything was functioning properly.

The next few months passed very slowly. My four- and two-year-olds would ask questions like, "Can we name the baby 'House'?" and, "Will he come out in two pieces?" or, "When are the puppies in your tummy going to come out?" We played together and talked to the baby. I managed my RA and tried to keep my stress levels as low as possible.

As I approached my due date, for each sigh of relief I felt there was an equally increased tension on my nerves. I looked forward to saying goodbye to the pregnancy insomnia (not at all helped by the steroids I was taking), not needing to get up to pee every seven minutes, and no longer having to waddle around after my toddlers. With each passing week, I became more worried that this baby was going to fall out of me. The downward pressure was amplified when my little man turned head-down into the ready position.

At one of my last prenatal appointments, my midwife sat me down and gave me detailed instructions on what to do if I could not make it to the hospital in time. Alarmed, I promised her and myself that I would leave ample time to make the 20-minute drive to the hospital and hopefully avoid giving birth on the side of the highway. Around midnight, I woke up with minor cramping and started listening to my body. As I stood in the hot shower trying to notice repetition or a pattern to the cramps, I realized that my body was most certainly going into labor. I had done this twice before, but I was still petrified. I knew the pain that was coming and just the thought of it made me change my mind about wanting another baby. Clearly, it was too late to take back such decisions now.

I woke my husband after throwing a few items into a bag. I was sure to include some snacks, since I remembered starving while in labor with my first and being given a plain cracker. During my first labor, my husband actually opened and ate one of my crackers, and I nearly punched him in his cracker-chewing mouth. Don't you dare eat the snacks of a laboring woman! My in-laws had flown up to our house in anticipation of the baby arriving, so he went to wake them up. We made our way to the front door after calling my midwife to let her know that I was in labor. She said she would meet us at the birthing center. It was baby-birthing time!

The contractions intensified quickly, and all I could think about was the midwife's explanation about self-delivery if we couldn't make it in time. In his excitement, my husband jumped into the car, closed it, and started it, while I leaned on the outside of the passenger door, breathing through a painful contraction.

He yelled, through the unopened door mind you, "GET IN!"

What? Seriously? In his haste, he had forgotten to open the door for me as I stood there nearly having a baby fall out onto our driveway.

We arrived at the hospital around 2 a.m. The pain was intense at that point, and I asked for gas almost immediately. I just wanted to sit on the exercise ball in the shower with my happy gas.

By the time I was dilated enough to push—possibly after an entire tank of gas—I moved to the birthing stool. My husband sat on the bed behind me, and I sat perched atop a wooden stool with a hole cut in the middle to allow for the baby. Just as I was ready to push all of a sudden my contractions stopped. They 100% altogether just stopped. Nothing. Here I sat naked on this birthing stool, completely ready to birth my baby, and my contractions stopped. I looked to my midwife for answers. Her face was blank.

Then her face lit up and she suggested, "Stimulate your nipples!"

What? I'm sorry, what? So here I am holding myself up, perched on a stool, doing the longest wall sit ever in history, my legs are shaking, and I'm trying to push a baby out, and now I was being told to also play with my nipples? I'm no contortionist, so I looked to my husband, and in what might have been the most awkward moment of our couple's life, my husband reached around and followed the midwife's orders. Three awkward seconds later, my body was back to pushing. I pushed without contractions and made progress. Once the head was out I could have collapsed with excitement. I pushed again, and she caught the baby. Still perched on the stool with shaking exhausted legs, the midwife hands me the baby. He wasn't breathing and looked slightly blue.

I remember panicking slightly and repeatedly asking her, "Is he alright? Is he alright?"

That's when she told me to rub him. She gave him a few pats and went to call for the doctors. In the meantime, there I am, holding up my body weight after pushing out a human, holding onto said slippery human, and trying to stimulate him to cry or breathe. I'm sure my husband was doing something through all of this, but honestly, I felt very much alone in that moment

Jackson started to cry and the whole room relaxed. It was then that I looked down at his fingers and both my husband and I said, "What's wrong with his hands?" His pinkie finger looked like it was bent downwards and sideways touching his wrist. The midwife began counting, "One...two...three...four...five...six. And the other hand...one...two...three...four...five...six! It's okay, he just has extra fingers."

I guess I was slightly relieved, but my mind was thinking, *what the hell?* The midwife explained that it is a relatively common genetic birth defect, and both my husband and I immediately checked the outside of our own palms to see if there was anything our parents had forgotten to tell us.

Several doctors on duty examined Jackson for a few minutes. Meanwhile, I needed to birth the placenta. My legs were beyond fatigued, and I just wanted to change positions. My midwife asked if the contractions had returned, which they had not. I said, "I'll just push it out," and before she could interject, I pushed, and the placenta flew out.

She looked at me, slightly shocked as it flew past her, her gloved hands scrambling to catch it, and asked, "You don't want to keep it, do you?"

No, thanks. Although I have heard of people keeping the placenta, planting it with a tree, or thinking of something else to do with it, I just wanted my baby.

Jackson was born at 4:31 a.m.

Our little man weighed in at 8 lb. 5.5 oz. (3,780 g). His palate had been thoroughly checked, and he was fine despite our previous concerns. The feeling of relief was wonderful and calming. His stats were excellent, and he was booked for an ultrasound later in the week to check on his kidneys.

I cleaned up a bit and climbed into the double bed. I was shivering, shaking, and could not get warm. Layers and layers of warmed blankets were placed over me in the bed, but I was trembling fiercely. They kept trying to hand me the baby but I knew that I wouldn't be able to hold him until I stopped trembling. As my teeth chattered together, I huddled under the blankets, desperate to get warm. Several minutes later, my body calmed down, and I was able to hold and nurse my beautiful new baby boy. His extra fingers had been taped to his hands, as they had just been dangling there.

It was Wednesday, and the pediatric surgeon clinic was just down the hall. Once Jackson had nursed and I had showered, we walked with him down the hall into the clinic. Unlike our quiet birthing suite with a hot tub, kitchenette, large bed, and a patio, the clinic area was packed with people, bright lights, children's play equipment, and kids running everywhere. We sat down for a couple of seconds and then realized we needed to get out of there. Jackson was only an hour old and we wanted to keep him somewhat insulated from all of the little kid germs flying about. We decided to see the surgeon privately at his office later in the week.

We headed home when Jackson was only five hours old.

We pulled into our driveway and looked at each other. We had left only earlier that morning and now here we were, back home with a new family member within the same calendar day. Introducing our new baby to his siblings was heartwarming. Nanny and Poppy were there too, and that was a great feeling. We put the baby bassinet on the dining room floor, and I sat at the breakfast bar on a stool, eating a sandwich that my mother-in-law had made for me. Every few minutes, I would turn around to look at our gorgeous sleeping little man, and it did not feel real that he had only just come into this world, and here I was, at home eating a sandwich.

The week following his birth, the surgeon tied off each finger, and Jackson screamed like nothing I had ever heard before. The fingers were meant to turn black and fall off but a week later they were still there—being held on by a bone at the attachment area. The surgeon snipped off each finger, and Jackson was booked for another surgery to remove the bone and nerve bundles when he turned one. I still haven't taken him into that surgery, as it is purely aesthetic. To this day, Jackson still has extra nubs on each hand as a reminder of those extra fingers.

My rheumatologist reminded me that I would only be breastfeeding my son for a couple of days before introducing him to a bottle so that I could start the treatment for my RA. Already emotional due to the pregnancy hormones and coping with chronic pain, knowing that my son and I would both miss out on the benefits and bonding of breastfeeding broke my heart. Tears rolled down my cheeks in my appointment with my rheumatologist, and there was a lump in my throat that I could not swallow.

I knew going into this pregnancy that I would most likely not be able to breastfeed and that a flare up after delivery was expected. Many women can enter into remission during pregnancy, with their symptoms decreasing or diminishing all together. Unfortunately, I never experienced this. Rather, my first symptoms had been noticed only after I became pregnant with my first son. I was 25 years old. I would not have ever thought that I was developing an autoimmune disease, and it was not evident to my obstetrician or regular doctor. The sporadic but severe shoulder discomfort disappeared after giving birth, so it was thought that the pregnancy hormones has caused my ligaments to stretch. I had no other symptoms until I became pregnant with my second child. The shoulder pain came, and again, it was thought that my body must be producing excess ligament-stretching hormones. My OB/GYN sent me to a physio, which exacerbated the problem. On my first visit, I drove to the physio and complied with their requests. By the time I left, I was unable to use my arm. I sat in the car park and cried. I was in pain and frustrated. I listened to my doctors, and now I could not move.

At one point late in my second pregnancy, my foot swelled to three times the normal size, and the pain was overwhelming. It was a Sunday, so I visited a walk-in medical clinic. The doctor was stumped as it looked as though I had a severe case of gout, extremely rare for young women. I was given a large dose of steroids and some crutches. That was when it became evident that I am terrible at using crutches. Once I got the hang of using them, I attempted to go down my front steps and catapulted my heavily pregnant body through the air, several feet above the ground. Luckily I landed, on my good foot, but from then on I hobbled much more slowly down the five steps to the driveway. The steroid treatment eased the pain but did not answer any lingering questions about what caused the swelling and pain. The questions, however, were pushed aside with the business of life with an almost-two-year-old.

My daughter was born. I was relieved, thinking the pain would go away just as it had with my first. However, it kept lingering, and the cases of random but severe pain continued. When my daughter was five months old, I went to my primary care doctor and asked the questions, "Why has it not gone away? Are the pregnancy hormones still out of balance? How can I fix it?" When she answered me, my world changed. Something along the lines of, "I think we need to rule out autoimmune diseases. It is possible that you might have lupus or a similar condition." My head spun. What? It did not make sense. I was always so healthy and active. I rarely got sick, not even a cold.

I was referred to the rheumatology department at the public hospital. At that time, there was no private rheumatologist in my city. The wait-list was lengthy. It took one year to be seen by a specialist. In the meantime, the tests for lupus and similar conditions came back negative, and my general practitioner tentatively diagnosed me with seronegative arthritis. I did not test positive for RA, but not everyone who has it does. I lived for that year just as I had been living all along. Enjoying my babies, coping with the strange and unpredictable episodes of pain, and taking pain medication when absolutely necessary. I had a newborn and a 20-month-old, so life was demanding but beautiful. My stress levels were high as we owned our own family business, and looking back now, I realize how damaging stress can actually be on one's health and overall life.

My husband and I, with our small children and one growing, visited America to see family. We spent a week in Orlando and went to Pennsylvania. My family got to see how painful my disease was, but they did not quite understand it. I needed daily steroids to be able to walk. It was nice to be able to break the pregnancy news to my family in person, for the first time ever. I opted to stay a couple of days longer than my husband, so my journey home consisted of me, with a four-year-old, an almost-two-year-old, and a growing bump, with several legs and 30-plus hours of travel. I thought I might die.

Easily by far the hardest part of living abroad for me is being away from my family. Something happened when I became a mother. I don't know if I suddenly appreciated my parents more or the fact that I gave them their first grandbabies, but we appreciated each other even more. The physical distance between us became more menacing. And traveling overseas with a family of five is five times more expensive than just traveling alone. A trip home will easily cost my family $20,000, which is not pocket change, especially with our currently diminishing Aussie dollar against the US dollar. When I am sick, I want my own mommy. When I see a grandfather holding his toddler, I yearn for my own dad. When I see my children run to their Nan and Poppy (my husband's parents who live a 20-hour drive away), I wish they had that relationship with my parents too. We talk on Skype, but seeing them in person is much different, and of course it takes a bit to warm up to them. My littlest boy has never met my mom and dad. He is three years old.

Our financial situation these past three years along with my health just haven't allowed us the opportunity to travel home. The guilt I feel is immense. I feel guilty that I am depriving my own parents the chance to know their grandchildren. I feel guilty that my children can't cuddle their grandparents regularly. I feel guilty that so much time passes between my visits home to see my family. I feel guilty that my parents are aging, and I am not there to assist them. I want to be there for them, but I also have a family and a life here that currently requires all of my attention, energy, and presence. I hope that as my children age, I am able to achieve a greater balance between living our life here in Australia and allowing my children to become acquainted with their family and culture in America. Perhaps that will happen once they are able to carry their own belongings and their little legs can make the 30-plus-hour journey without needing to be carried or dragged through the airports.

Parenting isn't straightforward or easy, but neither is life. Because of the storms, I thoroughly appreciate the rainbows. Not having family here has meant I had to create my own village, for it really does take a village to raise a child. We need people to confide in, bounce ideas off of, and relieve stress over a cup of coffee. Someone to call in times of emergency or, say, when you need to rush off to the hospital when you go into labor, and you need to rely on your neighbor to look after your children. We need other moms, too, who will happily listen to poop stories or lend a sympathetic ear when you have a baby that won't let you put it down for a second. I am happy to be an American mom in Australia. It is one of the most difficult and rewarding journeys of my life.

Demi Jones still lives in North Queensland, Australia with her family of five. They enjoy the beautiful Australian weather, countryside, and of course, the beach.

CHAPTER 18

BIRTH EXPECTATIONS

Sherah S. Haustein
Nationality: USA
Birthed in: Israel, USA, and Germany

I grew up hearing legendary stories about my own birth. My father was in the service in Greece in the later months of my mother's pregnancy. My mother threatened that if he didn't arrive home in time for my birth, she would name me Mephibosheth. Fortunately for me, he did arrive in time, and I didn't need the nickname "Mephy." Thank you, Dad! I arrived into the world within 20 minutes with no complications and no pain medication. Mine was a birth for the storybooks, especially when you consider the fact I was the firstborn of my family. My brother, born five year later, was born after 13 hours of hard labor. I clutched onto my mother's first birth experience and believed with all my heart my experience would be something similar. Her experience became my ideal image for my future births. Little did I know how amazingly unrealistic this ideal was going to be for me to reach.

As a teenager, I always had a desire to leave my home country in the US and try life abroad. At the age of 23, I embarked on a new adventure far from home. Ultimately, I chose Israel. Israel seems like an odd choice for a non-Jewish Northwesterner, but to me it made sense. I spent my high school years in the history library learning everything I could about the Holocaust and the birth of modern Israel. My curiosity about Israel led me to seek out a way to live there for an extended period of time. I chose to study a bachelor's degree at Bar-Ilan University, and this allowed me to stay in Israel for four years without having to deal with immigration. At the end of this degree I met my husband, Herman, and ended up making Israel my permanent home.

Some months after we married, I became pregnant with our first baby. My husband is an Israeli citizen, and after our marriage I had to go through a long process in which to receive residency. At the time of my first pregnancy, I was still turning in the paperwork to begin the process as a resident of Israel. This created a bit of a problem with health care because, I was not yet covered by an Israeli health fund or *kupat holim*, as it's called in Israel. For residents of Israel, all pregnancies are covered by *kupat holim* and births by the National Insurance Institute (*Bituach Leumi*). I was not going to be covered by a health fund until after the birth, so all of our initial check-ups had to be done privately. Therefore, we had to find a doctor who worked privately and had to pay everything out of pocket. For this reason, we kept our doctor check-ups to a bare minimum. We only saw a doctor twice during the entire pregnancy—in the beginning for a pregnancy test and for the big anatomy scan done around the 20th week. That was it. Two visits.

This may seem too few doctor visits to people who are used to the regimented monthly visits you usually have in most other places. Actually, we didn't need to see a doctor more often because Israel has another service for pregnant women called *Tipat Halav* or "a drop of milk." *Tipat Halav* has centers all over the country for pregnant women, babies, and young children. As a pregnant woman, you go to *Tipat Halav* to talk with a nurse about your pregnancy and have urine and blood pressure tests. If any of these tests show signs of complications, the nurse sends you to a doctor. This was much simpler and much more cost-effective than having to pay for private doctor's appointments each month.

As I began to consider the birth I wanted to have, I gravitated toward the idea of having as natural a birth as possible. I wanted to birth in a natural environment without drugs and without medical interventions. This philosophy of birth led us to pursue a home birth. Israel is not a country where home births are the norm. We knew of a few people who had home births, but no one personally. Most of our family and friends in Israel thought we were taking an unnecessary risk choosing to birth at home. Some family members even begged us to reconsider our choice. In addition to this backlash, around the same time, the midwives' insurance company decided to withdraw their coverage. Many midwives decided they would no longer perform home births whatsoever. As we looked around for a still active midwife, we finally found one who had a clinic next to her house. She had the necessary equipment to handle most complications that could arise during a home birth, and was only a five-minute drive from the hospital. These details were comforting to us, especially considering the concerns of our family and friends. We felt we were making a good decision as the midwife seemed competent and friendly, and decided to hire her after just one meeting.

A few weeks later, on my due date, the birth process started with cramps and the initial signs of labor. As a first-time mother, no one can convey to you what you are going to feel physically when you go into labor. Some women report agonizing pain, and others feel like they float through it on little clouds. You just don't know what to expect. I was hoping for little clouds, and when I began to feel tiny contractions, I interpreted them as full-blown labor. To say I was naive is an understatement. That evening my "contractions" were about five minutes apart, and we headed to the midwife's clinic. The clinic was about an hour and a half from our house. I honestly don't remember suffering very much during the drive. This should have been my first indication that we had come too early.

The midwife met us at the car, and the first thing she said to me was, "You don't look like a woman in labor!"

I immediately felt put off by her attitude toward me, but we followed her into her clinic anyway.

Looking back I can see that she was absolutely correct in her assessment; I wasn't in full-blown labor. There are just nicer ways to go about letting a woman who thinks she's in labor know that she is, in fact, not as far along as she thinks. I guess she knew she was stuck with us, since we had an hour and half drive to return home. In spite of her irritation, she showed us all the things we could use to help with the contractions. She then left us and went to her house to get some sleep. She was probably cursing all the way there about how stupid and inexperienced we were. Well, we were definitely inexperienced. She told us to call her if we felt the contractions gained any momentum. It was at this point my contractions slowed and stopped. I was very frustrated with the midwife because I felt she was antagonistic toward us. It's no wonder that after such a cold reception my body decided not to cooperate at all. We tried to encourage it along: We tried to sleep, we tried walking, but by morning we all realized my labor had stalled. We finally decided, with the encouragement of the midwife, that we should leave and come back when labor picked up again.

Since we were far from home, we chose to go to a friend's apartment closer to the midwife's clinic. I only had to sit in the car for around 15 minutes before my contractions kicked in again. Our friends live in Tel Aviv, where traffic is always a problem—and sure enough pretty soon we were stuck in it. I couldn't take the combination of contractions and traffic, and I jumped out of the car to walk past traffic instead of sitting in it. When we finally arrived at our friends' apartment, I escaped to their guest room while everyone else socialized. It only took an hour or so until my contractions became unbearable.

The removal of the midwife had been the key element to getting my contractions going. Now we had to choose whether we should abandon the home birth and go to a hospital, or go back to the midwife's clinic. In the end, we decided to return to the midwife's clinic and finish what we started. We did make one important addition to our party though. We decided to bring our friend along for moral support and to balance out the negativity of the midwife. Once we were back in the midwife's clinic, it was clear my labor had progressed quite a bit. The midwife suggested we use the Jacuzzi to see if that would help with pain management. I didn't feel it helped much, but I was in shock at how painful my contractions had become. As I was progressing into transition and in a lot of pain, the midwife decided to return to her house because she needed some rest before the delivery. It is possible that we had hired the sleepiest midwife ever. This caused me to panic, so we insisted that she stay. Begrudgingly, she sat down on the bed and started catching up on her paperwork.

When I felt the urge to push, the midwife suggested I get out of the tub and try the birthing stool. We moved from stool to bed and back to the stool, but the baby was reluctant to descend through the birth canal. This was frustrating for both me and the midwife. I kept pushing and pushing wanting to see the baby, but also getting more and more exhausted as things dragged on. After two hours of pushing, she finally made her way down.

As the baby's head was crowning, the midwife said, "Oh, that's why she didn't want to come down. Her head is facing sideways."

It turns out this was why my contractions had been so painful: I was having full-blown back labor.

Earlier in our pregnancy, when we went for the anatomy scan, the doctor asked if we wanted to know the sex of the baby. We didn't want to know, so he suggested writing it on a piece of paper in case we changed our minds. He said he was 90% sure he knew the sex, which made us suspect it would be a boy. Even with that piece of paper sitting in my wallet, begging to be opened, we didn't change our minds. When the baby came out, we were very eager to find out what sex it was. As it turned out the doctor was right—we had given birth to a baby girl.

After the birth, we moved back to the bed, and I tried to nurse the baby. From here on my memory begins to fade because I was losing a lot of blood. I remember the midwife being very concerned my placenta was not detaching. She was reluctant to call an ambulance at first, possibly because she felt this reflected badly on her skills as a midwife. We tried nursing, and she tried to manually encourage it to detach, but I just continued to bleed out. When she realized this was turning into an emergency situation, she decided to call an ambulance after all. We waited for the ambulance for over 20 minutes, even though the hospital was only five minutes' drive away. By the time they arrived the midwife was already very upset. The ambulance team had not understood it was an emergency and had taken their time to get there.

As they were trying to put me in the ambulance, I had been bleeding for around 40 minutes, and it was getting close to midnight. When I tried to get up, my husband said I suddenly turned white, and he began to worry for my well-being. I blacked out a few times on the way to the operating room. Somehow I got the message across to them that I am allergic to latex. As they got me to the operating room and began to prep me for a dilation and curettage, they had to wait for someone to find non-latex gloves. With most of the staff off-duty for the night, they could not find them anywhere.

The last words I remember hearing before I lost consciousness were: "I can't wait anymore; we have to just go ahead with latex gloves."

In the meanwhile my husband was running all over the hospital trying to fill in all the necessary forms and declarations, the whole time not knowing whether he would ever see his wife again and wondering where his new daughter had ended up. In the hustle of being rushed off to hospital, the newborn baby, still wrapped only in a blanket was handed to our friend, with these brief instructions, "Follow us to the hospital."

After the procedure, I was transferred to a recovery room where I was hooked up to all sorts of wires and had to wear an oxygen mask. This is not the ideal picture of birth I was imagining. After two blood transfusions and some rest, I was feeling better and able to spend some time with my new beautiful little girl.

With all of the post-delivery chaos, we didn't name the baby right away. It wasn't until after we left the hospital that we agreed to name her Yaheli, meaning radiance in Hebrew.

I was extremely disappointed and depressed after Yaheli's birth. I felt like my expectations for an easy and smooth birth had been completely decimated. I needed to rebuild everything I knew about pregnancy and birth from the ground up. The birth wasn't quick like my mother's had been, it ended in complications, and it had been extremely painful because of the back labor. Who am I kidding? Most labor is extremely painful, back labor or not. My traumatic experience during my first birth affected my decision-making going forward into my second pregnancy.

We knew we wanted more children, so right around Yaheli's first birthday we bravely decided to try to get pregnant again. Fortunately, it didn't take long for me to conceive, and this time I was eligible for National Health Insurance and full health fund coverage. There wouldn't be any issues except minor participation fees for the anatomy scan.

As the pregnancy progressed, we realized my husband was going to be at a conference in the United States for a week after our due date. Rather than have him travel alone and leave me by myself with a toddler and a newborn, we decided instead we would all travel to the US for an extended period of time. I would give birth in the US instead of Israel. Due to the complications I experienced last time, this time we planned a hospital birth.

When it came time for the birth, we ended up at a hospital in Texas where midwives handle all the non-complicated births. We didn't have any control over which midwife we would have, so we just trusted it would be a better situation than the previous one. This time, we arrived at the hospital when I was already five centimeters dilated, and I was put into a birthing room fairly quickly. Fortunately, we had a wonderful midwife who was very understanding and supportive. We asked her about our birthing options, and she explained that the only option was the traditional hospital approach: on my back and on the bed. Since I was more open to pain management after the previous birth and there wasn't the option to move around, I asked for an epidural.

This birth experience was so different from the first. Everything was calm, and the midwife handled everything to perfection. At some point during the pushing stage, the baby's heart rate dropped suddenly. Instead of rushing to some rash intervention, she had me rest for a few contractions to get the baby's heart rate back up and then I pushed him out quickly. He did have his umbilical cord hooked over his shoulder, which explains the drop in heart rate during the final pushes. This time we had found out that the baby was a boy, and named him Yoash intending to call him Yoshi. Yoash is a bit of an old-school name in Hebrew, which belonged to a Judean king from the line of David, and it means "God is fire."

After I recovered, I was taken to a room shared with two other women. I didn't move from the bed during my two-day stay, other than to go to the bathroom and shower. This was very different from my experience in Israel, where they encourage you to get up and move around quite soon after the birth to promote a speedy recovery.

Overall, Yoshi's birth was completely different from my first one—much closer to my original birth expectations. Besides his heart rate drop during the pushing stage, the birth went quickly and easily.

Two years and two months after Yoshi was born, I was ready to deliver our third baby. This time we were in Israel again, but in the process of moving to Germany. We planned another hospital birth since the last one had been so successful. I was unsure whether I wanted pain management or not, but was open to either way, as long as it was in the hospital in case of complications.

My contractions began a few days before my due date, my husband's parents took the children to their house, and we drove to the hospital. The birthing room had a large tub in the bathroom and some additional tools for coping with natural labor. We knew that if we wanted to, we could choose to have a natural birth without an epidural. However, as my contractions intensified, I was scared of the pain, and we elected to have another epidural. Despite this, my labor steadily progressed to the pushing stage. When I began to push, we had the same issue as we did with my first birth—the baby wouldn't fully descend. The midwife would see the top of his head emerging every time I pushed but without any further progress. This began to frustrate her, and we feared medical intervention. Fortunately, she asked my husband to help me sit up so we could use gravity to help him descend. This approach proved successful, and as he crowned, the midwife saw that he was facing the wrong way. He was a stargazer. This was again the cause of the difficulty in descending and the intense back labor. It also caused quite a big tear that had to be stitched afterward. By the time our third child, who we called Yishai, was born, it was around two in the morning and we couldn't be transferred to a room for the night.

After the birth, I was starving and really just wanted to eat and sleep. My husband went to find food since the hospital had nothing to offer at such a late hour. His only option was a Coke and a granola bar from the vending machines. I downed them, and they immediately came back up, all over the floor. The nurse came in and called me crazy for thinking I could drink something carbonated after pushing a baby out. Somehow that hadn't occurred to me, though now seems perfectly logical. We live; we learn.

Yishai's birth was not a quick or easy birth since he was a stargazer, and the recovery was also more difficult. By now, I had begun to accept the fact that birth is not easy, and that no two births are the same. Each one has its beauty, its difficulties and its memories, even when things don't go as planned.

Shortly after Yishai was born, we moved to Germany for my husband's work. We were sure we wanted another baby, but not sure about the timing of another child. We were also not sure we wanted to have a baby while we were living in a different country. Every new experience in Germany had been a learning curve for us, and we weren't sure we could handle another lesson in cultural norms. We waited for a few years, and when it was clear we weren't going back to Israel anytime in the near future, we decided to go ahead and have another baby.

Since this was my first pregnancy in Germany, I had to learn a whole new medical system in terms of pregnancy and birth. I also had to learn quite a lot of new vocabulary. I made monthly trips to an obstetrician down the road. There they did blood tests and checked my blood pressure. On several visits the doctor did an ultrasound or put me on a heart monitor to check how the baby was doing. Because I was under 35 at the time, they didn't ask to do any further tests like the triple marker test or an amniocentesis.

As in Israel, Germany also uses midwives to attend uncomplicated births rather than doctors, but usually midwives attend births in the hospital. In our area, home births were more popular than in other parts of Germany. I think this may be because of the proximity of our town to the Netherlands, where home births are very common. Since there was also better infrastructure to support home births, we decided to pursue another one. For me, I wanted to try to have the birth I was hoping for with our first child. It was almost like I was looking for healing in the experience. In Hebrew, this is called a *chavaya metakenet* or a "corrective experience."

Fortunately, I had a very good friend who knew of a midwife who prefers home births to hospital births. My friend had hired her and had a good experience with her. After meeting with the midwife, we felt we could put all our fears aside. She had a warm and friendly personality and understood why we wanted another home birth despite our previous experiences. Meeting with the midwife periodically in our home, I was able to express my concerns about the upcoming birth. As she listened to the baby's heartbeat and checked his position, we communicated in a mix of basic English and German.

I continued to see my obstetrician throughout the pregnancy, where all the general tests were done. She wasn't thrilled I had decided to do a home birth, but she wasn't totally against it either. We lived quite close to the hospital, so she encouraged me to register just in case we needed to go there.

As the due date drew closer, I met with the midwife more often, and we began to talk about the preparations for the birth. I had a list of supplies I had to buy, such as a plastic cover for the mattress and special receiving blankets for the baby.

The week before my due date, I began to get agitated. Waiting for labor to start was a difficult thing for me because I knew it was going to be tough, and I just wanted to get it over with and meet my new baby. Two of my previous births had been five days early, so I expected this birth to be early as well. As the week dragged on and I got closer to the date, I became more and more upset the baby wasn't coming. Two nights before my due date, I was awoken by labor pains in the night. They went on for some time but weren't very intense, so I decided to go back to sleep to rest as much as possible before the birth.

When I woke early in the morning, my contractions had stopped. Realizing I had started labor but then the labor stalled was even more frustrating for me. I was also very nervous about the prospects of this birth, since I was to have the baby at home without any option of pain relief. By my due date the contractions hadn't returned, and I began to panic about the baby's reluctance to enter the world. In Germany, the policy was to induce once you are a week overdue, and induction had always been a curse word for me. To speed things up, I decided to go on a long walk around my neighborhood, hoping the walk would help my labor restart.

It must have helped somehow, because that night my contractions returned. We timed them for a long time, and when they were close together we called the midwife. As I concentrated on my contractions by walking in our back yard and rocking on the birthing ball, the midwife began to set up her equipment. Even with all of my walking and rocking, the contractions weren't big enough to move the labor forward. Around 2 a.m., the midwife told me she was going to go and rest, and she would be back in the morning. She asked if I wanted her to check me. I told her I did. She checked and saw I was only one centimeter dilated. Oh! It was a big discouragement, but she didn't think it was a big deal.

She told me encouragingly, "You've had three babies already; don't worry, your cervix can dilate in one big contraction if it wants to."

My first birth experience had traumatized me, and I think my midwife understood that. She was extremely sensitive to the whole situation. She knew she needed to give us space so I would relax and thus the contractions would intensify. She suggested we rest and said if we needed her, she would come right away. I am so thankful for her in so many ways, but most of all for knowing how to approach our birth on a spiritual and personal level. Some midwives know how to catch babies; other midwives know how to lead you through birth.

With the intention of resting as much as possible, my husband and I got into bed, but he was the only one able to sleep. At around six in the morning I got up to go to the bathroom, and as I got up, my water broke. It was the first time my water had ever broken before the pushing stage. I didn't say anything about what had just happened to my husband. I just returned to bed and tried to rest some more. My contractions gained momentum soon after that point, and I woke my husband. The other children were starting to wake up, and they needed breakfast. Before the birth, we had talked about sending them to a friend's house, but by time they were all up and dressed it was too late. My contractions were intensifying very quickly. My husband called the midwife, and then stayed with me through the contractions.

The midwife arrived 20 minutes later, and it was clear I was in transition. My husband asked if he should take the children to our friend's house, but both the midwife and I told him there was no way he was leaving. Instead we decided to let them watch a movie in another room. The midwife moved me to the bed, and I started to push. As with all my births, the pushing wasn't so easy. I pushed for a long time, and the baby slowly made his way into the world. I ended up pushing for around an hour to get him out, which is rather long for a fourth birth. These are the times when I envy my friends who can deliver a baby in two pushes. That's definitely not my experience. This last midwife later told me she thinks there may be a physiological reason for the pushing difficulties, as I've had them in almost all my births.

After the baby was born, we left him attached to the placenta until after the placenta was birthed. My husband cut the umbilical cord and I was left to rest with the baby for a little bit before they weighed him and cleaned him up. We had already decided to name him Yizrael, after a valley we both love, with the intention of calling him Izzy. The most peaceful time for me was after the birth. No one rushed around to do tests or move me to another room. Eventually, I went to the bath to get cleaned up, and the midwife left us for the day. It was all slow moving and not hectic at all.

The next day our pediatrician came to the house to check on the baby. He did all the checks they would have done in the hospital. Later in the day, the midwife came to check on me. She came several times during the first two weeks and would have done things like the laundry and the dishes, but I felt uncomfortable asking for these things. Overall, it was a very good birthing experience. The only drawback was that my husband forgot to feed me, because he was so busy taking care of the children, which wouldn't have happened in the hospital.

And so, as I think about my own birth that led to my expectations of my children's births, I can only conclude one thing. As wonderful as my own birth was, I may never have an easy birth like my own, as much as I would love to have one. Every birth experience is different, and when we come to the time of giving birth, we can only accept what we have and deal with it accordingly. Ironically, this is mostly because you just can't quit a birth in the middle—there is no way around it, you have to birth your baby one way or another.

Although my births were nothing like my expectations, I am extremely proud of my experiences, my courage, and the decisions I made approaching each birth. When it comes to birth, I have experienced both natural and medical approaches.

One of the benefits of being a modern woman is being able to approach birth on our own terms. But even so, in birth we can't control the outcome, and that's where our expectations and our realities don't always meet. Whether it's our own stress and baggage, the approach of the doctor or midwife attending us, the physiological limitations of our bodies, the policies of the hospital, or the culture and country in which we give birth, there are so many factors that mold our outcome and add up to our own unique birth experience.

Sherah S. Haustein was born and raised in Montana and Texas in the US. She has a bachelor's degree in non-formal education and musicology from Bar-Ilan University in Ramat Gan, Israel. She is married to a South African-born Israeli and has four children. You can find her working as a freelance writer and podcast host for http://hebrewpod101.com. Sherah and her family are currently living in Israel.

CHAPTER 19

MY BIG APPLE BABY

Katarina Holm-DiDio
Nationality: Finland
Birthed in: New York City, NY, USA

My husband and I lived on the Upper East Side of Manhattan for the first few years of our marriage and we were living and working in Manhattan when the attack on the Twin Towers happened on September 11, 2001. Like for so many other couples, the attack prompted us to think about the future, question our values and goals and as we were in our mid-to late thirties we decided it was time to start a family. Serena is one of those 9/11 babies—born in 2002 about 15 months after the terrorist attacks on New York City and Washington, DC.

I moved to the United States from Finland in 1998 to spend the first year of my post-master's degree studies at the State University of New York in Albany. My husband and I had met in Finland a couple of years earlier through a mutual friend, while he was there for a wedding. We stayed in touch, dated the year I was in Albany, and the rest is history. As for so many others who have moved across cultures, the initial few years were a roller coaster of emotional highs and lows. The thrills of living in New York, the sadness of missing my friends and family, happiness with my new life and family, and overall, major culture shock. There was a time when I compared everything in the US with Finland, and Finland always won. I would drive my husband insane by starting many statements with *"in Finland we do X, Y, and think Z...and it's much better."*

Being pregnant with your first child has both excitement and anxiety wrapped up in a round hormonal bow. Your mood and your body changes, as does your relationship with your partner or spouse. Living in a country and culture different from the one you grew up in or call home adds a layer of complexity. Not only do you have to learn to care for yourself as the pregnant mother-to-be, but you also have to do it without your own family and childhood friends there to support you.

I was lucky to have an OB/GYN who had worked with women from Finland before. She was aware of differences in health care and especially prenatal care. She was also extremely calm and professional. This was a whole new experience for me. I was being cared for the whole nine months by the same OB/GYN who would deliver our daughter. Such an arrangement is unheard of in Finland, where midwifes deliver babies while the OB/GYN is available for emergencies, and where pre- and postnatal care is also provided by midwives and nurses. I felt like a queen. We also paid for it like royals compared to my friends in Finland who pay almost nothing for their delivery and care. The price of having a child in the US was an eye-opener for me regarding how the American health insurance system works and how much it costs.

When you're pregnant you learn quickly that everyone wants to give you unsolicited advice on what to do and not to do. What to eat and what not to eat. For example, I was told not to color my hair nor drink coffee while pregnant by some well-meaning Americans. I shared this with friends and family back home in Finland, and they disagreed. Yes, you can color your hair, the new products are safe, and you can drink a moderate amount of coffee, but decaf is preferred. My husband's family on his mother's side lives in France. From the French family I heard that it is healthy to drink half a glass of wine or wine diluted with 50% water daily while pregnant. With so many mixed messages of advice, what is a first-time mother in a foreign country to do?

I did color my hair, gently, and I eventually switched to decaf coffee because I noticed the baby would kick more energetically after I had my coffee, but I did not drink any wine. Not even French-approved diluted wine.

My husband and I attended Lamaze classes and learned how to

change diapers on a doll. Neither of us had ever changed diapers before, and it was intimidating—even on a doll. I had never babysat children in my teenage years as I wasn't that interested in babies and children when I was young. So this was all new to both of us.

Honestly, I wondered how I would ever be able to care for a squirming infant if I could barely manage a diaper change on a stationary doll. My husband showed more talent for the diaper change initially, which proved very useful later.

As was suggested during the Lamaze classes and in books I read about giving birth, I selected the music I wanted to listen to while in labor. I chose U2, a long-time favorite, and the new Icelandic band, Sigur Ros. We had heard them play during a weekend in Iceland a couple of years earlier, a band that played hugely melodic and mystical, almost hymn-like music with lyrics in Icelandic. My goal was to create a serene, relaxing, and encouraging atmosphere for the birth of our daughter. My husband took this task very seriously. We had the delivering-baby playlist ready very early on.

We couldn't wait until the birth to know the sex of our baby, so we knew she was a girl, and we had decided to name her Serena after Serena Williams, whom we both admired. Most of my friends and family back home in Finland prefer not to know the sex in advance. They prefer to be surprised. I am more pragmatic. It's not about preferring a boy or a girl. I simply wanted to know the sex so I could prepare for her arrival and avoid buying only gender-neutral (yellow, green, and such) clothing and blankets.

The big day arrived! Her arrival was scheduled for a Friday in December. Yes, she was scheduled because my blood pressure had been rising dangerously the final few weeks, and my OB/GYN feared complications. It fit me well; I was nervous and preferred to know when it would all happen so I could plan and prepare. I also opted for the epidural. While I hail from a stoic stock of Finns where *sisu* (often translated as determination, perseverance, guts, and resilience) is admired, encouraged, and instilled into children from an early age, I was not sure I could handle a birth without pain medication; another factor to consider was my high blood pressure. The commotion over the option to get pain relief through an epidural or not puzzled me. Most pregnant women I spoke to were wrestling with the question. Again, everyone seemed to have an opinion they wanted to share with you. Finns are more private about such matters, and we refrain from imposing our opinions on others.

I soon learned all about the extremely competitive culture of the northeast US and especially of New York City when it came to birthing methods. Just like when you meet someone for the first time in the US and after they learn your name they ask you what you do for a living, mothers would ask you if you had a natural delivery or not. Like there is any other kind? The questions initially confused me until I understood they were asking if I took *the epidural.* Implying that having delivered my daughter nearly painlessly while being medicated through my spine was somehow less of an accomplishment and unnatural. Why this was of any concern to others, I'll never know. Is childbirth supposed to be awful and full of suffering? Did they prefer that I suffer instead of enjoying this beautiful birthing experience?

In the end, I *took* the epidural and it was beautiful, except for the one scary moment when my blood pressure went through the roof and I thought my head would explode. So Serena arrived without too much pain, to the harmonious and serene melodies of Sigur Ros, while my mathematician husband was counting my breaths and pushes. We fell in love with our daughter, and looking back I wouldn't have wanted her birth any other way.

We were sent home within a couple of days. It felt as if it came too soon. How am I supposed to keep this little girl alive on my own with only the help of my husband? I was convinced I would never be able to sleep peacefully again. Ever.

Serena was born about a week before Christmas. We had just moved across the street from one Manhattan high-rise to another only a month earlier. This apartment was on the 25th floor with plenty of natural light and more room compared to the previous, dark one on the third floor, facing the inner garden and with hardly any natural light. We brought her home to our beautiful views of the City and East River. We celebrated a very quiet Christmas, just the three of us with occasional friends visiting. I had decorated our home in the traditional Nordic fashion with the electric candle lights that resembled menorahs, lots of little wooden Christmas elves, and a real Christmas tree. I don't seem to otherwise remember a lot from our first Christmas. It's a haze of sore breasts, sitting on cushions, and lack of sleep. I do recall slowly recovering from the birth and getting up to speed on breastfeeding. My husband's employer gave him some paternity leave, so we were all cuddled up in our bird's nest high above the big apple.

New Year's Eve came. She was only two weeks old, so we took it slow. When midnight rolled around, it was time to nurse her. My husband lay asleep next to me, while I was sitting up against a heap of pillows with her in my arms. I had a southwestern view out the bedroom window over the City. I could hear the fireworks explode and see the lights flash and some of the higher ones cascade down in a rainbow of colors over the dark gray rooftops of the City. It was such a moving, peaceful, and also lonely moment in the City that never sleeps that it remains burned in my memory despite all of the sleep deprivation. The world was transitioning into a new year, I was learning how to be a mother, and we were slowly finding our way as parents with different cultural backgrounds and with no family nearby to guide us.

We were very attentive parents. Most of our time was spent making sure she ate, slept, pooped, peed, and was warm. As it happened, a pediatrician of Swedish origin was working at the hospital were Serena was born, so we continued to visit her for checkups since she shared my cultural background. I felt I could trust her immediately as she understood my values and expectations as a new mother. She also served as a cultural informant for me, explaining what the American customs are.

The focus was on making sure she ate enough and gained enough weight. The pediatrician would ask me how much she ate and pooped and peed. In my sleep-deprived, hormonal state of mind I found it difficult to recall precisely. My statistician/mathematician husband was very pragmatic about the whole thing and developed a poop and pee chart for her. Every day we recorded what she did and when. We recently found the chart, to much amusement. Needless to say, we had no such chart for our son when he arrived two years later.

The Upper East Side of Manhattan has the reputation of being posh and filled with old money. Not so much any longer, and we lived on the border to East Harlem. But we were within walking distance to world-class art museums—the Met, Guggenheim, and Whitney Museum of American Art—something I enjoyed immensely as spring and summer arrived. However, it was still winter, and a cold and snowy one. I found it difficult to get around with a stroller, and I often worried if she was cold in her drafty but cool stroller. The well-insulated and sturdy ones that Nordic children sleep in for hours outside in below-freezing temperatures were not available in New York. I was soon as eager to exit my 25th floor apartment as Rapunzel was to exit her tower in the traditional fairy tale told by the Brothers Grimm.

Serena's godfather is an artist, and the Whitney was showing his art for the first time that year. We were invited to the opening, and I really wanted to go. The problem was that it was only three weeks after her birth. I was still very tired, didn't look my best, and Serena was obviously very small. We did not have a babysitter yet and no family nearby. I decided I would go, at least for a short time. I walked the 20 minutes it took to get there, in the freezing wind, and met my husband who was already there. Whitney was warm, trendy, and noisy. I can't say I felt and looked the part in my post-birth body and loose practical clothes that allowed for easy breastfeeding. But I was among adults in an artsy world.

I felt alive.

Serena certainly was the youngest gallery visitor that day. As the noise grew louder with Serena and breastfeeding among the trendy crowd didn't seem appealing, I soon fled home, exhausted, in a taxi. The whole excursion seemed a bit unreal as we arrived home to our bird's nest full of diapers, blankets, and laundry. I decided to take it easy with the social calendar for a bit longer and perhaps find some more infant-appropriate activities.

With my family an ocean away and my husband's family a five-hour drive away, being new parents can be a bit lonely. There were no Sunday family dinners. No grandparents to babysit those first few months when you are an overprotective new parent and distrust strangers to care for your child. Friends become your family.

My husband's best friend is Korean-American. He and his wife were one of the few couples we knew who had children, so they were a major early influence. From them we learned that in Korea they traditionally arrange a celebration (*Baek-il*) at the time when the child reaches 100 days, to mark that the baby has survived this first period.

Coming from a country with one of the lowest infant mortality rates among industrialized nations, I didn't first really grasp the significance of this celebration. We certainly did not have such celebrations back home. However, while her baptism at the Finnish Seaman's Church in New York during my parents' visit had been a family event, we now felt ready to introduce our daughter to a larger group of friends.

We decided to arrange a *Baek-il* celebration for Serena, complete with a traditional Korean dress and headpiece in pink tulle rented from the catering company that provided the Korean food for us. The staff did look at us with wonder as we strode into the store with our blonde and blue-eyed daughter. It was probably just as well that we didn't understand what they were talking among each other. Obviously none of us were of Korean origin. But in the multicultural society that is New York City, nothing is impossible, so we got the traditional Korean dress and food and celebrated our daughter's first 100 days. The party was a success even if some quietly wondered why we had a Korean celebration for our daughter. Why live in the nation of immigrants and in the cultural melting pot that is the US if you can't borrow some customs and make them your own? Serena was now officially introduced to our New York as a blond-haired and blue-eyed Korean girl of Finnish/Italian and French ancestry.

I would lie if I said that those first four months being a new mother in an anonymous city and in a new country were easy. My husband traveled with his work and left me alone for days with Serena. I did miss having my friends and family close by during these periods. And I probably called the pediatrician a few too many times during those weeks, making sure our daughter was fine as she had caught a cold during this very frigid winter.

As spring came, it was time for me to get some time to myself and leave Serena in her father's care for longer periods of time. I enrolled in a full-day career coaching class that met on Saturdays. I pumped and froze breast milk for my husband to give Serena while I was away and then hurried home to her and the breast pump after the class was over and I was dripping of milk. Not the most relaxing and comfortable experience, but I enjoyed being among adults and having adult conversations about matters of my interest.

My husband was a doting father for his young daughter. But with a demanding job in finance he did not have a chance to spend much time with her. So putting the responsibility of her care into his hands during Saturdays was a chance for him to bond with her. He seemed to take it easy, bringing her with him to lunches and other activities with his friends, having her in the small city stroller and enjoying the attention from women of all ages. Manhattan is famously full of strollers, well-toned mothers, and an army of nannies. These days I hear of hair-braiding classes for active Manhattan fathers of dual-career couples, to help them care better for their daughters. That was not the case 15 years ago when we lived there.

While I am a planner and an attentive caretaker who prefers to have a diaper bag full of everything you possibly might need, my husband is quite the opposite. He does things last minute and improvises. When it comes to caring for an infant, these two characteristics are rather different. Being in an intercultural marriage, we have often explored if the origins of our differences were personal or cultural. Probably both. As a mathematician, he is definitely a cerebral man who sees the world in patterns and equations. But managing the daily routines of a household is not his forte. I used to lovingly call him "the professor" because of his tendency to be so internally occupied.

It can cause some strains in the relationship when two people with such different personalities share the responsibility of caring for a child. One Saturday when he was caring for Serena, he forgot to strap her into the stroller as he ventured out into the city with a friend. Pushing her in the stroller on the uneven sidewalks of Manhattan while talking to a friend, he hit something, and the stroller turned over with her in it. As he picked up the stroller, our five-month-old was lying on the sidewalk with a scraped and bloody nose. He cleaned her up using some very unorthodox and primal ways to wipe away the blood.

I feared the worst as I made my way home that afternoon after receiving a phone call from his friend John telling me something had happened, but it wasn't serious. Seeing my beautiful daughter with a swollen nose covered in dried blood made me rethink the Saturdays-with-Dad arrangement. But I gave him another chance, and the children are now 12 and 10 years old, respectively.

The big question for me was if I should stay at home full time for a longer period or return to work. This is a question with personal, cultural, and societal dimensions to it. My friends back home in Finland could stay home for up to three years and still have a guaranteed job to return to. Maternity leave is 18 weeks, parental leave is 26 weeks, and paternity leave approximately nine weeks. It adds up to almost a year, and while you are home with your infant you are paid 70–90% of your previous annual earnings. After the first year you can choose to stay home on paid parental leave until your child turns three. During this time you receive a childcare allowance. After your child turns three, he or she is guaranteed municipal childcare services until it is time to enroll in school. These benefits make it easier for parents to care for their children while also continuing working.

I worked in higher education when I became pregnant. As I was exploring different childcare options, I soon realized that most of my salary would go to cover the pay for a full-time nanny. After taxes there would not be much anything left. Affordable and high-quality childcare centers were far and few between, so I decided to resign my job and stay home for a while and explore new opportunities later.

Then the United Nations called, the same week I had resigned from my job at the university. Working for the UN was a childhood dream. I had successfully completed a recruitment exam for young professionals a couple of years earlier, and now they had found a suitable post for me. Was I interested? Yes I was, but how could I leave my young daughter? I wrestled with the question, but decided to interview for the job. I was selected and scheduled to start working three months later, giving me time to arrange for childcare.

Had I lived in Finland, I would have more easily trusted the quality care of the nurseries there. I knew and trusted the education and training childcare workers receive, and I would not have even considered hiring a nanny. Very few have private nannies in Finland.

But I lived in New York and was about to launch my career with an organization I'd always wanted to work for. A dream come true for me, but I needed my daughter to be safe and well cared for. I looked at childcare centers but didn't care for most of them, and others had 12-month waiting lists and college-level tuition. What an ordeal.

A former colleague came to my rescue. She had a friend who was a full-time nanny looking for a new family to work for. She was 58 years old, had raised two children herself, and had four grandchildren. She had emigrated from the Philippines to the US in her thirties. She was loving, reliable, and highly skilled. She was a perfect match for a young immigrant first-time mother.

On my first day of work, I was nervous both for the new job and for leaving Serena. I called home anxiously to find out how they were doing. Our nanny assured me everything was fine, they had a good time, and Serena was doing well. She ended the call by urging me to stop worrying and focusing on my new job. She was the doting and loving grandma we needed, even if she was a paid one. I took her advice and focused on my work. Thanks to her I excelled at work. When we moved to the suburbs and she couldn't work for us any longer, my work-life balance became much more difficult as the younger nannies we hired were not as reliable and caring.

As a working parent, your happiness and success rests upon quality childcare.

Now years later and with my children aged 12 and 10, I look back at my younger self struggling with all these decisions and questions. Why was it so difficult? At the time I didn't realize it, but being a first-time parent in a new and strange country and culture without the strong social network of support that deep friendships and family provides is a challenging and stressful phase of life. I was then still adjusting to and acculturating to my new home country in addition to learning to be a parent and finding my identity as an immigrant and wife.

Today I call the US my adopted home, and I would not wish to move back to Finland. I am happy I have the opportunity to raise children with a global awareness and multicultural identity in a country that celebrates diversity.

Kat grew up in Finland but currently lives in New Jersey, US. She enjoys travel and exploring the diversity of her adopted home country and is an avid reader and film enthusiast. She writes about global leadership, cross-cultural matters, and living and working globally. Kat has published in The Wall Street Journal's Expat blog, Trade Ready Canada, and Bloomberg BNA, and regularly contributes articles for Est Elle Norden/USA, a monthly magazine printed in Finland with a global reach.

Kat's day job is as a corporate trainer, consultant, and writer on matters pertaining to managing global careers, transitions, and change, and doing business in a diverse world. She specializes in the role of culture and communication for organizational success and for individuals working and living globally. Kat launched her career in the USA at the Columbia University School of International and Public Affairs (SIPA) before she joined the United Nations in New York City.

She still consults with the UN and regularly works with major relocation service and corporate training providers as a trainer, expat partner support consultant, and expert adviser. Kat has two master's degrees: one in mental health counseling and one in political science.

SECTION III

PARENTING ABROAD

CHAPTER 20

THE DEFINITIVE GUIDE TO PARENTAL LEAVE IN SWEDEN

Jonathan Ferland
Nationality: USA
Parented in: Sweden

Hey there!
   This book is about…[checks notes]…babies? Ah, okay then. I can work with that.

But I imagine that you are asking, "What does this guy, an obviously handsome, intelligent, red-blooded American *man* know about birthin' babies? He never went through 40 weeks of pregnancy in the hot Atlanta sun, or through hours of labor."

And luckily for me, you are *exactly right*. I never went through all of that uncomfortable stuff—if we're being honest, it doesn't seem like much fun to me (biology limitations also applied). But what I have been able to do is spend over six months raising my daughter without that having any negative effects on my career.

"Impossible!" you say.

I say, "*Nej.*"

"You lie!" you say.

I say, "*Not about this!*"

Finally, before this starts getting heated and you say something we'll both regret, you acquiesce and ask "How did you do it?" (I'm going to spend the rest of the chapter posing a lot of hypothetical questions, so thanks for bearing with me.)

Well, don't worry, that is the precise question I'm going to answer. I am about to give you, Dear Reader, a step-by-step guide so that you too can enjoy the trials and tribulations of the famed "rumor from the North"—Extended Parental Leave!

And so, to begin, it's probably good to start at the beginning. Not all the time of course, and sometimes it's probably even better to begin at the end. But this time, for this story, we'll begin at the beginning.

Without further ado:

Step 1: Work for a small, niche consulting firm that gets acquired by a large Scandinavian multinational company after you've worked there for a few years.

Okay, so this one might be a challenge for you. Not really in your control as much, but I'm not really sure how to make that more generic. It is what worked for me, so I'm going to put it out there.

Step 2: When a solid job transfer opportunity comes up, jump at it.

Now we're back in control—a little bit. Basically when the mother ship wants one of those hardworking Americans to come over and shake things up a bit, you have to throw your name into the hat. Volunteer to take the road less traveled as they say. We had heard rumors of Stockholm being some sort of Nordic paradise and figured it was worth the risk of moving to it sight unseen. After a long series of interviews—including hours doing online IQ tests on Thanksgiving morning—it was go time.

Step 3: Move.

Uh, I'm pretty sure my wife and I had some sort of a nervous breakdown/stress-induced blackout during this period, so I don't have much advice here. Moving on...

Step 4: Get acquainted with your new land.

I'm guessing you might not be completely aware of all that Stockholm has to offer. It's not a city like Paris or London that tourists flock to like the salmon to Capistrano. So as a quick primer, I'll catch you up on the things we learned those first few weeks, for instance:

Did you know that not everyone talks like the Swedish Chef? Shocking, I know.

Did you know that not every meal involves meatballs? They also really like salmon.

Did you also know that not everyone is tall, fit, and gorgeous?? Just kidding, that stereotype is 100% true.

To figure these things out, we spent the first few weeks of our time in Sweden exploring all the various islands that comprise the city of Stockholm. We would spend 30 minutes making sure that our nine-month-old son was fully protected against the February snowscape that is Scandinavia that time of year and then go out on our expedition trek for the day.

While we were doing this, we were enjoying all of the "European" things, such as buildings older than America and really good lattes. In addition, though, it really jumped out to us how family-friendly the whole city was. Bus rides were free if you had a stroller with you. Every bathroom (men's included) would have baby-changing stations. And most interesting, they had a *lot* of male nannies pushing strollers at all times of the day.

Wait.

It turns out, they actually aren't male nannies, but dads! They are just Viking dads spending their days with their children. Most of the time, no moms were in sight—just dads taking full responsibility for their kids for hours on end every day.

This was very different from what I was used to seeing in the States. A lot of this is due to the Swedish parental leave policy. I had heard only rumors, whispers really, by that point, but I knew that dads were "expected" to take months of extended parental leave. I still wasn't exactly sure how a country could operate when it frequently loses one or two parents to an extended leave of absence, but that wasn't my problem to solve.

So now that we know this is a possibility, you're probably asking, "What's the next step? How do you actually take all of this time?"

This is a great question. I'm glad you asked!

Step 5: Figure out how you actually take this time.

I immediately started digging into this more. The way it works (this is a simplified version) is that for each child you have, Sweden gives both parents 480 days of paid parental leave. The trick is that one parent must take at least 60 days of this leave. Sweden tries to ensure that both parents have equal share in childcare and that it is not only the women who take time away from their careers to spend time with children. It turns out that most of the men I worked with actually did take their parental leave. Some people deliberately spaced out their time, taking off every Thursday and Friday for two years, some used it as a supplement by adding a week or two to their summer or winter holidays, and some took big chunks of time—one of my colleagues was planning a nine-month leave soon. This certainly wasn't like my American job where we were discouraged from taking sick or vacation time; Sweden, my company, my boss, and my coworkers—they all expected me to take this leave.

My company helped out with this a lot because while the Swedish system is very generous, it does not come close to fully replacing a salary, which would be a major issue for us, obviously. So my company "tops up" the salary to a certain level—assuming the days are all used by the time the child is 18 months old. This encourages employees to take the leave while the children are young. It also lit a fire under me to figure out the details and make a plan to actually take this leave. With this newfound information, we started planning. We read up on all the details, filled out all the forms and then finally, we were ready for a test run that July, adding two to three weeks of parental leave onto my vacation time. I was ready to go parental.

Now, as the old saying goes, "If you fail to plan (or rely too much on Google Translate for official documents), you plan to fail!"

When we got that first pay stub in from the government, I opened it up and my jaw hit the ground. Evidently we had missed some fine print and I wasn't eligible for *any* payments because we were so new to the country. So back to work I went!

Test Run #1: FAIL

The dream wasn't dead yet, though.

A little over a year later, we were blessed with our second child, and this time we were more prepared. My wife had been right when she said that if I didn't take the maximum amount of time allotted to me that it would be an insult to the kids, to her, and to all the folks back home who don't have the opportunity to take such a long parental leave. It seemed like every week I saw a post from a new American mother on Facebook who was really upset because she had to go back to work after having a baby six weeks prior. For me, as a father, to have a whopping six months of paid parental leave was such a surreal and unique situation. I had to take this time off to be with my family.

So with this in mind, we floated another "trial" parental leave. Beforehand, we spent a few days trying to figure out how much our income would drop, but because we don't have advanced degrees in theoretical calculus, we ended up having no idea at all. For this leave, we planned out a six-week trip, including the Tour de Lucy in the US during Thanksgiving and Christmas. This time when we checked our bank balance online, we turned out not to be totally destitute.

Now we were emboldened. We had financial data. We had a successful trial. We had a calendar. We were ready to *do this*.

Step 6: Tell your manager, with a straight face, that you will be gone for six-plus months.

It was game time. All I had to do was tell my manager. All I could think about before that meeting was how nervous I was to take off five days when our son, Calvin, was born, and now with Lucy, I was going to take off for six months! This was insanity!

Despite my nerves, the conversation went shockingly well. We made sure that I was still there for the really high–priority deadlines and deliverables and that there was a good handover plan to make sure no important items fell through the cracks, but outside of that, it was simple and uncomplicated.

My goals for the handover were two-fold: to make sure that I didn't put any undue stress or pressure on my friends at work, and also that they had no reason at all to contact me for the next six months.

This actually seemed to be easier than I had expected. When you are going on a one-week vacation, your projects sit there collecting dust until you return. But when you're gone for six months no one waits for you to come back. They weren't going to rely on me to handle any deliverables, so the plan was that outside of a few short phone calls and emails, I would be able to go the rest of the time blissfully unaware of what was happening at the office.

Step 7: Paperwork. *So much* paperwork.

This part was horrible. I will spare you the details, but when you get to this step yourself, let me know, and I can walk you through it.

Step 8: Get into a routine.

During my parental leave the first few months went perfectly. We started with a picture-perfect Swedish summer—enjoying sunny, mid-70 °F (24 °C) days by biking to the beach or to the forest every day to pick blueberries. Then we traveled with friends and family around the world a bit. Swinging by neighboring Norway, France, and Italy before an extended trip to the great state of Texas and the rest of the American southwest.

Seeing all those great places was a once-in-a-lifetime experience, and I wouldn't change any of it, but it was hard to get into a routine with Calvin and Lucy during that time. When you are living out of a suitcase or in a constant state of packing or unpacking, it's tough to really get into a good flow like I wanted to with them.

We had anticipated this, so we had wisely decided not to travel at all over the second half of my leave. Yes, we decided to leave Sweden during the three warm-weather months and stay in Sweden during three of the worst months of the year weather-wise. We may have planned it a bit backwards, but hey—no one is perfect, okay?

Once we did get into a routine, though, we had a blast.

After we had gotten all those pesky passport stamps out of the way, it was time to get down and dirty. It was time to look my daughter in the eye and let her know that we are in this thing together. We started off slow (mostly because she could barely walk) and would play at the house for a while or go visit the library for a little bit after dropping her brother off at preschool. Then it would be just Daddy and Lucy time. At first, I had little to no idea what to do. I would bring five juice boxes but no snacks. I would put 20 diapers into our little diaper bag but no wipes. We'd go outside to play and have to come back in 15 minutes later because she wasn't dressed appropriately. I made all of the rookie mistakes.

Luckily, Lucy was very patient with me and sternly but lovingly corrected me after every misstep. Like any great boss, she saw the potential in me and worked really hard to help me reach it. Eventually, we were a well-oiled machine and had such a good routine that my wife would ask me how to handle her on weekends! She was normally the expert on our children, and now she was asking me for advice?

As part of our normal day, we would leave the house around 9 a.m., both fully confident that we were about to have a blast. We would always discuss the day before what grand adventures we would go on. Maybe the forest? Maybe the playground with dragon statue? One day, after talking it over the day before, we decided to visit the library the next morning.

And you'll never believe what happened next...

Step 9: Make some friends!

Hanging up at the library entrance was a flyer for local activities. Looking at that, we found a great little *öppna förskola* (open preschool) near our house. Basically, because so many parents are taking long extended stretches of time off and subsequently going stir crazy, as a public health measure (I assume) Sweden instituted a public "open daycare" system. In a city like Stockholm, this means that every day of the week, a different church would open their doors and let parents show up with their kids. There is a range of toys available—everything from rattles for newborns to cars and action figures for four- to five-year-olds. They also have teachers there who chat with the parents, get to know the children, refill the refreshments, and lead song time. The children are never left unattended—parents must stay with them the entire time—but it allows parents to socialize with other adults, allows the kids to play with other kids, and lets everyone enjoy a different location for a bit. And did I mention it was all provided free of cost?

Because we lived in a suburb of Stockholm, there wasn't the range of *öppna förskola* available, but instead we had one location within walking distance. I realized pretty quickly that this was even more fun. As an expat who is very lazy and has been slacking at learning the language, this situation was perfect. Everyone at our *öppna förskola* was Swedish. This was very different from my international office where my colleagues are used to speaking English. At *öppna förskola* it was just casual, toddler-level Swedish all of the time. On good days, I was able to follow along and possibly contribute slightly to Swedish conversations. On sleep-deprived days, I was the weird deaf-mute guy in the corner.

And I was definitely the weird guy for a bit. But eventually some very patient Swedes helped me learn a bit of Swedish, and after a while I was able to hold very basic conversations. Toddler-level conversations, but here I was, speaking Swedish! I had imagined these Swedish dads were probably talking about awesome stuff at *öppna förskola*: Swedish league hockey, moose sightings, whiskey tastings, and that sort of thing. It turns out though, that when groups of dads in charge of toddlers get together, they talk about the same stuff moms would—how their baby was sleeping, eating, and pooping.

This time was really special to me, because in addition to learning Swedish, it was my one-on-one time with Lucy. Every day after dropping Calvin off at school, Lucy and I would walk directly to the *öppna förskola* and arrive just as they opened the doors. We would have the playroom to ourselves, and she would have a blast with the dragon pull toys (*drakar*), horses (*hästar*), and stacking toys (uh, never learned this in Swedish).

An hour later, things would start getting a bit more crowded as parents filed in, and the teachers would come and organize song time. We would sit in a circle with children in our laps and have fun sing-alongs to Swedish nursery rhymes. Some of these I was familiar with (same tune, just different words), but most I had never heard before (like "Watch out, little snail"). Luckily for me, they had the words printed on the wall behind the instructor, so while I was still a beat or two behind, I was able to practice, practice, practice. After doing this day after day, week after week for all of October and November, I was feeling pretty comfortable. Finally, I was able to sing along without stumbling over every word. I was feeling, dare I say, even confident!

Then we switched to unfamiliar Swedish Christmas songs, and I started from Day One all over again. Oh well.

Step 10: Treasure every minute.

At this point in the chapter, Dear Reader, we have covered a lot of material, from advising you to somehow get your company acquired by a large Scandinavian firm to singing Swedish Christmas songs. And while all of these steps are important, the only essential part is this step—treasure every single minute. Whether parental leave is five days, six weeks, or six months, it goes by so quickly. It is never enough time, and when it ends, it hurts.

Watching Lucy every day as she transitioned from a non-crawling blob to stumbling around like a drunken sailor was such a blessing to me. I hope that she got a lot out of it too. I believe that it also helped my marriage, because I was able to understand what it's like to be home all day with only a baby to talk to and how it feels to have your only project deliverable entail getting rid of a dirty diaper.

When I walked into work that Monday after my six months of parental leave, I quickly realized that nothing had really changed. Business had grown, but not as much as we had hoped. The strategic issues had been researched but not solved. The same annual conference needed preparation. I just sat down and stared at my computer screen for 10 minutes trying to figure out what I was doing back at the office.

Walking back into the house a few hours later, I found out that Lucy had started "reading" books to Lisa and Calvin. It was the first time she had done that. So in the six months I was gone from work, nothing had really changed. In the eight hours away from my 16-month-old daughter, I had already missed out on a special moment. It was a moment I'm not sure I would have appreciated before my parental leave, but after spending so much time with her and investing so much energy reading books to her every day, it was a milestone that I cherished.

That's when I really took a minute to think back and reflect on how lucky and blessed I was, especially as the dad, to be able to take any parental leave—let alone the extended one that I did. I know most cultures (to say the least) don't have opportunities like this. In comparison to how our life used to be, it doesn't really seem fair that I could take so much time, but I am so glad my wife was able to convince me to embrace our adopted local culture and take on the role of a stay-at-home dad for an extended period of time.

Truly, taking the road less traveled made all the difference—to my wife, to my children, and especially to myself.

So that's it! As I promised at the beginning, I gave you a simple, step-by-step guide to extended parental leave. Now it's up to you, Dear Reader, to follow the guideposts I laid out, and you too will hopefully land in a society that is family-friendly and open to foreigners butchering their language. Easy, right?

Jonathan Ferland grew up in Rhode Island and went to college in upstate New York before thinking he had escaped the cold weather for forever by moving to Atlanta, Georgia. He now lives in Åkersberga, Sweden with his beautiful, amazingly talented wife, one Teenage Mutant Ninja Turtle, and one Pippi Longstocking.

CHAPTER 21

PRESCHOOL PARENTING ON A CARIBBEAN ISLAND

Clara Wiggins
Nationality: United Kingdom
Parented in: Saint Lucia

My youngest daughter, still a baby really, clung to me like some sort of newborn koala bear desperate not to lose sight of her mother. Outside and down the hall, in another classroom, I could hear my oldest daughter's screams. As I tried to get to her, the baby still refusing to lessen her grip and moving along the corridor with me, the voice of one of the teacher's boomed out.

"No Mrs. Wiggins, don't go to her. We don't allow parents in the classroom!"

She was four years old. It was her first day at her new preschool in a new country, surrounded by people she didn't know. And I wasn't allowed to comfort her. Welcome to parenting—Caribbean style!

To say we were hit by culture shock when our two children started preschool is Saint Lucia would be as much of an understatement as saying that beautiful but tiny island had a mildly warm climate. In fact, we were continuously sweating from the stifling heat—and constantly negotiating some bizarre rule, regulation, or requirement from the day the girls (aged almost two and four at the time) started at the school.

Take the school uniform, for example. Bearing in mind it was usually around 90 °F (32.2 °C) in the summer months, with humidity levels through the roof, one would have thought that the clothing chosen by the school would be made out of a nice, light cotton. You would have been wrong: In fact, we were instructed to dress our school-age daughter in a thick, almost wool-like material pinafore dress, with a white shirt underneath. So two layers. And under the dress—modesty pants. Modesty pants? It took us several hours of hunting the shops to work out what this might mean—in the end we bought a pair of boy's white boxers and hoped they would do. Apparently, the school was nervous that the boys might see the girls' pants while they were on the play equipment or sitting on the floor. Back home in the UK, the boys and girls were still getting undressed together for physical education.

Then, after school started and we had survived the initial few hellish days of screaming and clinging, we realized something else slightly odd about the school. There were no toys.

At this point, I should mention that this was a Montessori school, and we attributed the weirdness of the school to just a different school system as opposed to specific Caribbean culture. Other oddities such as the developmental milestones of using knives at the age of three and learning to pour water from a jug were also interesting quirks that we later learned were part of the Montessori system. Although, not having experienced another Montessori school before or since, we will never know how much of the strangeness was a Saint Lucian thing and how much was a Montessori thing.

But whether this was the norm or not, having no cars or dinosaurs or dressing-up clothes or tea party sets was quite different from what we had experienced back in the UK. There were beads to thread and blocks to count, little mats to sit on to do school work (which needed to be rolled up and put away at the end of the session), and total quiet from all the children when they were working. This was all great for their development—but also all seemed so serious at such a young age.

However, as we quickly worked out, schooling was a serious business in Saint Lucia. When we attended a parents' meeting for three-year-olds and found earnest fathers questioning exactly what the children would be learning in the coming months, we quickly realized that academic achievement wasn't something left to chance in this country. We sheepishly wrote down notes, encouraged our daughter to start practicing her letters and numbers at home, and eventually we started feeling the same pride as the rest of the parents. We were very proud when it was declared she had learned enough reading and writing to move on to the next level. She may have only been in preschool, but it's amazing how caught up you can get in academic achievement of your just-out-of-diapers child when everyone around you is comparing notes on their child's achievements.

But the academic side was really only the start of it. Just when we thought we were getting used to the strange ways of teaching, the school threw a whole new curveball at us: dress-up days.

We hadn't long arrived in Saint Lucia when the first such day presented itself to us. It had been a difficult, sticky, tiring first few weeks on the island, so it was a huge relief when the school was finally open and the girls had somewhere to go and other children to socialize with. This was despite the horrible settling-in period when my older daughter screamed and clung to me every morning. But I knew we had to get through this phase—if they didn't go to "school" then what on earth was I going to do with them all day? Yes, it was definitely for the best.

But they'd only been there what seemed like a few days when we were told that the next week was the La Marguerite festival. Now we had to sort out clothes for my older daughter, who had been chosen to be the Marguerite Queen and lead the parade.

The *whaaaat* festival? The *whaaat* parade?

Saint Lucia is an island with a lack of the sort of shops I was used to back in the UK. No fancy-dress places, nowhere was I likely to be able to pick up a quick queenly dress, the right size, oh, and yes, the right color. Didn't I know that the Marguerite colors were always blue or purple?

And so this was the start of my love/hate affair with the peculiar dress-up days and the strange rituals on this slightly eccentric island—rituals which go back centuries and are actually very interesting once you start reading in to them. But these rituals, at this point, simply caused me a massive headache as I tried to procure the right dress for my Queen.

La Marguerite (known colloquially in the local creole as *La Magwit*) was one of two societies in Saint Lucia—the other being La Rose (*La Woz*). The societies originated from the time of slavery and had started out as cooperative groups for mutual support in difficult times. Probably the closest we can get to them in the UK is the Freemasons—although I am not sure that the Saint Lucian versions have the same funny handshake. However, there are other rituals that go with La Marguerite and La Rose that involve singing songs and parades.

This is all well and good and understandable. But what I never quite understood was why the schoolchildren did not only sing and parade but had to also dress up. Sure they dressed as queens and kings but also as lawyers, police officers, and (it seemed) old ladies. And then they paraded around waving flowers and singing the creole songs. In the 110 °F (43.3 °C) heat. In their finery. We certainly got a nice, big dose of culture shock right there and then.

If you're wondering, I did manage to find a dress for my daughter—or rather, I found some suitably colored (and suitably shiny) material and a dressmaker, living on a patch of land, surrounded by chickens down a back road in the middle of nowhere. Which I would never have known about if it wasn't for my housekeeper who at that point was more or less the only person I knew on the island.

These dress-up days seemed to come around fairly regularly during our time on the island—or maybe they just caused me so much stress that they seemed to be more of a regular occurrence than they actually were. A year after the first one, we had to come up with not one, but two Marguerite costumes, as now my youngest daughter was old enough to join in. But in the meantime, I had to source outfits for *Jounen Kweyol* (Creole Day) for them both, which involved hunting round the back streets of the capital, Castries, for a particular dressmaker who I had been told specialized in children's costumes. I found her in the end, and luckily she had what I needed, in the right size. But it certainly wasn't the easiest way to kit out the kids.

And then there was sports day.

Since our Saint Lucia days, I have had to sit through plenty of sports days at our UK primary school, so now I know what it's all about. In the UK, there are a few races per child, no medals or even announcements of who the winner is, and a little uncompetitive throwing. It's all a bit of fun and everyone goes home happy.

Was it similar in Saint Lucia? Was it hell? Again, bearing in mind these were tiny little children we're talking about (aged between three and five), you would have expected the school to be at least gentle with the youngsters. No one wants a child to cry because they not only have lost a race but have come in last in every single category they were entered for. We're taught in the UK that children can't cope with competition and that they'll probably be scarred for life if they're never first.

Well, this isn't how they feel in Saint Lucia. Before arriving in Saint Lucia, I hadn't attended any sports days in the UK, so it wasn't really culture shock that hit me at first (and only) so much as genuine, human shock.

Each child was entered for a number of races. Parents not only cheered them on from the sidelines, they screamed and shouted and cajoled and hollered and then ranted and raved when they didn't win. Each child was given some sort of badge for taking part—but the first, second, and third places were all color-coded, so it was very obvious who the sporty children were. Remember, again, some of these children were three years old. Three!

Not only did the "competitive" spirit of some of the parents shock me, but the day itself—which lasted from early in the morning until well into the afternoon, all taking place in the blazing sun—was also a little, should I say, unusual. When I heard friends back in the UK complaining about their little ones being made to spend a couple of hours under a shaded tent at the first sports day I attended after we returned home, I thought back to our Saint Lucian experience and bit my tongue. Perhaps children are a little tougher than we think (and in fact I haven't yet seen any lasting damage from my daughter not winning any of her races at the age of four—if anything, it has given her a competitive edge over some of her contemporaries).

School trips were another learning curve for us all during our time in the Caribbean. These trips did have the advantage of allowing the children to visit the beach (although sadly no swimming in the sea—I guess even in Saint Lucia there were health and safety standards). But on another occasion my older daughter's class was all taken to the local boat yard. The only reason for this, as far as I could tell, was that the father of one of her classmates worked there—not because they were studying boat building or marine biology or anything (although, after the evening with the competitive parents, I wouldn't have put it past them).

I happened to accompany the class on this trip—mostly because I was the only parent to volunteer, but also because I rather wanted to keep an eye on my own child. The reason for this was because I knew that boat yard—and a children's playground it was not. The couple of teachers on the trip did their best to keep the children in line, but it was certainly useful to have another pair of hands and eyes to stop some of the more "active" children running under a 10-ton yacht hanging above our heads in a dry dock or a hefty mast being winched from one side of the yard to the other. I'm glad to say they all made it back to their classroom alive and unharmed.

The "interesting" parenting issues we faced while living in Saint Lucia didn't end at the school gates though. Children's parties represented a cultural minefield that we had to carefully tiptoe through, lest we unintentionally offend someone. We were mixing with so many different nationalities and cultures that it was hard to know exactly what to expect every time we turned up to another birthday celebration.

At one house, men dressed head to foot (including full coverage of their faces) as superheroes and ran around the garden terrifying the children. I don't think my then two-year-old has ever been able to look at Superman the same way again. In another, the bouncy castle was totally free-range, with children bouncing off the floor, walls, and each other in alarmingly carefree style. Food was always hit-and-miss for my fussy children—although I was pleased to see that birthday cake seems to be a worldwide phenomenon.

Most worrying of all, though, was the party at our own house when my eldest turned five—and we realized it was perfectly normal and acceptable for parents to leave their very young children at a total strangers' house for the afternoon without more than a quick wave goodbye. Bearing in mind we had not one but two swimming pools in our garden and had no idea which of these children could swim (surprisingly few—for a nation of island dwellers, swimming lessons weren't always a priority). This resulted in a fairly stressful afternoon for those of us adults remaining at the party.

But it was only at the end of the day when things really got what I would term "island-like," when we realized that one little girl had been left behind—and no one had come to pick her up. We had no contact number for her parents, and it was only because someone knew her aunt and offered to drop her there on their way home that we didn't end up with her moving in with us! This may sound like a joke, but one of my other friends did end up with one of her daughter's school friends staying the night when no one came for her at the end of a play date. Oh yes, they do things a little differently in the Caribbean!

Sports day, dress-up days, strange developmental activities, singing in Creole, class trips to the beach...all of these were part and parcel of our slightly surreal experience of living on the island of St Lucia. I still wake up at night in a cold sweat after dreaming about trying to find the outfits for *Jounen Kweyol* with just a couple of days' notice. But I wouldn't have swapped it for all the Biff and Chip phonics, book days, Red-Nose days, non-competitive sports days, and all the other things our children have to go through in this country. It was part of the charm of living on that tiny Caribbean island, and it was, in the end, one of the most memorable things about it.

I can't say I ever really *enjoyed* the last-minute scramble to find the right costume for yet another strange event I had never heard of, but it certainly made me a stronger person. I also have no idea whether my daughters remember much from their time in the Caribbean. It's not important if they learned anything from the Marguerite parades, the visits to the boat yards, the beading, and the competitive sports days. But, if nothing else, it was certainly different from the sort of experiences they would be getting back home at a British preschool. And for that alone, I am glad we participated in all of those very unique Saint Lucian rituals.

Clara Wiggins was born in Cuba to British diplomat parents. She started traveling as a baby and hasn't stopped. She has lived in 11 countries on five continents and visited nearly 70. Along the way, she has picked up a husband and produced two daughters. As a family they have lived in Pakistan, Saint Lucia, and are now enjoying life in South Africa. Here, she spends her time managing the International Journal of Birth and Parent Education, looking wistfully at the blue sky outside, writing a blog, and marketing her book for "trailing spouses"—"The Expat Partner's Survival Guide." To find her blog and book, please visit http://www.expatpartnersurvival.com.

CHAPTER 22

ADVENTURES OF A STAY-AT-HOME DAD IN SWITZERLAND

Sten-Ove Tullberg
Nationality: USA
Parented in: Zurich, Switzerland

My journey as an expatriate parent came as not just one, but two life-changing experiences at once. Not only was I experiencing what it was like to be a parent in a country far from home, but our third day in-country was also my first day as a stay-at-home dad. This made some minor dilemmas easier, for example answering the sometimes paralyzing question of "What are we going to do today?" early on yielded a default answer of "Exploring!" However, managing a stroller, a basket of groceries, and perhaps a cranky 13-month-old while remembering enough German to order the right meat, cheese, or bread made some of my new solo-dad experiences just that much harder.

The first two months of our stay in Zurich were in my wife's company's corporate housing in a not-quite-central but still very close district of the city. To get to the downtown heart of the city was a 10-minute tram ride or a 20 to 25-minute walk (depending whether we stopped at the mini-skate park to do stroller tricks on the ramps). Most of these two months Nellie and I settled into figuring out each other and our new home. While I had always been an involved dad, weekends often deviated from the Monday-to-Friday routine with errands, traveling, or other adventures. Figuring out and sticking to a meal and sleep routine was the number one challenge as I was now Director of Calories, Nutrients, and Naps. The second challenge was figuring out how many activities I could fit into Nellie's day between nap and meal times. Grocery shopping at my preferred store 800 yards away could slot in easily before or after the two naps, but not in between. Laundry meant four or five trips across the building to the shared laundry facility and a morning or afternoon at home plus "folding" with Nellie's help. A trip to the city was long and required food and nap on the go, and so on. I did not really think of myself as an expat during this time, because everything still felt like an extended vacation. I had some nice chats with people, for example at the Mexican grocery, at the laundry room with another expat with a seven-month-old, but it had yet to sink in that I was an expat and this place was home. The newness of the Stay-at-Home Dad experience and the tourist feel delayed that realization for those first two months.

The third month saw us moving into our new apartment in a small town that was a 15-minute train ride away from the *Hauptbahnhof* station in downtown Zurich. This is where my expat experience truly started. I was in my rhythm as the primary caregiver, and after a couple of days I no longer had my explorer and tourist activities to fall back on, or not as easily, given the distance and expense of getting to the city. With the new apartment came all of our things from the US, and Nellie was thrilled to have all of her toys and books back as well. After a couple of days, though, it was clear that we needed to establish a new routine. I had some trepidation about integrating with the local expat or stay-at-home parent groups though. First off, other than swinging by the community playground, where was I to find them? MeetUp, Facebook, and the Internet in general did not have much. Second, would I be welcomed at the Moms of Smalltownville group, or would my presence change the dynamic of the group? Sad to say, I let my apprehension get the better of me, and I never found out.

So Nellie and I ended up keeping to ourselves for the most part.

She made friends quickly and happily at the playground, playing along with the other children without any worries. The moms never really spoke to me though, and whether that was a function of the more closed Swiss culture or a function of my dadness I am not sure. I did run into one very nice Puerto Rican mother, but she was only at the park with her school-age girls on a no-school afternoon. It is difficult to be objective, but in a culture where being a stay-at-home mom is still viewed as typical, I always felt as if I was viewed as a bit of an intruder or as a passer-by just doing dad duty for the day. I cannot say that it was easy primarily conversing with a babbling toddler during the day for half a year, but Nellie and I had a blast anyhow.

Another facet of my expat parenting experience that deserves mention is free time. With a night owl for a wife who likes to sleep as late as possible even on work days, I was "on" from approximately 6:30 or 7 a.m. every morning when Nellie woke up on through to whenever we sat down for dinner. Part of successful integration, given the assumption that we are in this for the long haul, meant learning the language. It was also a potential prerequisite for returning to work, depending on the company. Even as Nellie shifted from a two-nap to a one-nap schedule, she gave me two to three hours of free time during the day. In that time I could: learn German, research companies and jobs, clean up after the morning's activities and play (thus reducing my chances of a sprained ankle), do the general cleaning, do laundry, or maybe even do something I enjoy, like eating lunch. Perhaps I could attribute my early on weight loss to an improved diet, or to all of those walks around Zurich, but I am pretty sure it was due to forgetting to eat or just not really having time. Anyhow, balancing all of those activities was quite the challenge. It became easier (and lunch became a regular event) when Nellie shifted to one longer nap rather than two short ones. I could breathe and set my focus just once versus sometimes having just gotten things put to order, having had a quick bite to eat, and then started a German lesson right before hearing "Tataaaa" echo from Nellie's bedroom. Not that I will ever tire of hearing that, but it slowed down my productivity just a bit.

Being a new arrival to Switzerland definitely added another head to the hydra assaulting my schedule. Settling into Zurich was another dimension of activities that we had to deal with, and thankfully my wife speaks fluent German or that would have been a nightmare. The time drain that is searching for a place to live (in one of the most expensive cities on earth), outfitting a newly found apartment, navigating health/home/car insurance, converting our car to Swiss standards, registering it and ourselves, and more definitely occupied a lot of our free time. As much as possible we attempted to isolate these activities on weekends or late evenings, but Nellie definitely watched me do some work on the car from her stroller; if (when?) we move again in a few years, at least she'll be able to hold the flashlight for me.

By late spring, Nellie and I had settled into a great rhythm, just in time for the travel season to hit and the impulse to visit everywhere kicked in. She was a trooper through flights to Porto, London, Vienna, Warsaw, and DC, and a great road trip buddy on short or long journeys to Munich, Nuremberg, Konstanz, Zug, Lucerne, and more. The demands of travel did not seem to alter her schedule too much, and we usually recovered pretty quickly on site and back at home afterward. I would not change a thing about how often we packed up and went places, but we certainly devote more time to random playgrounds and wandering in parks than we used to. Plus, I am building a fabulous collection of "Nellie in castles" pictures.

September was the start of Phase Three for my expat-dad experience. Nellie started daycare at a *Kinderkrippe* in our small town, and while it is not intentionally an international daycare, it may as well be with Swiss, German, British, Russian, Indian, Spanish, and now Polish-American children. Not only does she have other children to play with all day, a great Swiss emphasis on outdoor time (rain, snow, or shine), and all the other benefits, it is also exposing Nellie to a great range of people, places, languages, and cultures. With her in daycare for a few hours each day, I now have what feels like a massive amount of free time in my day. However, it is still easy to fill with structured German lessons (plus the commute to get there and back), applying for jobs at a much higher rate than I was previously capable of, and keeping up with the cleaning, shopping, and cooking much more easily. If I were not an expat and spending half of my day in language lessons, I would definitely have too much free time though.

With Nellie in daycare I am getting my first experience in providing supplementary activities and education rather than being the person responsible for everything. She gets great time outside, good food, plenty of play time, some art time, and more at daycare. However, my wife and I feel like she could use more story time and books in general, more practice with letters and numbers, and more time building things without the ever-present threat of structure collapse from overenthusiastic toddlers. So we will do our best to ensure that she is well rounded and progressing with her education. This will continue to be a challenge, as we will likely sneak books on American and Polish history onto her reading lists, provide Polish language exercises, or possibly encounter philosophical differences regarding curriculum and pace as she goes into Swiss schools.

One obstacle that has spanned our time in Switzerland is our distance from American family and friends. I cannot imagine what living abroad with small children was like before the advent of video chat. Skyping with my parents makes the telephone seem like sending smoke signals. That they are able to see each other on a regular basis has made the decision to move to Switzerland that much easier and better. Without that capability, I would feel like an entire segment of her life is missing.

We have lived in Switzerland for only eight months as I write this, but already I am certain that those months will be some of my favorite times in my life. The opportunity to stay home with Nellie as she develops and learns at such a time of change in her life is amazing. Working American dads do not get this opportunity, and I certainly did not during her first 13 months. Being a full-time dad in a foreign country has been extremely enjoyable. Though she may not remember much of these early times, I know that she is being raised in an environment that is much more kid-friendly and encourages her independence. Amid the other stressors that living abroad brings, I take comfort in knowing that she is being raised in this multicultural, nurturing environment. While not an easy or simple experience, the most rewarding things in life are hard earned, and I would not change a thing.

Sten-Ove Tullberg was born in Maine to a Swedish father and American mother and was raised in Maryland, US. Later, he made his home in Atlanta, Georgia, Chapel Hill, North Carolina, Chicagoland, Illinois, and Washington, DC. He is married to Kasia, a Polish citizen, and together they have one daughter, Nellie. Currently, they live in Zurich, Switzerland, where he is pursuing a career as a digital technology strategist with PwC. Sten enjoys reading, gaming, and cooking, as well as getting outside in his newly adopted country.

CHAPTER 23

MEAN CLASS MOM

Sarah Metzker Erdemir
Nationality: USA
Parented in: Istanbul, Turkey

No one elected Mean Class Mom as far as I know. I've seen her elbowing her way around the various gossip circles in the playground after school, staging her takeover after the former class mom, Bossy Teyze became too ill to do the job. She's saved in my phone as Mean Class Mom so when she calls I don't accidentally mistake her for someone nice.

Bossy Teyze was the boss of first grade. Mean Class Mom is the boss of second grade. She regards this as some sort of privileged position and was even driving her car onto the playground through kids running around playing, right up to the front door the kids leave through, until the principal told her to cut it out. Her daughter has tight, immaculate handwriting. The girl's copied poems are always at the center of the bulletin board displays. She doesn't make mistakes. There are never grubby fingerprint marks in her pasted flowers. She's the girl always chosen to read a poem to everyone on report card day, which she does in a high, breathless voice. Mean Class Mom always sits up next to the teacher on report card day, smiling benevolently down on everyone.

Bossy Teyze is someone's grandmother. *Teyze* means "maternal aunt" in Turkish, and it's also used as a respectful and somewhat affectionate term of address to any older woman. Even though she was bossy, at least she was nice and sat crammed into the kids' little desks with everyone else.

Mean Class Mom is more of a bully. Her cowed husband tags along behind her as she circulates around waiting parents, hustling money for things like Teacher's Day gifts or to hire a cleaner to come tidy up the classroom over the weekend. Her eyes bulge out a bit, so it feels weird to look her in the eye. I'm not one of the moms who stands in clusters whispering about secret women's problems and the people in the other clusters while dandling babies and small children, sharing recipes and weight-loss tips and cures for mild ailments with herbs and artichokes. It's not that these kinds of conversations are a linguistic challenge for me anymore. It's just that they bore me. Sometimes I hang out near the one small group of dads with my earphones in and the music off, eavesdropping while they discuss work and politics and football.

I can't tell if I'm the only single mom around. I'm the only foreign parent in a school of approximately eight million kids. I'm in the increasingly smaller minority of moms who don't wear a headscarf. I'm in an even smaller minority of moms who work full time in official, over-the-table jobs. A lot of the moms are housekeepers or nannies, which is unofficial and under-the-table work because they don't get social security and no one—not even the government employment statistics—thinks those jobs count as real work. Once my kid told me his best friend's mom worked at my university. She was a cook in the cafeteria. That kid moved away, and we were sad.

So I'm pretty much in the demographic of just me.

Mean Class Mom schedules class parent meetings during the day on weekdays. She's unclear on quite why my job should prevent me from coming to these meetings, or why I can't send someone in my place. The entire system here assumes every home has a cadre of unemployed women with nothing better to do than look after children, or bake things, or change bedpans for sick relatives in the hospital, or receive mail. Once a postman was furious with me for not being home when he was trying to bring me a letter from my grandmother. When I finally got the letter, my grandmother had been dead for three months.

So Mean Class Mom isn't the only one who seems somewhat unsympathetic to the fact that my household is just me and the boy. It's just that she is often the face of this lack of sympathy. "Oh that's right," she says when I tell her I can't come to a weekday meeting. "You don't have anyone else."

Yes, that's right, Mean Class Mom. Thanks for your help.

Sometimes school is canceled with no notice. When this happens, I've instructed my kid to go to the nearby daycare where he stays in the morning, and call and let me know where he is. Because the school is so crowded, the kids go half day—middle school in the morning and elementary in the afternoon. My kid objects to going to the daycare—a preschool really—because he's so much bigger than the other kids there. When he arrives in the morning they gather around babbling "Ender! Ender!" and trying to touch and hug him. He's like the King of the Babies. He hates it when I call him that. During the day, the little ones annoy the hell of him. They cry and yell. They poop their pants. They hit and push and snatch toys and there's not much Ender can do about it because he's big.

We tried to get a sitter earlier this year, but it didn't work out. She talked way more than I could deal with first thing in the morning before work, nosing through my stuff, asking how much things cost and why I got divorced from my husband. Did he beat me? Or cheat? Plus she had a small child starting first grade. In the beginning of first grade, mothers stay at the school hovering outside the classroom or bursting in periodically to wipe their little bunnies' faces or push food into their mouths. This is meant to help the kids get used to being away from their mothers. Mostly they all cry a lot, mothers and children both. Many of the mothers don't have much schooling themselves, and they're as intimidated with the new institutional surroundings as their children are.

The sitter's husband was supposed to be in charge of taking their son to his first week of school. The sitter came over to sit with my boy, and within 15 minutes her husband started phoning her every three minutes to holler at her that the kid was crying. There was no other possible solution to this problem than for her to go sit outside her son's classroom so her husband could go sit at the *kıraathane* (a teahouse that only men go to) and commiserate with his friends about how hard it is to raise children. I had to get to work, so she took Ender to her son's school up the hill, where she sat in the hallway to be there when her son cried. My son sat there with her for several hours, bored silly until it was time for him to go to school. At some point he and the sitter called me at work, and all he could tell me was how bored and hungry and thirsty he was. The boy can rarely go more than a couple of hours without eating, and it's hot in September. There aren't water fountains because city water isn't exactly drinkable. Public schools don't have air-conditioning, and the worried mothers outside the classroom door would naturally insist on keeping the windows closed because air moving indoors is a surefire way to catch all manner of serious illnesses.

So that was the end of the sitter, and Ender went back to daycare. This was fine with me, because the sitter tried to get a monthly salary of about five times more than a half-day sitter would normally get. People seem to think foreigners all have a money tree hidden somewhere. I paid her for the few days she'd failed to look after my son properly, plus a bit extra because I felt bad about firing her for needing to look after her own child.

Look, school in Turkey is a problem. The school system is a shambles, designed by politicians and not educators. For shits and giggles, the whole system is changed on a regular basis to suit some political end, which most recently has taken the form of injecting more Sunni Islam into classes at younger ages. The curriculum is out-of-date, nationalistic, and narrow-minded. Memorization and regurgitation of unanalyzed information is central, critical thinking not so much. The kids march around a lot and bellow their love of the flag and Atatürk, the founder of the Turkish Republic. All of it leads up to a single high-stakes exam that determines not only which university a kid can attend but also his or her major. High school is not much more than preparing for this exam, and the kids have to attend outside night or weekend courses called *dershane* because the exam contains more material than can possibly be covered in class.

Classes can have up to 40 kids. The facilities are bare bones and shabby. The bathrooms smell really bad, and there's no toilet paper. Lots of days my kid comes home desperate for a poo because he refuses to do his big jobs in those bathrooms, and I don't blame him. When they decorate their classrooms for holidays, it's the teachers who spend their prep time cutting out a bunch of identical construction paper shapes to put in all the windows, where they stay until the next holiday, slowly curling and bleaching gray in the sun.

But despite all this, there isn't much allure to private school, either. Smaller class sizes, yes, and fancier facilities. The curriculum is basically the same, and the way they avoid the *dershane* trap is to assign hours of homework every night. Generally the parents do the homework. English lessons are one of the bonuses of private school, which doesn't do much for us. Plus, I figured that because Ender is half Turkish and I'm in a situation of relative privilege compared to people around us, sending him to private school would further push him into a rarefied environment. And anyway, many of the university kids I teach are products of private school—entitled and lazy and scornful. They're the ones who had several years of English-medium education but still can't pass an exam that says they're borderline proficient in English. I don't want my kid growing up thinking it's normal to have drivers and buy good grades.

Not paying 15,000 lira ($5,200) a year for school also helps. It means I have more money for booze and expensive foreign cheese, and a small chunk left over to change to dollars so we're not left penniless as the lira devalues. And Ender still has an English class once a week. His English is much better than the teacher's. In class, he speaks English with a Turkish accent, in short broken sentences, so everyone can understand him. Every week his team wins the chocolate in whatever English games they play.

My ex-husband and I agree on very few things, but one thing we agreed on was that our son should go to public school.

Each year, schools organize a *kermes*, which is like a bake sale or fundraising event for the school. They set up little stands in the playground and sell things. One day when we were walking home from school, Mean Class Mom stopped me on the street. She always looks a bit frazzled, with hair dark at the roots springing free of their band, and of course there's the thing with her bulging eyes. Being Mean Class Mom must be a really hard job.

"You didn't come to the meeting yesterday," she said.

"Yes," I said. "Sorry. I was at work and I couldn't get away."

"We're planning the *kermes*," she said. "I asked Ender if you could bake something, cake or *poğaça* maybe, something like that."

"Um, I don't really have time for baking, unfortunately." This is not strictly true, actually. It's just that I have about ten thousand other things I'd rather do than learn how to bake.

"Yes," she said. "That's what Ender said. He says you're a lazy mom," and she laughed.

I often tell Ender I'm a lazy mom and that's why I don't bake or iron his underpants like the other moms do, so he was merely reporting facts. He's glad I don't fuss over him constantly, plus he knows he gets to do a lot of things the other kids don't get to do, like painting snails and tasting wine and skipping school to ride every form of public transportation we can think of. We even managed to avoid most of the tear gas in this year's Gay Pride March, when the police suddenly decided to attack using TOMAs, which are armored riot control vehicles equipped with water cannons that contain water adulterated with pepper spray or tear gas to make it hurt more. Despite the TOMAs and riot police all over blocking the escape routes, I still got us root beer at one of the few places in all of Istanbul that sells root beer. We'd researched it ahead of time where to find root beer, because no way was he going to another Gay Pride March without getting root beer at the end.

"Lazy mom!" she continued. "Aren't we all lazy?" she said, patting my arm conspiratorially.

This is one of those jokes in Turkish pragmatics that's not really a joke. It's a way of insulting someone and pretending it's a joke. My Turkish is pretty good, but not good enough to turn these jokes back on people. Plus I'm not skillful at being mean in any language.

"Ender!" I said to him in Turkish. "Am I really lazy?"

"No," he replied in English. "It's just that you have better things to do than bake."

"Good man," I said, reaching to tousle his hair, but he ducked away because lately he's become very sensitive about how his hair looks. Being eight is not easy.

"Whatever," Mean Class Mom said. "Why don't you just buy some socks or underwear from one of these little shops around here? It'll only cost a few lira."

"No problem," I said, hoping my smile didn't look smarmy. "I'll do that."

On the way home, Ender and I talked about other stuff, though he did apologize for the lazy mom thing.

"Fuck it," I said. "We'll show them lazy mom."

I've been learning to knit. I have this really dear friend who's great at knitting, and she's been doing it forever, plus she's an awesome teacher and whatever she hasn't taught me is on YouTube. I had a short work break coming up, so in lieu of baked goods I decided to knit some stuff for the *kermes*. Simple things, because I've barely mastered scarves, but I figured some headbands would do, and perhaps some simple bracelets. Nothing fancy, but I had fun with it, and I'm never quite sure what to do with myself during work breaks anyway when I have the days free, but the boy is still in school, so it's not like I can go anywhere. Ender was pleased that we would have something cooler to bring for the *kermes* than store-bought socks and underwear.

And then one day, he came home from school saying Mean Class Mom had told him I needed to send 20 lira ($7) and some cheese for the *kermes*.

"Is this in addition to the socks and underwear she wanted, or is this another thing?" I asked.

"I think it's just the cheese and money," he replied.

So I sent him to school with a round of cheese and the money and the things I had knitted. At pickup time a few days later, Mean Class Mom wove her way through the gossip circles and barreled over to me. I took my earphones out before she was even near. She pulled out her checklist.

"You gave cheese, right? And 20 lira?"

"Yes," I said. I wondered if she would say something about the other things I sent.

"Just that small round of cheese, right?" she asked. Her pen wasn't poised on the paper, so I assumed that was a barb about the size of the cheese.

"Yes," I said, faintly baffled as to why the size of the cheese was a thing, and why selling cheese at what was essentially a kids' bake sale was a thing, and why she didn't mention the other stuff I'd made. It's not like I was expecting heaps of praise for my amateur knitting, but maybe a veiled snarky comment about it would have been nice.

"Thank you," she said, and toddled off.

And then Ender came out and it was all hugs and "what are we having for dinner?" and "can I have ice cream?" and "why won't you buy me ice cream?" and "look, it's the cute guy selling the ice cream!" so I pretty much forgot about Mean Class Mom. In fact, we both pretty much forgot about Mean Class Mom until the end of the week, when Ender's dad was due to come pick him up. I was digging through Ender's backpack to make sure all his books were there for the weekend and to see if he'd drawn anything cool. At the bottom of his backpack was the bag of things I'd made for the *kermes*.

I got kind of upset. I just assumed he hadn't given her the knitted things because he was embarrassed. There are times when my kid is embarrassed about my Turkish (because it's fraught with mistakes), or my behavior (like when I kiss him too much on a Monday because I missed him after the weekend, when he was at his dad's), or my English (because everyone in the schoolyard stares at him for being bilingual in a prestige language). It felt like this was one of those times, that knitting stuff for the *kermes* was wrong, or the knitting was crappy, or whatever, but I was just kind of sick of him being ashamed of me. It's not like I'm going to stop being me to appease this rather narrow-minded view of what it is that mothers do, and I'll be damned if he starts thinking that mothering is limited to baking stuff and wiping his face all the time.

"What's this?" I asked. "Why didn't you give this to Mean Class Mom?"

He didn't answer.

"Why is this still in your bag?" I asked. "What's wrong with it? You know, you're not going to be like all the other kids all the time."

And then I realized the reason he didn't answer was that he was crying. Sobbing. I kicked myself a thousand times for getting mad and went to cuddle him up by his back and knees, because he's too big to cuddle him up like I did when he was small. "What happened, little man?"

He didn't want to tell me. He didn't want me to be mad or sad, and clearly I was now both. But it turned out that Mean Class Mom had taken the things I'd made along with my money and too-small round of cheese, and then brought back the knitted things the next day and told Ender they didn't need that stuff. And he was so crushed he didn't say anything about it for the rest of the week. He'd just stuffed it in the bottom of his backpack and hoped I wouldn't notice.

It made me remember this one time when I was about his age and my dad put this kind of cheese I didn't like into my lunch. I didn't want to tell him, because he thought I liked it. I even forced myself to eat the cheese the first few times it was in there because my dad had put it there. But then I told my friends, not friends really but the mean girls I hung out with, that I didn't actually like the cheese. Somehow they got ahold of the cheese and started kicking it around. I got really upset, thinking of my dad popping the cheese into my lunch believing that I liked the cheese and that it would make me happy, but now it was getting ground into the dirt.

So I cuddled the boy and tried to tell him he'd done nothing wrong. I kissed each of his dirty little knees. I invited him to join me in my invectives about this stupid petty woman who would do such a thing to a little boy, and he let fly an excellent stream of all the bad words he knows, ending with "bitch-head." I tried to high-five him for coining "bitch-head" because I'm pretty sure that's a new one, but we always miss on our first few high-fives and that got him calmed down again.

But I wasn't calm. I wanted to punch Mean Class Mom in the neck for being such a horrible person and for making my kid cry. I wanted to call her up and tell her she was a horrible person. Ender's dad came to fetch him for the weekend, and Ender made me promise not to tell his dad why he was upset, so I made him promise to tell his dad when he was feeling up to it. I talked to his dad later that night, after he'd discussed it with the boy, and his dad advised against both the punching and the phone call. He advised against even mentioning this to anyone at the school, ever.

So I bitched to all of my friends whom I'd kept apprised of these events as they unfolded. I think my friends like these stories.

As always, the mother guilt eventually began to set in. That's actually a thing, according to the Internet, how mothers always find a way to turn things on themselves. It was my fault somehow, that my kid got treated this way. I thought about how Mean Class Mom and the other moms must see me. Maybe they actually do bear some animosity toward me? And maybe it's not misplaced? Let's look back on what I've written these last few pages:

I've referred to the playground women's "gossip circles," which I apparently hold myself above and can't be bothered to participate in because I don't give a shit.

I've been nasty about the women's topics of conversation.

I'm too busy with more important things to do than bake and do other household chores.

I think my kid is more awesome and interesting than their kids because he's bilingual and bicultural.

I've belittled their mothering.

I think my life is better than their lives because I'm not held to Turkish norms the way they are. I have quite a lot more liberty because of being foreign, plus I have money and a good education and a fancy university job, and there I am with my earphones in the schoolyard every day, not doing what everyone else is doing, and they don't know why.

I've pretty much failed to integrate as a woman here, which I see as an advantage to both my kid and me but that doesn't mean they see it that way.

Can you blame them? It doesn't matter that I'm kind of shy, or that language is sometimes a barrier, or that I have very little in common with anyone on the playground other than being someone's mother. It matters that I lead a privileged life full of liberties that they don't even know about, earned by nothing more than the luck of having been born female somewhere that isn't here.

"Who does she think she is?" they might ask. And they're right.

Who do I think I am?

I didn't even know Mean Class Mom's real name until the other day when I asked my kid. He knows everyone's name and I don't. Still, I'll leave her saved in my phone as Mean Class Mom because despite all my failings, she's definitely mean.

And to be honest, it's not that hard to rise above it. Some people make it really easy to be the better man. Woman.

Whatever.

Sarah Metzker Erdemir moved to Istanbul on a whim in 2002, and has been there ever since. Her son Ender James was born in 2007, and he is now in 3rd grade with the same Mean Class Mom. Sarah is getting better at believing her fake smiles are real, and Ender is getting better at arguing about everything. Follow her stories at http://istanbuls-stranger.blogspot.com.

CHAPTER 24

WHERE IS HOME?

Candice Cabutihan-Cipullo
Nationality: USA and Philippines
Birthed in: Japan
Parented in: Japan, Canada, and Philippines

I was leaving the parking lot of a store in Winnipeg when I noticed a man was trying to figure out how to take a grocery cart out of a line of carts. He didn't know that you have to put a loonie (one dollar coin) in, push the key chained to the cart, then pull out the cart. I was too far away to help, and he figured it out eventually, but I saw his frustration and felt it. I've helped a lot of people who couldn't figure this out, and they've all been relieved that someone cared enough to show them how to do it. I've asked around about this system, and they said that it's an incentive for people to always return their carts, especially in the winter months (because a buck is a buck!), and stealing grocery carts has been rampant. I recalled the first time I tried to do it, and I felt so stupid that it seemed like a simple thing to do (there were even written directions) but I couldn't do it.

Seeing this man, helpless over a simple grocery cart, with nobody helping him made me very emotional. As I was pulling out of the parking lot, I started crying, and I couldn't stop! I realized that for many years, that's what I've been doing! I've been figuring things out...everywhere I've lived, since I got married. I felt tired and homesick. It was a cold and rainy day after all, and the wind just made me feel sad.

At that moment, I wished I were somewhere familiar, where people didn't look at me differently, where people just assumed I was from there, where I spoke the language—without having to think first if I am making any sense. At that moment, I felt disconnected, and felt that every place I've lived in, I've struggled to belong.

When I first moved to the States, I had to get a driver's license and a job, figure out public transportation and process my citizenship. I had to speak English every single day. When one is running out of English words to say, we Filipinos use the term "nose bleed," and I bled a lot. I learned to go to the airport early enough because inevitably, I would be pulled out of the line for "random" screening.

In Tokyo, I needed to get another job, figure out the crazy train stations, and speak the language as best as I could when I got lost or stopped by an immigration officer, or tried to order food in a restaurant. I learned to be comfortable being naked in a public bath or hot springs. I learned to pour alcohol for my husband and never allow his glass be empty. I learned not leave my chopsticks standing upright on a bowl of rice. I learned that I would never be able to make perfect sushi, *o-nigiri* or ramen in the eyes of a Japanese *obachan* (grandma).

In Canada, my children and I got kicked out of a playgroup for bringing peanut butter sandwiches and got yelled at for not wearing socks in the play area of a mall. My car was towed twice, for parking illegally where the signs were unnoticeable, got cursed once or twice for following the speed limit in a residential area, and got rear ended by a texting 16-year-old. I've learned to cope with the cold—and it gets really cold in Manitoba.

Now in Manila, I am extremely happy and grateful that I have the opportunity to give back to my country through my various outreach activities and spend a lot of time with my family and friends, but Manila for me has changed. It is not home anymore.

Life can surprise you in many different ways. It can take you out of your comfort zone and, using love as bait, take you to places you've never been, make you blend in with cultures you're not familiar with, and allow you to realize you're resilient. Life as a parent can make you discover a part of you that is selfless and overflowing with unconditional love and show you how strong you are in the most challenging moments. Life in the Foreign Service forces you to be tough in dealing with change and still create positive experiences for your family.

As I recalled the past 10 years of my life abroad, I felt how grown up I'd become. I realized how much I'd thought of only myself before I had children, and now I needed to make a conscious effort to think of myself, and my well-being. Now it seems like a luxury to have alone time in the bathroom, uninterrupted sleep, non-stop conversation with adults, or the ability to just do nothing.

I never dreamed of traveling, living, giving birth, or raising kids abroad. For the first 26 years of my life, I lived in my own little world in Manila, enjoying my life with family and friends, doing what I loved, teaching, and making music. I came from a big family of seven, and we only really traveled domestically, visiting relatives or meeting my dad when he was on out-of-town business trips. My parents worked extremely hard to send us all to private schools. We always had food on the table and things we needed, but we never had enough money to take leisure trips to explore the other parts of the world. I limited my worldview to pretty much my own country, and I remained oblivious that things were happening in other parts of the world while I was living my life in my own bubble.

In 2005, I met a man who changed my life forever. Tim was working as a political officer at the US embassy in Manila, and I was a teacher for a private foundation that provided free education to the gifted but poorest children of Manila. The embassy put together a conference about civic education, and I was invited to be one of the participants. Tim had to attend as an organizer. The rest, as they say, is history. We had a State Department gunshot wedding after only nine months of dating, and I don't regret it for one second. We have been married for 10 years.

Leaving your home country, family, friends, ministry, and your job, moving to a country with an entirely different culture, and living a newlywed life was pretty overwhelming, as it all happened in a span of a year. I am grateful that we were assigned to Washington, DC, as it was a good introduction to American culture for me. We loved living in DC—going to work, exercising, and grocery shopping together, and experimenting on new recipes in our small apartment. On weekends, we enjoyed sleeping in, having brunch, strolling in the beautiful parks, kayaking along the Potomac, then a movie and a gourmet dinner to cap a Saturday night. Sundays were usually spent reading, doing volunteer work, and watching our favorite TV shows until bedtime. Whenever we visit DC now, having had children, we marvel at how things are so different than they were during those early carefree days.

Our second tour was in Tokyo, and it was a great place to start a family. Japan has excellent health care, one of the best in the world, so we knew we were in the right place. During our first month there, I got a teaching job at an international school. Ready to commit to three years of work, I found out I was pregnant on my first week on the job! My boss was very supportive and was truly flexible all the way till the end of our assignment.

And so the journey began. I read about giving birth in Japan and was worried about one thing only: no pain medication! Most Japanese women don't take any form of pain medication because of the *gaman* (suck it up) attitude. Also, "beliefs about the effect of anesthesia on the baby and the mother-child bond, as well as the commonly held notion that painkillers are 'like cheating' (particularly as their mothers didn't use any) also serve to discourage their use," according to an article in the English-language newspaper The Japan Times.

In Japan, birth is a natural process the woman has to go through, and so there is no other choice but to push the baby out, in the most natural (and painful) way. I say this with so much respect for Japanese women. The mothers that I've met in Japan and eventually became friends with were the most dedicated mothers I have ever met. Their elaborate *bento* boxes for the kids' lunches, the multiple dishes they serve their husbands for dinner after a long day's work, their utmost dedication to make their humble homes clean and cozy are some of the beautiful things I witnessed there. Walking up the streets of Roppongi where I lived, I would see countless mothers on their bikes, riding up the hill with two of their preschool children in tow. I found it striking that these women—tired from a day's work, breastfeeding their little ones and volunteering for their communities—still had a sense of fashion, a graceful disposition that was so unusual and at the same time admirable. How could they, in their busy lives look so put together from head to toe while chasing their toddlers at the playground? It must be the Zen gardens. I only wish I could exude the kind of calmness that Japanese mothers displayed everywhere.

Childbirth was one of the most beautiful things I have ever experienced in my life. Yes, it was the most physically difficult thing I have ever gone through in my life (and yes, I did get an epidural eventually, for both births), but I think it was by far the most memorable and transforming one. From conception to developing in the womb, to the process of labor—this was the work of a genius. My whole body was ready to give it all in order to gracefully make way for another life. I gave birth to another person. How amazing is that? At a time in my life when I was struggling with my faith (I was born and raised Catholic), the whole process of childbirth made me firmly believe that there is someone truly greater than all of us. Thinking about it now still gives me goose bumps and makes me teary-eyed.

When Kevin was 18 months old, we had to have him admitted for the first time to a Japanese hospital. At first, we took him to the health unit at the embassy, and the nurse said that it could just be sore throat. After three to four days of continuous flu-like symptoms, including a low-grade fever, we took him to his pediatrician at the Tokyo Medical Clinic. The doctor suspected it to be strep, and prescribed antibiotics. After three days of medication, Kevin got worse. This time, he was more lethargic and just wanted to sleep all day. His eyes, lips, and tongue were getting red, and his fever was over 40 °C (104 °F).

I was 36 weeks pregnant with our second child when this happened. While sitting in the emergency room, I kept on praying that Kevin only had some kind of flu and could go home the same night. I was hoping that we wouldn't have to stay in the hospital and we could resume our lives the next day. However, after waiting for about two hours for the results of the blood tests, the doctors came back with a worried face—they suspected Kevin had Kawasaki disease. If there is a place in the world that could best treat this disease, it is Japan. After all, the disease was discovered and studied there. This is a serious though treatable condition. It is an autoimmune disease—in Kevin's case, his white blood cell count shot up to 20 times the normal amount. Doctors do not know what causes it, or what we could do to prevent it, and it is a pretty rare disease. They admitted him and hooked him up to a saline IV and heart monitor. He was treated with IV gamma globulin for 24 hours. The risk of complications during treatment was small, but the risks of not treating included heart damage.

I felt numb when I heard the news. I had to deal with so many things at the moment, and I honestly did not feel a thing initially. I looked at Kevin, his frail and delicate face. I looked at my belly, my tired and heavy body and all I could think of was, *I hope I don't give birth this week.* I looked at Tim, who remained strong despite the news—but I knew he was dying inside. This was the first time our son had something major like this, and his broken tibia when he was one suddenly felt like it was just a splinter. I took deep breaths as we were about to go into the children's ward, and I thought, *there is no other way but through, and we will get through it.*

On our first night in the hospital, I asked for an extra bed for my husband. The nurses looked puzzled and said only mothers could stay in the room. I showed them my belly, and in my broken Japanese I said I was pregnant and I would need help. They said they would help me, but my husband had to go home. I was too tired to call the Emperor of Japan, and so I just nodded, stroked Kevin's hair, and took a nap. After 18 nerve-racking hours, and waking up every hour to check on Kevin, the drugs started to work. He was discharged three days later and was cleared of the disease after a year of heart monitoring. Tim and I were both relieved and grateful that he overcame this without any long-term consequences, but for several months afterward I was extremely cautious of every sickness that came his way. We're back to normal now, but those dark days really scared us as parents.

Three weeks later we came back to the hospital again, this time for the grand entrance of our second child. Nina came on the last day of 2010 at 11:45 p.m. Yes, we got a tax break.

One typical day, I took two-year-old Kevin to the playground, put him down for a nap, then breastfed two-month-old Nina at home. I headed out to do some shopping and left them with our helper. Before I closed the door I heard Nina crying again, so I came back to feed her some more. The ground started to shake, and as earthquakes are pretty common in Japan, we thought it was just one of those 10-second ones that would soon be over. It shook more than usual, and my helper and I looked at each other, terrified. It was the biggest earthquake we had ever experienced. I ran toward Kevin's room, and picked him up from his crib. We all went under the dining table and waited for the shaking to end. We thought it would never stop. It was a good three minutes of escalating, worsening trembles. We must have sang "Row, row, row your boat" to the children more than 40 times before the quake finally stopped. Luckily, we were safe. Tim was at work, and although the US embassy was built to withstand Japan's earthquakes, it was a 35-year-old building, and they felt it shake. Tim thought it was the last day of his life, and so did many of his coworkers.

I took my kids to the empty parking lot across our apartment for safety. Our neighbors were all out there too. In silent nods and smiles, we took comfort in seeing each other safe. We waited there until I finally got a text message from Tim, saying that he was a bit shaken (no pun intended) but he was fine. The US embassy immediately set up a crisis center to monitor the casualties, to look for Americans who need help, and to help the Japanese government in any way possible. After several aftershocks, we went back to the apartment, swept up the broken glass from the floor, and turned on the TV.

What I saw was heart-wrenching. A lot of my family and friends were trying to find out if we were okay through email and Facebook, and relative to what I saw on the news, we were perfectly fine. I cried alone in my bed as the images of the devastation of the tsunami flashed before me. I wept for the thousands of Japanese people who could not contact their families, who were stranded in the trains, and who were helpless.

We opened our home to several friends who could not get out of Tokyo. I remember clearly to this day how happy I was to cook dinner for all of them that night, and prepared beds to provide them a comfortable night's rest. One of them was our American friend, Steve, whose wife is Japanese. They have just built a house in Ibaraki, and after trying to get in touch with his family for two days he learned that his family was safe, but their new house has turned into rubble. The tsunami hit their area.

After the earthquake, the tsunami damaged a nuclear power plant in Fukushima along the coast, 149 miles (240 km) away from Tokyo. For the first several days, the country was gripped with the concern that the reactors would melt down, spreading radioactive fallout over Tokyo and other cities. While the Japanese government was trying to gain control of the situation, along with all of the other countries that had pitched in to help, there was talk about other embassy families leaving Tokyo. Families of American embassy staff stayed for six more days. However, one night, my husband called and asked me to pack whatever we could as we were leaving for Osaka as soon as possible. He said it was safer for us to leave than be trapped in Tokyo if everyone was trying to get out. He had to stay and work at the operations center, but the kids and I would fly to Manila, where my whole family was waiting.

The journey out of Tokyo was chaotic, long, and tedious. We had to take a bullet train to Osaka, as the airport in Tokyo was very busy. We were not sure what the radiation levels in Tokyo would do to our two-month-old, so it was better to be safe than sorry. Traveling with both kids was challenging, but motherhood brought me so much clarity at that moment, and I had to get my kids to safety. I remember changing Kevin's diaper on the moving bus while Nina was strapped in the Baby Bjorn onto my chest. I remember running through 34 gates at Incheon airport in Korea to make it to our flight to Manila, carrying a diaper bag, a suitcase, and two very worn-out children both in my arms. I must have had an extra shot of adrenalin because I still had the courage to scream at the crew who were closing the airplane door, "We are on that flight! Please help me!"

We had been traveling for more than 15 hours, and all I could do on the plane was cry. I felt so many emotions all at the same time. I was relieved that we were finally getting out, grateful that we were going to be safe, but at the same time fearful for my husband and all the other "essential" employees who had to stay to monitor the situation. I was so exhausted, both physically and emotionally, but I knew I had to get it together. I was moved by the acts of kindness I experienced during that whole process—friends from Osaka who had us stay for a few days while we waited for the evacuation announcement, bus drivers who compassionately carried my bags while Kevin was having a temper tantrum, co-passengers on the flight who, upon seeing me sobbing, took the kids gently out of my hands and gave me a break. It was almost as if people knew what I was going through.

Coming back to the loving arms of my family, I felt relief to have the support of my loved ones in Manila during those trying times. We were able to see Tim again after six weeks, and we came back to Tokyo to pack our things and head out to our next assignment in Winnipeg, Manitoba. It was not the ideal way to end our tour in Japan.

I decided to be a stay-at-home mom when we moved to Canada. Kevin was two and Nina was seven months old. They were still too young for a preschool program, and it was a new place to explore, a new place for a new life. I feel like our approach to life always gives us a chance to start with a clean slate, and it is such a blessing to have this opportunity to allow our children to thrive in this environment of change. We accept our new environment and adapt accordingly. Winnipeg was ideal. We had a large house, a very safe neighborhood, access to all things American, and we had a pretty great community. Our routine was very predictable: We would go to a playgroup in the morning, take a nap mid-afternoon (while I did all the household chores), and go to the playground in the afternoon. Eventually, Kevin and Nina were ready for a two-hour program in the morning, while I set up an online graphic design business and got involved in a lot of volunteer work in the community.

Though it is deemed to be the coldest city in Canada (yes, there were winters with three weeks of -40 °F/-40 °C temperatures), one thing we learned from Canada is that life goes on. I met the toughest people there, including Filipinos, who I thought would never think of moving there. Canadians never cancel anything, even school at -50 °F (-45.5 °C), not even if the water pipes have frozen. The kids loved the snow. We were living just a few steps from a lake. In the summer, we would canoe around and have picnics. In the winter, the kids would sled and ice skate in the frozen lake.

We all have our crosses to bear, we all have our struggles, and what I've learned through the years is to forgive ourselves for the things we do wrong. It is only then that we can move on and strive to have a better day tomorrow. As my kids were growing up, there were definitely times when I would question our way of parenting. Are we raising our kids the right way? What is this whole nomadic lifestyle doing to them? We are witnesses to how they are growing up, and I could see how different they are from each other. While one is very sensitive, looking for arguments and reasoning all the time, the other one is very laid-back, compliant, and contented. While one is gifted with music, the other is gifted with art. Journaling has helped me deal with motherhood a lot. I find that when I write down my feelings, I am able to identify the root of my misery and deal with it. Most often than not, I am conscious of what people will say about my kids, as there is always judgment in the way that we are raising them.

But as I wrote in my journal one Christmas we spent in New York,

"I have resolved that every time I am having a bad day, I should always look at the bigger picture and choose my battles. What matters is that my children feel loved, secure, safe, and always forgiven. What matters is that I give them the best care that I can provide. What matters [is that] I strive to correct them and constantly remind them of respect and honesty.

People around me will always judge, and mothers around me will always make me feel that their children are far more perfect than mine, and look down on me while my children are at their worst behavior. Non-parents will always think how ridiculous I am for raising such bad-mannered, spoiled brats. And random ladies will always think of me as a mom who never puts on winter gloves on the kids when it's just a couple of degrees below freezing. (We live in Winnipeg, you know…) All the chaos of traveling actually made me realize how sensitive I am and how senseless my thoughts have been about parenting. I thank God for time for family and for blessing me with new realizations. I pray that I may never judge other parents or look down on other families who can't seem to put their act together."

I am in Manila as I write this, thankful for the opportunity to be back in my home country. We have been here for almost a year now, and the kids have experienced so many of my childhood memories—the food, the parties, the beaches, my friends, and my family. Adjusting here was tough at first as they absolutely loved our time in Winnipeg, but now they are flourishing, only to move again in a few months. Many have commented that we are destroying them, that they won't ever have a sense of normalcy, or that they won't ever have roots and strong friendships. Some have praised us that we are exposing them to what the world has to offer, and that their understanding of the world will be so different from other kids their age. But seeing how strong and brave they are despite their occasional meltdowns, how understanding and patient they are, and how resilient they are becoming, I think we are doing okay. We sent letters to their friends from Winnipeg and the US, Skyped and sent videos to their best buddies, and made them feel that the world is small enough now that we could always get in touch. I've shed a lot of tears these past few months trying to be patient with them and trying to understand where they are coming from. We are moving again, as our next assignment will be in Madagascar. I continue to struggle, but I know that there is no other way but through.

I have learned to choose my battles while parenting—especially abroad. Tomorrow is a new day. Breathe. Just breathe. These have been the statements that have helped me through the past six years of parenting. I feel blessed to have healthy, beautiful children, and I can't wait to share every minute of their childhood as much as I can.

A while ago, during one of our home leaves spent in Colorado, Kevin had a really tough time adjusting to the move. One morning, he woke up sobbing and asked to go "home." Then he looked at me and asked, "But Mommy, where is home?" It was difficult to explain the concept of home to a two-year-old who endured the chaos following the Japanese earthquake, had consequently moved back and forth to different countries, flown numerous times, and slept in several beds in a span of less than six months.

Tim and I looked at each other lovingly.

In that small apartment we were renting out, we opened the curtains, watched the sunrise, and told him, "Home is where you, Mommy, Daddy, and Nina are together."

That is what my children's definition of home is now.

Wherever we are, wherever we are moving to, we will always be together.

Candice Cabutihan Cipullo has a degree in child development and education and was pursuing a master's degree in educational administration at the University of the Philippines before getting married and moving to the United States with her American husband in 2006. For six years, she was a teacher at a school for the gifted in the Philippines. Her husband's job as a diplomat paved the way for her to share her passion for education to the world. In Washington, DC, she taught in an elementary school, as well as volunteered to help design the curriculum and mentor teachers for Paaralang Pinoy, a school aimed to cultivate Filipino language and culture to children in Virginia. She taught in an international school in Tokyo, and volunteered in parenting programs in Winnipeg, Canada. After a year in Manila, she established enrichment classes for caregivers of children under five. She wrote "Kaya Mo Maging Super Yaya" ("You can be a Super Nanny") in Filipino and English, aimed at teaching basic child development concepts to nannies and parents alike. She and her family are moving to Madagascar at the end of February, 2016. Follow her adventures at http://www.travellingmaybahay.com.

ACKNOWLEDGEMENTS

I am extremely thankful for all of the amazing contributions from the writers in this book. It has been a pleasure getting to know each of you. Thank you for trusting me with your personal stories. I loved watching you embrace the idea and help it flourish all while juggling families and babies of your own.

My sincerest gratitude goes to Lauren Reeves, who sent me feedback in the middle of the night while reading early drafts and rocking her newborn baby back to sleep. I rarely make an editorial decision without first seeking your input. Similarly, Emelie Cheng, who designed the cover art, you are an amazing designer, and I am so fortunate to have you as a close friend. Let's grab dinner soon! Thank you to Melinda Lipkin for strengthening my editorial decisions, providing precise edits, and empowering me throughout this project. Sandra Jolly, you have an amazing talent at making me feel comfortable and eliciting a genuine laugh (and smile) out of me in an otherwise very awkward photo shoot situation. I'm much more accustomed to life on the other side of the camera. Christine Kite Kelly, I couldn't function without your expertise, opinion, and wit guiding me through some of the larger creative decisions. Thank you to all of the ladies in the LC who provided their opinions and feedback. You provided an emotional outlet when I needed it the most. I am so grateful to be a part of such an amazing network of mothers.

To my family, thank you for supporting my decisions even though they have taken me geographically far away from you all. Without your love and support, I wouldn't be as bold and self-confident as I am. I wish we could visit more.

Specifically, to my parents, Julie and Don Dwyer, who have always encouraged me to stretch beyond my comfort zone, even if that meant going to places and doing things that made you nervous.

Your guidance helps me navigate through this foggy haze of parenting and life decisions.

Joann Ferland, you have earned a special spot in heaven for listening to me read every chapter over the phone. I looked forward to our daily readings, and your feedback was instrumental in shaping the order of the chapters.

Samantha Eells, who is always available to chat (thank you, time zones!) and who, at the drop of a dime, will book an airplane ticket to come and visit. My best friend, you are. Eternal thanks, you have.

And finally, I'd like to acknowledge my amazing husband, Jonathan Ferland, who not only kept me on task but also made sure I could focus entirely on the book. You took over many of my normal responsibilities with the children and the house so I could continue clicking away on my computer. Truly, without the decisions we have made together, we wouldn't be where we are today, and I couldn't imagine being anywhere else. Thank you for always supporting my dreams and aspirations. Without you, I'd never be knocked up abroad.

To continue the Knocked Up Abroad experience, learn more about the contributors, or submit your own story, visit our website at www.knockedupabroadbook.com.

53661249R00167

Made in the USA
Charleston, SC
13 March 2016